Michigan Public Recreation Lands BILLION DOLLAR BONANZA!

A History of the Michigan Natural Resources Trust Fund

By
Jack R. Westbrook

"Broader public access to plentiful, quality outdoor recreation opportunities plays a central role in Michigan's economy and quality of life for residents and visitors. The Michigan Natural Resources Trust Fund continues to support active, healthy lifestyles for people of all abilities and has done so for nearly 40 years, funding recreational opportunities in every county in Michigan."

Rick Snyder
Michigan Governor
March 2011

"The Michigan Natural Resources Trust Fund has put more than a billion dollars in public land acquisition and development projects in all of Michigan's 83 counties. Every high-value access to every high-value natural resources in this state came from the Michigan Natural Resources Trust Fund. Many people say it is the only thing state government got right since 1976."

Keith Creagh
Department of Natural Resources Director
December, 2014

ON THE COVER:
A sample view of MNRTF sites against a background of Wayne County's William G. Milliken State Park in Detroit, Michigan's only state park in an urban area clockwise; the tip of the Keweenaw Peninsula and a hiker along a trail in Roscommon County's Mason County's Mason Tract River Retreat.

Michigan Public Recreation Lands BILLION DOLLAR BONANZA!

A History of the Michigan Natural Resources Trust Fund

Jack R. Westbrook

JACK R. WESTBROOK ORSB PUBLISHING

Mt. Pleasant, Michigan

ISBN: 10: 0984036180

ISBN 13/EAN 13: 9780984036189

Library of Congress Control Number: 2015903434

Published by Jack R. Westbrook ORSB Publishing
POB 16, Mount Pleasant, Michigan, 48804-0016
E-mail: jackrwestbrookorsb@charter.net
Phone: 989-773-5741

First Printing March, 2015

This book is especially dedicated to Michigan Oil And Gas Association President Frank L. Mortl and the late Tom Washington, former Director of the Michigan United Conservation Clubs, who hatched the idea for what was to become the Michigan Natural Resources Trust Fund on a drive from Lansing to Clare, Michigan, for the Annual Pere Marquette Hunting and Fishing Club Banquet.

Further dedications are devoted to former Michigan Senator Kerry Kammer, whose determination brought the Fund into legislative reality and to all those who have served faithfully on the MNRTF Board of Directors through billion dollars in grants awarded for Michigan public recreation venues.

Contents

Smokey Bear sez: "Only YOU can prevent lack of knowledge about the Michigan Natural Resources Trust Fund."

Introduction

By Erin McDonough, President and CEO
Michigan Oil And Gas Association

Millions of people are well aware of Michigan's one-of-a-kind natural wonders. Of its abundant resources, its amazing landscapes, its top-notch facilities and recreational outlets.

But far fewer know about the fund that made so many of these treasure possible: The Michigan Natural Resources Trust Fund.

The MNRTF, derived from oil and gas revenues from state-owned mineral rights, has enabled the acquisition and creation of many of the public recreational lands and facilities that make our great state the envy of the nation.

I feel fortunate that my career path, first as Executive Director of Michigan United Conservation Clubs (MUCC) and now as President and CEO of the Michigan Oil and Gas Association (MOGA) as well as Vice Chair of the Michigan Natural Resources Trust Fund Board, has allowed me to play a small role in the history of this historic and vital program.

For more than 75 years, MUCC has served as a unifying voice for Michigan's hunting, fishing and trapping interests. Comprised of hundreds of affiliate clubs and tens of thousands of individual members, MUCC has been long considered the premier champion for conservation in Michigan.

MOGA brings together the crude oil and natural gas interests of our state to further policy and practices that ensure resource use and extraction is done with sound conservation principles at the forefront.

In 1976, MUCC and MOGA joined forces to spearhead the movement that ultimately resulted in the creation of the MNRTF.

I am honored to have served all three organizations.

Conservation is the wise use of natural resources. It is about sustainable, responsible use.This is a mantra that is revered at both MUCC and MOGA.

Thanks to the creation of the MNRTF, we have been able to show that we can have a thriving oil and gas industry while maintaining Michigan's status as a premier outdoor recreation destination.

In fact, because of the MNRTF, we have been able to enhance our public recreational holdings and facilities in a way we otherwise could not.

"Serving A Great Industry In A Great State" has long been MOGA'S motto and never have we served more proudly than by helping bring to the people of Michigan the outdoor recreation opportunities chronicled on the following pages.

This same motto would apply equally well to MUCC and the MNRTF. To all three, it's the resource that matters most. It's conservation that is the focus. I know because I've lived with all three.

In the following pages of this book, you will learn what the MNRTF has accomplished in every county in Michigan and odds are high you'll recognize many of them. It's likely you've long reaped the benefits of the MNRTF and likely didn't even know it. This book is not just a guide to MNRTF projects throughout the state, it's a handbook of Michigan history.

This is not just the story of the MNRTF. It's the story of conservation, of cooperative effort.

It is a uniquely Michigan tale.

Foreword

Grab your hiking boots, your bicycle, your fishing pole, your picnic basket, your swimming suit, snowmobile or all-terrain vehicle ..... we're headed to a Michigan Natural Resources Trust Fund-funded public outdoor recreration project near your home. Oh, and don't forget your saddle, horse, riding clothes, bow and arrows and golf clubs.

The new breed likes to say "There's an app for that."

To paraphrase for the Michigan Natural Resource Trust Fund (MNRTF), it can be said that no matter what your outdoor recreational interest, "There's a project for that." Besides all the standard activities you think about as outdoor recreation *(camping, hiking, biking, fishing, etc.),* Michigan's network of public outdoor venues include MNRTF projects for equestrian, archery and golf activities.

In this book, we will visit 1,874 of active and completed MNRTF projects in all 83 Michigan counties, chances are one of them is close to your back yard. Many of the properties would not have been acquired or developed for public use without the help of the MNRTF, founded in the wisdom of industry government leaders almost four decades ago as a unique in the nation solution to a seemingly hopeless stalemate.

Since 1976, more than a billion bucks has been earmarked for your outdoor pleasue and almost 900 million dollars in completed and active projects await your recreational use. I'll tell you where. Just include this book on your next drive. Have a good time.

I am asked "how long does it take you to put together one of your books?" In this case the answer is simple : "42 years and four months."

I started working for the *Michigan Oil & Gas News* magazine in March, 1973, at the beginning of the northern Michigan oil and gas drilling "boom" that would percipitate the Pigeon River Country State Forest controversy, which in turn percipitated the controversy's solution with the founding of the Michigan Natural Resources Trust Fund in 1976. So it might be said I was covering the Trust Fund from the marriage of north woods and oil drilling, through its conception to its adulthood.

After my retirement from the magazine in 2001, I continued following the MNRTF as a semi-retired special reporter until 2007 and have kept updated ever since. The 2010 record lease sale and the resulting "topping out" of the mandated fund balance cap, ended the era that saw Michigan oil and gas revenues from state-owned mineral properties principally fund MNRTF. This, combined with the MNRTF 35th birthday, prompted me to gather materials from a career of articles, photos and notes to launch this project that led to my first MNRTF book in 2011 and now, after more than a billion dollars in recommended grants, this update. Thanks for your continued interest.

Jack R. Westbrook – February, 2015

Michigan Natural Resources Trust Fund Project Map

The back cover of a Michigan DNR Campground Guide illustrates the 83 county distribution of Michigan Natural Resources Trust Fund projects. No matter where you are in Michigan, you are near an MNRTF-funded public recreation facility.

Michigan Oil & Gas Drilling Map

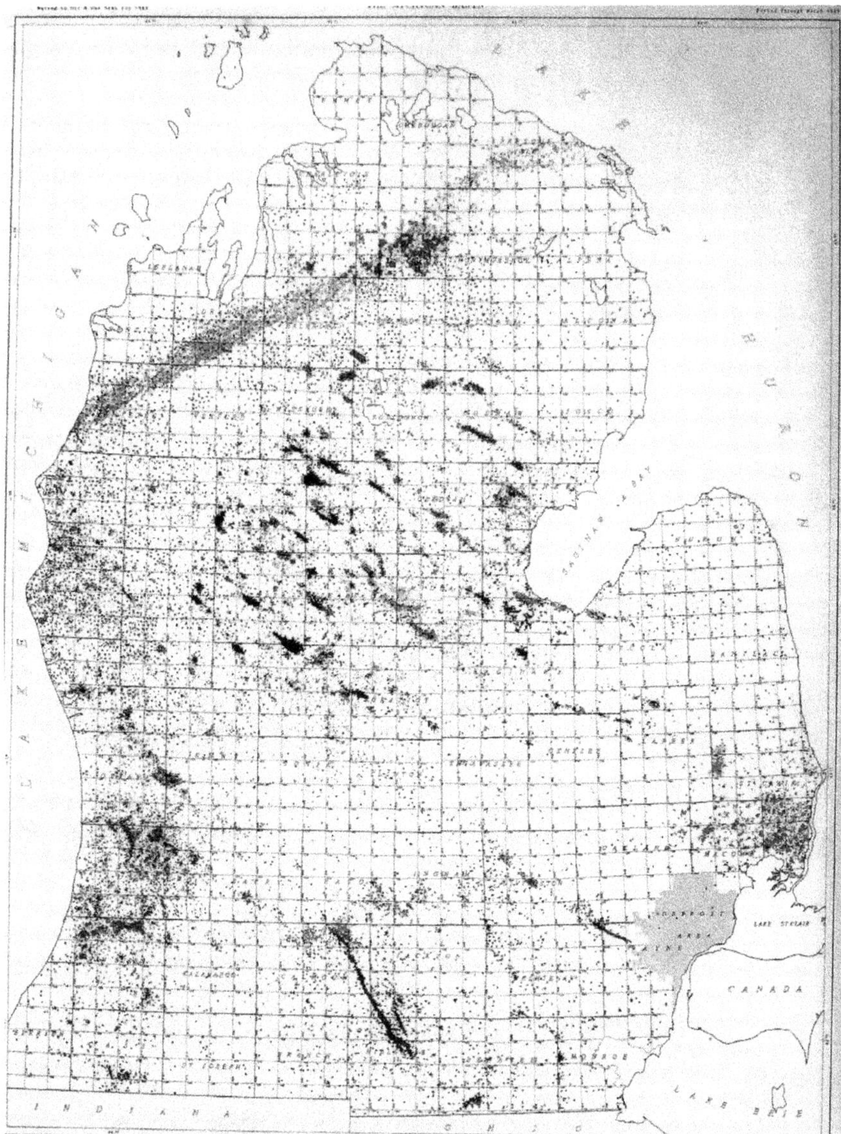

A modern Michigan oil and gas well map shows the result of drilling more than 50,000 holes in the search for oil and gas, with more than half of those holes dry, or non-commercial. Michigan oil and/or natural gas is produced from 64 of Michigan's 68 Lower Peninsula counties. The lack of significant sediments make the Upper Peninsula an unlikely petroleum potential, though 20 holes have been unsuccessfully drilled there.

Neat Things to Know about MNRTF

- In 1976, Michigan became the first state in the nation to establish a land trust fund specifically subsidized by revenues generated from the oil and gas industry.

- The smallest MNRTF grant is a $6,795 acquisition for Marquette County's Champion Township Wetlands and Mangers Creek.

- The largest MNRTF grant is a $20 million acquisition grant for Detroit's William G. Milliken State Park.

- The 15 counties of Michigan's Upper Peninsula, with 3.34% of the state's total population, has received $73,574,317 in 247 MNRTF active, completed and 2014 recommended grants, representing 8.18% of the total grant monies to individual county or smaller government entities and 13.1% of total grants to counties.

- The 68 counties of Michigan's Lower Peninsula, with 96.66% of the state's total population, has received $825,703,250 in 1,627 MNRTF grants, representing 86.9% of the total grant monies to individual county or smaller government entities and 91.82% of total grants to counties.

- MNRTF all-time active or closed (completed) and 2014 recommended grants through 2014 total $899,277,567 in 1,874 projects in all 83 counties.

- Oakland County has received 122 MNRTF active and completed grants, the highest number of involucel county grants.

- Luce County has received the least amount of MNRTF grant dollars in 3 grants totaling 130,800.

- Wayne County has received the most amount of MNRTF grants, totaling $76,444,618 in 90 grants.

- Missaukee and Oscoda Counties have received the fewest MNRTF grants – one apiece.

Prelude to MNRTF: Pigeon River Country State Forest Controversy

By the mid-1960s Michigan oil and gas exploration was increasing in northern Michigan with widespread anticipation that significant pools of oil and natural gas were waiting to be discovered.

On July 1, 1970, Shell Oil Company announced a major find in the area. Shell's discovery began a long battle over drilling in the area that would last for over a decade. Ford Kellum, a wildlife biologist employed by the state's Department of Natural Resources, was inalterably opposed to drilling in the Pigeon River area. The Pigeon River area was a roughly 500 square mile area in the northeast corner of the Lower Peninsula. In the early years of the twentieth century, P. S. Lovejoy, Administrator of the State's Department of Conservation, conceived of creating a "wilderness tract" in the area that would become much like the pristine forest that had existed before the logging era. As part of the project, in 1917 and 1918 wild elk from the Rocky Mountains were released in the forest, to recreate the elk which once lived in the region but had become extinct. Until his death in 1942, Lovejoy was devoted to the "Pigeon River Project."

Kellum inherited Lovejoy's fierce devotion for preserving the area as a "Big Wild" as well as to protecting and enhancing the re-established elk herd and other wild animals which lived in the area. Kellum became the central figure opposing drilling in the area. In the early 1970s, Kellum found sympathetic ears among a few northern Michigan newspapermen, who took up his cause, and he organized opposition among groups such as the Audubon Club chapters and the Michigan Bear Hunters Association. In 1971, Kellum resigned his DNR position to spend all of his time opposing drilling in the area. He organized the Pigeon River Country Association to create a group to promote his vision for the forest and to oppose oil exploration in the area. The

Pigeon River Country Association organization eventually proposed creating a 148 square mile tract of land to be kept completely free of development. For the next decade, newspapers, the legislature, the courts, the governor, and the public would argue over the fate of this 148 square mile tract.

State government was unable to speak with a single voice on the matter. Some elected officials and state employees supported drilling while others opposed it. The Department of Natural Resources (DNR) was internally divided on the subject and its staff spoke on both sides of the issue. The DNR's on again, off again pronouncements and policies angered all parties.

From the industry perspective, the state had auctioned mineral rights under the Pigeon River Forest for record prices, then balked at issuing drilling permits, sometimes imposing temporary moratoriums on new lease auctions or on all new permits and in some cases denying requests for specific drilling permits. This action was unprecedented. In the past drilling permits had always followed leases. Although in 1977 the State Supreme Court affirmed previous lower court rulings that found that state law did not require the state to issue a drilling permit for land where the state had previously leased its mineral rights, the "change in the rules" led to confusion and anger among oil explorers.

The Pigeon River Country Association believed that no drilling was acceptable. The PRCA demanded that since the state had the authority to ban drilling regardless of whether or not it had leased the mineral rights, it should do so. If PRCA was angry with the DNR, the organization's anger turned to fury in 1975 when DNR Director Howard Tanner issued a proposed regulation which allowed significant drilling in the area. "Just one well, just one more, could ruin the whole forest," declared the president of the Pigeon River Country Association.

In northern Michigan, public opinion regarding drilling was divided. Some residents certainly agreed with the PRCA's position, but others saw the potential for economic growth outweighing the possibly environmental problems.

State representative Mark Thompson of Rogers City, for example, was blunt in his demand for drilling permits. Over the years, at a variety of public hearings held on the topic of oil exploration and exploitation, the industry, environmentalists, and the public all expressed themselves at great length. Attorney William A. Porter, representing diverse citizens of Otsego County at a Michigan Natural Resources Commission public hearing February 18, 1972, expressed the local, pro-development, opinion.

Kellum himself never fully appreciated the reasons for local support of drilling.

McClure Oil Company of Alma, denied a drilling permit on land it had previously leased, filed a test case in 1974 that would eventually find its way to the State Supreme Court in 1977. The controversy finally ended in 1980, with the passage of legislation allowing drilling in the southern third of the Pigeon River State Forest, while banning all drilling operations in the northern two-thirds of the forest for twenty years.

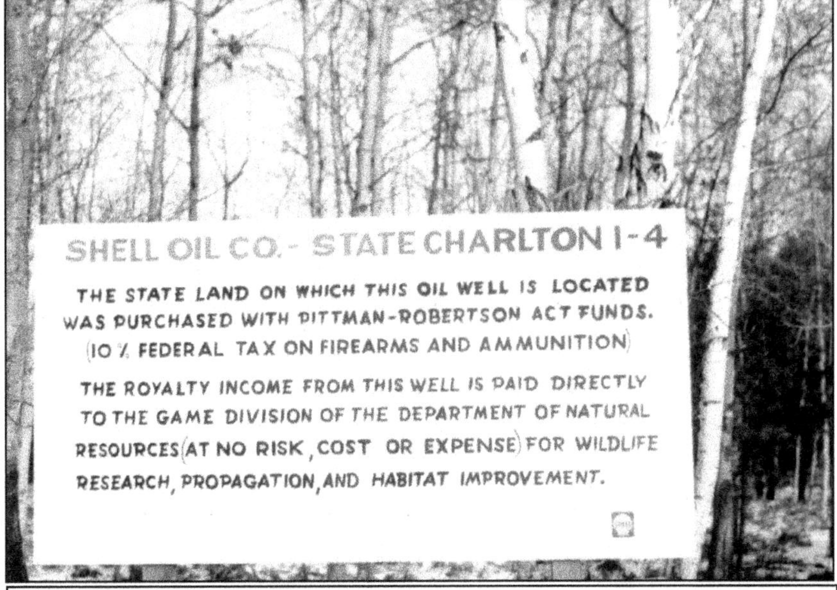

Michigan Oil & Gas News photo

This prophetic sign on a Shell Oil Company Otsego County discovery, telling of royalties dedicated to recreational purposes, foretold the philosophy of the Michigan Natural Resources Trust Fund.

Michigan Natural Resources Trust Fund

In October 1975 Tom Washington, the newly hired executive director of the Michigan United Conservation Clubs (MUCC), quietly began talking with Frank Mortl, executive director of the Michigan Oil And Gas Association.

Michigan Oil & Gas News photo

MUCC Executive Director Thomas Washington and MOGA Executive Director Frank L. Mortl in 1988.

Washington had decided it was time to abandon the environmentalists' "absolutely not" strategy in the Pigeon River Country controversy. "If we can't stop them," Washington said, "we should seek the most palatable plan and get all the concessions we can." Eventually an innovative and creative solution was reached that balanced the desire for economic development with the need for preserving the environment. MUCC and MOGA agreed that drilling should continue, however revenue the state realized from oil and gas leases and royalties would be used to buy more land for the use of Michigan's sportsmen. Although Washington was sharply criticized for this stand by some MUCC member organizations, he stood his ground going so far as to disparage the elk herd, which had often been the emotional heart of the discussion. "We are not," Washington said, "enamored with this species and do not feel this would be an irreplaceable loss to the state if, in fact, a total loss will occur." [1]

Governor William Milliken, in his 1976 state of the state address, expanded on the MUCC-MOGA solution, calling for all oil and gas revenues generated by the state to be placed in a "Heritage Trust Fund."

The Michigan Natural Resources Trust Fund was created by the legislature through Public Act 204 and was established on July 23, 1976, when then Governor Milliken signed Act 204 into law, creating the Michigan Land Trust Fund, known as the Kammer Recreational Land Trust Fund act of 1976[2].

Although Act 206 specified that "interest and earnings of the fund shall be used exclusively for the purchase of land or rights in land for hunt-

[1] Appendix A – MUCC's Tom Washington MNRTF history 1988 speech

[2] Appendix B – Kammer Land Trust Act of 1976

ing or fishing and recreation purposes including, but not limited to camping, hiking, picnicking, and swimming...and for any taxes owed by the state on the land". The Trust Fund Act 204 language dwelt a lot on oil and gas royalties from beneath the Pigeon River Country State Forest and talked about those monies being used to "improve the multipurpose use of the Pigeon River Country State Forest". Other mineral, oil or gas leases entered into by the State after the effective date of the Act provide additional revenues to the Fund.

The purpose of the legislation was to enable the acquisition (only) of land for recreational purposes, utilizing funding from the development of oil, gas, and other minerals from state owned lands.

The fund was the first in the nation that earmarked state revenue generated through oil and natural gas industry activity for the acquisition or improvement of environmentally sensitive land or for meeting community needs for outdoor recreation.

The 1976 Act established a five member board [3], including the Director of the Michigan Department of Natural Resources and the Chairman of the Michigan Natural Resources Commission and three citizens of the state appointed by the Governor of Michigan, specifying that one of the appointed members "shall be from a group representative of sportsman's

The 2015 MNRTF Board, here at their February 11, 2015 meeting l. to r.: Erin McDonough, Vice-Chairperson; Keith Creagh, Director of Michigan Department of Natural Resources (DNR); Brad Canale – Chair; Steve Hamp; and Samuel Cumming.

associations or interests". The sportsman's interest group represented on the board has traditionally been from the Michigan United Conservation Clubs (MUCC). The appointive member terms are for 3 years, with the initial three appointed member's terms designated as one for one year, one

[3] Appendix C – MNRTF Board Members 1977-2015

for two years and one for three years in order to establish a rotation among appointed members.

The Board reviews applications for Trust Fund grants and recommends them for legislative and the Governor's approval

Each year, one-third of the Fund's earnings in the previous fiscal year, plus the interest on the Fund's principal, up to $2.5, could be used for recreation land acquisition, with the remaining two-thirds applied to the Fund principal, which the 1976 Act capped at $100 million, excluding interest, without being specific about how funds in excess of the $100 million cap would be used.

The original philosophy of the Fund, as stated by the first MNRTF board of trustees, was:

- "To give major emphasis to the acquisition of lands or interests in lands which will provide the potential for recreation areas in or near urban areas;
- "To acquire lands or interest in lands which will provide access to and use of inland lakes, rivers, and streams or to preserve the natural characteristics of a floodplain;
- "To acquire lands or interests in lands which provide the potential for preserving or enhancing rare, fragile, or scenic areas or resources;
- "To acquire lands or interests in lands providing a habitat or protection for endangered or threatened species of fish, wildlife, and plant life;
- "To acquire lands and interest in lands to promote innovative and/or recreation opportunities;
- "To expand the public access to and use of the Great Lakes and connecting waters shoreline through the acquisition of land or interests in land;
- "To enhance the general values of the Pigeon River Country State Forest, and;
- "To acquire lands or interest inlands that will provide hunting and/or fishing opportunities."

After almost eighteen months of organization and establishing of guidelines, the Michigan Land Trust Board in January, 1978, recommended a list of 8 public recreation land acquisitions totaling $2.6 million. One of those first grants added 680 acres to the Pigeon River Country State Forest.

Gaylord Convention &Tourism Bureau photo
The first round of Trust Fund grants in 1978 included acquisition of 680 additional acres to the Pigeon River Country State Forest.

In the early years, the Fund also served as a means to help balance the state budget and fund the Michigan Economic Development Authority and other programs. Transfers were made to the Michigan General Fund amounting to $26 million in 1980 and 46.2 million in 1981. Another dip into the fund was a $5 million loan mandated to assist petroleum carriers in upgrading their double-bottom tankers.

Repeated "raids" over a period of seven years saw more than $100 million diverted to programs other than those in the original philosophy of the Fund.

Protests to the "raids" on the Fund grew louder and more widespread.

Voters in a statewide referendum election conducted in 1982 banned future "raids" on the Fund.

In the 1983 fiscal year, all revenues and interest went to appropriations to transfers for projects and 1984 to transfers and projects, with fiscal year 1985 seeing a return to an amount of revenues being added to the principal again and every year since.

Following a November 6, 1984, Michigan voter referendum at the polls which resulted in the Michigan Natural Resources Trust Fund Act 101 of 1985, implementing an amendment to the Michigan Constitution in 1985, assuring that funds would continue to be made available for lands acquisition. A quarter of the Fund's earning and interest were authorized for land acquisition and a quarter of earnings and interest would go to facility development by Act 101. Additionally, the Act raised the Fund's principal cap to $200 million, excluding interest, and allowed for the use of Trust monies to make some payments in lieu of taxes to local units of government.

Also, the 1985 legislation specifically earmarked $20 million per year "off the top" for the Michigan Strategic Fund.

While constitutional protection was provided to the MNRTF back in 1984, the Fund's future as a perpetual source of funds for public recreation land acquisition remained threatened by the annual diversion of $20 million to the Michigan Strategic Fund. The loss of revenue slowed the Funds' growth with the principal balance of the Fund standing at $88 million at the end of fiscal year ending September 30, 1994. At the end of the fiscal year September 30, 2005, the Fund's principal balance stood at $289,044,050.75.

Proposal P, passed by voters in 1994 amended the Michigan Constitution once more, implemented by Sections 324.1902 through 324.1908 of Act 451, Michigan's Natural Resources and Environmental Protection Act[4]. This prompted the end of any opportunity for future diversions from the MNRTF. Additionally, the proposal raised the cap on the Fund's principal amount from $200 million to $400 million and creating a Michigan State Parks Endowment Fund, which receives $10 million in MNRTF revenues each year for the operation, maintenance, and capital improvements of Michigan State Parks. Raising the cap to $400 million meant millions of additional dollars would be available under the program to protect the state's natural resources and provide public recreation opportunities far into the future.

Twenty-five years after MOGA and MUCC galvanized business, environmental and governmental groups into action to implement the Trust Fund, the two organizations spearheaded another campaign to sustain and augment the Michigan Natural Resources Trust Fund. MUCC and MOGA joined with the Michigan Chamber of Commerce, The Nature Conservancy of Michigan, the Michigan Municipal League, the Michigan Recreation and Park Association, the Michigan Natural Resources Commission and the Michigan Natural Resources Trust Fund at a November 26, 2001, press conference calling on the Michigan House of Representatives to take quick action to approve Senate Joint Resolution T.

The Senate Joint Resolution included in a "Funding for the Future" package, was a proposed constitutional amendment which would allow the Michigan Natural Resources Trust Fund to achieve higher earnings and make larger investments in Michigan's natural resources.

"Michigan oil and gas companies are committed to preserving and enhancing the natural resources that make Michigan so special, and this legislation will help that cause" Michigan Oil And Gas Association President Frank L. Mortl said at the conference.

Michigan United Conservation Club Executive Director James Goodhart echoed Mortl's comments. "We need to further the ability of the state to acquire prime lands for hunting, fishing and shooting range and 'Funds for the Future' provides a mechanism to do that."

---

[4] Appendix D – Excerpt from Michigan Act 451 of 1994

"After 25 years of success, we can truly say our state wouldn't look the same without the Michigan Natural Resources Trust Fund, " said Helen Taylor, State Director, Michigan Chapter of the Nature Conservancy. "Michigan needs a healthy and strong trust fund so that we can continue to protect Michigan's last great places."

In the August 6, 2002, primary election, state voters approved Proposal 2, the outgrowth of Senate Joint Resolution T. This voter mandate led to a September 22, 2002, Michigan Constitution amendment[5] which; raised the MNRTF cap on principal balance assets from $400 million to $500 million; removed the provision that when the MNRTF reached an asset total of $200 million, the state could no longer expend one third of the Fund's annual mineral resource revenues for public recreation projects; and allowed the state treasurer to invest MNRTF revenues in the same manner as is provided for in the Public Employees Retirement System Investment Act, a successful method of achieving a higher return on investment than other investment methods. The amendment further specified that when the $500 million principal cap was attained, "all revenue from oil and gas lease bonuses, rentals, delayed rentals and royalties received by the fund but for this limitation shall be deposited into the Michigan State Parks Endowment fund until the Michigan State Parks Endowment reaches an accumulated principal of $800 million. When the Michigan State Parks Endowment reaches an accumulated principal of $800 million, all revenues from bonuses, rentals, delayed rentals, and royalties shall be distributed as provided by law."

Any group, individual or unit of government can submit an application for land acquisition for management by the state or local unit of government. Development proposals may be submitted only by units of government or schools. All proposals submitted by local governments must be matched with a minimum of 25 percent of the total project cost.

The MNRTF board meets six times a year to evaluate applications, provide guidance to MDNR staff responsible for evaluating grant applications, and finally, to submit to the Legislature a priority list of lands recommended for acquisition and/or development.

Giving the board direction in determining how monies should be distributed are six program goals:

- Protecting natural resources;
- Providing public access to Michigan's waterways;
- Improving outdoor recreation in urban areas;
- Stimulating Michigan's economy through recreation-related tourism;
- Meeting community needs for outdoor recreation, and;

[5] Appendix E - Excerpt from State Constitution of Michigan

- Investing funds in projects that will yield the best long-term public recreation return.

The 12 criteria considered by the board and ranked by MDNR staff under board guidance until 2011 were:

1 Protection and use of significant natural resources.
2 Use of inland waters.
3 Population served.
4 Economic benefits.
5 Hunting, fishing and other wildlife related values.
6 Need for proposal.
7 Capability of applicant.
8 Site and project quality.
9 Special initiatives of the MNRTF board.
10 Financial need of the applicant.
11 Local match contribution.
12 Whether the county has oil and gas production.

In 2011, criteria # 12 was dropped by the MNRTF Board for reasons that will become apparent in the next chapter.

2010: The MNRTF Changes Forever

In 1929, the State of Michigan began leasing oil and gas lease rights to State-owned mineral properties at public auction. Until the dawn of Tuesday, May 4, 2010, more than 200 State lease auctions had taken place, producing $189.6 million cumulatively.

The May 4, 2010, State lease right auction, fueled by interest in an unproven Ordovician shale geological formation pushed the total bonus and rentals paid that day to $178,019,000.

In one day, all-time state revenues from auctioning oil and gas lease rights to State-owned mineral properties doubled .... to the shock and awe of industry and observers.

The initial "high-fives" in the face of such a tremendous shot in the arm the record influx of monies into the Michigan Natural Resources Trust Fund soon turned to head scratching contemplation and realization that such influx would push the Fund past its $500 million accumulated principal.

Unlike any previous time in the life of the MNRTF, there was no time to have the principal cap raised legislatively.

An October 1, 2010, amendment to Michigan Act 451, The Michigan Natural Resources and Environmental Protection Act[6] created a local recreational facilities fund to be administered by the Michigan Department

---

[6] Appendix F - Act 451 of 1994 – 2010 Amendments by Act 32

of Natural Resources as part of Michigan's Recreational Passport program and rescinded certain other parts of the act pertaining to the State Treasurer's duties in regards to the Michigan Natural Resources Trust Fund monies.

The record State Lease Auction made for a record MNRTF disbursement of grants at the MNRTF board meeting December 1, 2010.

"This is a historic meeting" 2011 MNRTF Board Chairman-elect said. "Future MNRTF grant funding will come from a formula that does not include oil and gas revenues from state-owned minerals, so MNRTF funding ability will be greatly abbreviated since we will be able to work with only the interest earned on the $500 accumulated principal. We have reached that principal and funded more than $900 million in public recreation projects in every county in the state thanks to the vision of those mid-1970s conservationists and our friends who produce oil and gas in our state."

That day the Board approved 117 grants (71 acquisition and 46 development) totaling $102,098,400, bringing the total appropriations numbers to 1,902 approved grants totaling $926,897,566. With the attrition of those totals brought about by withdrawn and not completed projects, the final number of active and successfully completed projects at the end of 2010 stood at 1,601 project grants totaling $816,682,867.

The MNRTF accumulated principal balance reached the $500 million mark in May, 2011.

How to apply for an MNRTF grant

For a listing of procedures and application forms, visit the Michigan Natural Resources website at www.michigan.gov/dnr then click on the word *Grants* on the left and, finally, click on the phrase *Michigan Natural Resources Trust Fund*. Those without computer access may contact Grants Management, Michigan Department of Natural Resources, P. O. Box 30424, Lansing MI 48909-7925, or call (517) 241-3687.

Application materials are generally available in January. With an April 1 deadline for applications to be considered that calendar year. Final grant recommendations are made by the MNRTF Board of Trustees late in the year (usually at their December meeting) after review and evaluation by the Michigan Department of Natural Resources Grants Management Division staff. After legislative approval of the MNRTF Board recommendations, appropriations are made.

MNRTF Signs of the Times

Signs designating Michigan Natural Resources Trust Fund projects have changed through the years. Above left is one of the earliest MNRTF signs at Devoe Park on Burt Lake in Indian River. Above right is the generic cast aluminum round logo most commonly used on MNRTF projects throughout the state. Below, left, is the sign adopted in 2008, identifying the principal source of funding for MNRTF and below right a rendering of the 2015 MNRTF project designation signs, genrally rendered in green with white lettering.

Alcona County

The area was a stop-off place for the voyageurs from the late 1660s. Alcona, meaning "Beautiful Woods", was designated a county in 1840, along with 12 other counties formally assigned that year. This brought Michigan's number of established counties to 48. The county, which is now Michigan's 75th most populated with 10,942 residents in 2010. Alcona County is Michigan's 30th largest county with 674 square miles and is bounded on the east by Lake Huron.

michiganfishingonline.com photo

MNRTF Acquisition Project TF70-86 South Bay – Hubbard Lake - $145,000. Originally Alcona Lake, was named for State Geologist Bella Hubbard.

Although natural gas was reported in 1892 test wells drilled near Alcona County's now defunct village of Killmaster, probably at the Berea or Antrim geological strata, 600 feet deep there. The county in modern times is the youngest of Michigan's commercially producing oil and natural gas counties. Since Alcona County's first commercial discovery was made in 1990, Alcona is Michigan's 32nd most drilled county with 551 holes drilled there in the search for oil and natural gas. Of the Michigan's 64 counties productive of oil and/or natural gas, with 2,387 barrels of crude oil production and 95.396 billion cubic feet of natural gas production through 2013, Alcona County is 63rd largest oil producer but 15th largest natural gas producer. Alcona County as an entity has received $520,400 in 3 Michigan Natural Resources Trust Fund grants, ranking the county 81st in number of grants received and 79th grant dollars awarded.

ALCONA COUNTY active or closed MNRTF Projects

CALEDONIA TOWNSHIP

TF12-015 Hubbard Lake North End Park	ACQ	$245,400

DNR - PARKS & RECREATION DIVISION

TF70-786 South Bay-Hubbard Lake	ACQ	$145,000

DNR - WILDLIFE DIVISION

TF70-890 Hubbard Lake Wetlands	ACQ	$130,000

ALCONA COUNTY TOTAL $ 520,400

Alger County

Alger County is named for lumberman Russell A. Alger, Governor of Michigan January 1, 1885, until January 1, 1887. Alger was a candidate for Republican Party Presidential candidacy in 1888, U. S. Secretary of War 1897-1899 and served as U. S. Senator until his 1907 death at 71. The county was set off from Schoolcraft County and officially organized in 1885. It's 918 square miles, make Alger County the 12th largest county and 77th largest in population with 9,601 residents.

MNRTF Project TF90-311, a $315,000 grant developed the Munising Municipal Marina, where tour boats depart for the Pictured Rocks National Lakeshore.

An Upper Peninsula County, Alger is one of those with no significant sedimentary geological strata, precluding the likelihood of the presence of oil and/or natural gas. Therefore no holes have been drilled there in the search for petroleum. The county has received $1,607,240 in 10 Michigan Natural Resources Trust Fund grants, ranking 58th in number of grants received and 65th in grant dollars awarded.

ALGER COUNTY active or closed MNRTF Projects

AU TRAIN TOWNSHIP		
TF10-076 AuTrain Township Heritage Trailhead	DEV	$246,700
BURT TOWNSHIP		
TF87-124 Carpenter Creek Beach	ACQ	$7,900
MUNISING		
TF06-082 Tourist Park Campground Expansion	DEV	$210,500
TF90-311 Munising City Marina	DEV	$315,000
MUNISING TOWNSHIP		
TF01-062 McQuisten Park Boardwalk	DEV	$174,640
TF03-024 McQuisten Park Boardwalk and Fishing Pier	DEV	$134,700
TF12-039 Munising Bay Universal Access Site	DEV	$86,200
TF13-142 Munising Tourist Campground	DEV	$200,000
TF13-141 Munising Bay Mountain Bike Trailhead	DEV	194,100
TF88-025 Munising Twp. Rec. Area	ACQ	$37,500

ALGER COUNTY TOTAL $ 1,607,240

Allegan County

Designated a county in 1831, Allegan County was established in 1835, two years before statehood was granted to Michigan. Allegan County is the state's 19th largest county with 828 square miles bounded on the west by Lake Michigan and is 18th most populous with 111,408 residents.

On the morning of April 23, 2011, Boy Scouts from Holland Michigan Troops 3044, 147 and 141 wave from the first landing Saugatuck's Mt. Baldhead Park Stairway, MNTRF Project TF07-036, $63,800.

Since oil was discovered in Allegan County in 1937, 3,385 holes have been drilled there in the search for oil and natural gas, making Allegan the state's second most drilled county of Michigan's 83 counties. Allegan County has produced 21,489,135 barrels of crude oil and 32.125 billion cubic feet of natural gas to rank 18th in oil and 32nd in natural gas production of Michigan's 64 counties productive of oil and/or natural gas.

There have been 30 Michigan Natural Resources Trust Fund grants totaling $20,349,772 awarded to Allegan County, ranking the county 15th in number of grants and 9th in grant monies received.

ALLEGAN COUNTY active or closed Projects

ALLEGAN

TF02-137 Brady Street/Riverfront Boardwalk Dev.	DEV	$300,000
TF10-096 Veterans Memorial Riverwalk Improvements	DEV	$45,000
TF90-235 Jaycee Park	DEV	$173,900

ALLEGAN COUNTY

TF00-076 Gun Lake County Park Improvements	DEV	$155,881
TF00-077 Dumont Lake County Park Improvements	DEV	$229,141
TF02-117 Bysterveld County Park Development	DEV	$500,000
TF05-001 New Richmond Bridge Park Development	DEV	$382,800
TF91-351 West Side Park	DEV	$96,800
TF95-126 Littlejohn Lake County Park	DEV	$96,000

TF13-042 West Side Park Improvements	DEV	$300,000
CASCO TOWNSHIP		
TF07-170 Lake Michigan Nature Preserve Acq. - Phase I	ACQ	$900,000
TF08-145 Casco Township Nature Preserve Phase II	ACQ	$668,800
TF10-066 Casco Township Nature Preserve	DEV	$154,900
TF10-167 Casco Township Nature Area Expansion	ACQ	$2,250,000
DNR – EXECUTIVE OFFICE		
TF127 Gate Property	ACQ	$450,000
DNR - PARKS & RECREATION DIVISION		
TF286 Saugatuck Dunes	ACQ	$650,000
DNR - WILDLIFE DIVISION		
TF560 Allegan Property	ACQ	$420,000
FILLMORE TOWNSHIP		
TF09-104 Fillmore Township Park Development	DEV	$201,000
LAKETOWN TOWNSHIP		
TF10-012 Wolter Woods Wildlife Corridor Acquisition	ACQ	$100,000
TF91-173 Wolters Park	ACQ	$225,000
TF95-024 Laketown Dunes Acquisition	ACQ	$600,000
TF11-007 Township Hall Park	DEV	$50,000
OTSEGO		
TF88-210 Brookside Park	DEV	$138,750
PLAINWELL		
TF97-040 Riverwalk	DEV	$321,000
SALEM TOWNSHIP		
TF95-197 Salem Township Park	ACQ	$23,600
SAUGATUCK		
TF07-036 Mt. Baldhead Park Stairway Renovation	DEV	$63,800
TF09-001 Saugatuck Harbor Natural Area Acq.	ACQ	$3,500,000
TF10-057 Saugatuck Harbor Natural Area Acq. - Phase II	ACQ	$7,000,000
WAYLAND		
TF05-047 Rabbit River Recreation Project	ACQ	$130,000
TF09-063 Rabbit River Park Development	DEV	$223,400

ALLEGAN COUNTY TOTAL $ 20,349,772

Downtown Allegan's Boardwalk and Veteran's Memorial Riverwalk, MNRTF grants TF02-137 and TF10-096 total $345,000.

Alpena County

Alpena County was originally named *Anamickee* County after an Ojibwa American Indian Chief when set aside from part of Mackinac County and unorganized territory in 1840. In 1843, Henry Rowe Schoolcraft renamed the county Alpena, allegedly combining Arabic and French words to describe the "thunder bird", or partridges populating the area. Alpena County was formally established in 1857.

With 574 square miles, Alpena County is 38th largest county and 49th largest in population with 29,598 residents.

On September 9, 2003, the Michigan Oil And Gas Association (MOGA) Award of Excellence was presented to City of Alpena for outstanding use of Michigan Natural Resources Trust Fund grants for the city's North Waterfront Park and Wildlife Sanctuary totaling $452,000. Present at the ceremonies at Alpena Island Park: were MOGA representatives from Gaylord Paxton Resources Mike Ryan, Noreen Klich, Becky Farmer, Chuck Simpson, Greg Vadnais, Jennifer Apsey, Bill Muzyl, Wanda Zaleski, Scott Lampert, along with Vernie Nethercut & Les Long - Alpena Wildlife Sanctuary Committee; Alpena Mayor Phil Ludlow, Deborah Pardike - Alpena Visitors Bureau.

Since oil was discovered there in 1973, 985 holes have been drilled in the search for oil and gas, making Alpena Michigan's 23rd most drilled county. Alpena County has produced 575,491 barrels of oil and 241.446 billion cubic feet of natural gas, ranking 55th and 7th respectively among the 64 oil or gas producing Michigan counties.

Alpena County has received $4,322,866 in 16 Michigan Natural Resources Trust Fund grants, ranking 39th in number of grants received and 41st in grant dollars awarded.

ALPENA COUNTY active or closed MNRTF Projects

Project	Type	Amount
ALPENA		
TF00-275 Harbor Breakwall Walkway Extension	DEV	$153,481
TF05-014 North Riverfront Park Heritage Improvements	DEV	$214,500
TF07-023 Starlite Beach Promenade Facilities Project	DEV	$443,300
TF596 Wildlife Sanctuary	ACQ	$237,500
TF87-016 Small Boat Harbor	DEV	$80,000
TF92-299 Thunder Bay River Plan	DEV	$195,000
TF95-180 River Plan-Phase 2	DEV	$279,800
TF99-353 Harbor Breakwall Walkway Extension	DEV	$155,685
TF13-022 NEST Alpena Regional Trailhead	DEV	$245,000
ALPENA TOWNSHIP		
TF02-128 Houghmaster Property Acquisition	ACQ	$1,392,900
TF99-262 Rockport Picnic Fishing Pier	DEV	$50,300
DNR - FISHERIES DIVISION		
TF952 Partridge Point	ACQ	$100,000
DNR - FOREST, MINERAL & FIRE MANAGEMENT		
TF571 El Cajon Bay	ACQ	$225,000
TF572 Hardwood Point-Lake Huron	ACQ	$450,000
SANBORN TOWNSHIP		
TF95-016 Sanborn Park Improvement	DEV	$26,800
WILSON TOWNSHIP		
TF11-124 Wolf Creek Park Improvements	DEV	$73,600

ALPENA COUNTY TOTAL $ 4,322,866

Sanborn Township photo

MNRTF Development grant TF95-016, $26,800 went to Sanborn Township Park for improvements.

Antrim County

Antrim County is named for a county in Ireland, not for the Antrim Shale geological strata that has been partially responsible for the bulk of Michigan's natural gas production in recent years. It was set off as a county in 1840 and was known as *Meigisee* County until 1843. Antrim County was formally established in 1863.

One of Michigan's smallest, Antrim County's 477 square miles make it 76th largest county and 61st largest in population with 23,598 residents.

Since oil was discovered there in 1972, 1,824 holes have been drilled in the search for oil and gas in Antrim County, ranking it 5th most drilled county. Antrim County has produced 2,846,425 barrels of oil and 410.417 billion cubic feet of natural gas, ranking 41st and 6th respectively among the 64 oil or gas producing Michigan counties. Antrim County has received $11,331,057 in 25 Michigan Natural Resources Trust Fund grants, ranking 18th in number of grants received and 17th in grant dollars awarded.

Antrim County photo

MNRTF grants TF03-160 andTF90-249, totaling $201,850, went to Antrim County for Barnes Park Development.

ANTRIM COUNTY active or closed MNRTF Projects

ANTRIM COUNTY

TF00-145	Grass River Natural Area Expansion	ACQ	$348,750
TF00-349	Antrim Creek Natural Area Dev. & Protection	DEV	$143,154
TF03-160	Barnes Park Improvements	DEV	$160,100

TF04-166 Waterfront Add. to Grass River Nat. Area	ACQ	$100,000
TF05-024 Grass River Natural Area Addition	ACQ	$50,000
TF06-014 North Shore Hunt Club Acquisition	ACQ	$2,093,000
TF07-113 Grass River Nature Center	ACQ	$400,000
TF07-163 Glacial Hills Pathway and Natural Area	ACQ	$162,000
TF86-186 Grass River Natural Area	ACQ	$45,000
TF90-249 Barnes Park	DEV	$41,750
TF95-051 Antrim Creek Natural Area	ACQ	$4,764,100
TF95-081 Grass River Boardwalk	DEV	$41,600
TF97-170 Grass River Natural Area Land Protection	ACQ	$243,178
TF98-269 Grass River Wetland Addition	ACQ	$86,925
TF99-436 Jabara Property	ACQ	$320,662
VILLAGE OF CENTRAL LAKE		
TF13-116 Thurston Park Improvements	DEV	$162,500
DNR - FISHERIES DIVISION		
TF592 Jordan River-Moorhead	ACQ	$120,000
DNR - FOREST, MINERAL & FIRE MANAGEMENT		
TF00-245 Sand Lake	ACQ	$675,000
ELLSWORTH		
TF06-092 Ellsworth Community Park Enhancements	DEV	$249,700
FOREST HOME TOWNSHIP		
TF00-165 North Arm Loon Nursery Acquisition	ACQ	$202,938
TF06-112 Glacial Hills Pathway and Natural Area	ACQ	$213,100
HELENA TOWNSHIP		
TF03-203 Coy Mountain Preserve Acquisition	ACQ	$93,000
TF1023 Chessie's Pause	ACQ	$180,000
TORCH LAKE TOWNSHIP		
TF91-340 Torch Lake Day Park	ACQ	$176,100
TF93-308 Torch/Bay Trail & Beach	ACQ	$258,500

ANTRIM COUNTY TOTAL $ 11,331,057

Torch Lake Township photo

Torch Lake Township used MNRTF grant TF91-340, $176,100, acquisition of the land for the William K. Good Day Park at the Torch Lake Nature Preserve at the Village of Torch Lake.

Arenac County

Named by Henry Schoolcraft by combining the Latin word "arena", meaning "sand" and Algonquin American Indian word "*akee*", meaning "land". Arenac County was set aside in 1831, annexed to Bay County in 1857 and formally organized in 1883. Arenac "sandland" County, with 367 square miles, is 81st largest county and 68th largest in population with 15,899 residents.

Since oil was discovered there in 1936, 988 holes have been drilled in the search for oil and gas. Arenac County has produced 55,247,558 barrels of oil and 49.126 billion cubic feet of natural gas, ranking 8th and 24th respectively among the 64 oil or gas producing Michigan counties.

Arenac County photo

MNRTF Project TF02-077, for $274,600, went to the Au Gres Point Arenac County Park.

Arenac County has received $2,140,700 in 5 Michigan Natural Resources Trust Fund grants, ranking 76th in number of grants received and 56th in grant dollars awarded.

ARENAC COUNTY active or closed MNRTF Projects

Project	Type	Amount
ARENAC COUNTY		
TF00-391 Arenac County Park Acquisition	ACQ	$900,000
TF02-077 Point Au Gres Park Improvements	DEV	$274,600
TF13-099 Point Au Gres Park Blue Water Trail	DEV	$126,100
DNR – WILDLIFE DIVISION		
F11 -0142 Wigwam Bay State Wildlife Area	ACQ	400,000
F14 -0141 Wigwam Bay State Wildlife Area	ACQ	440,000

ARENAC COUNTY TOTAL $ 2,140,700

Baraga County

Baraga County, formally established in 1875, was named for "the snowshoe Priest" Frederic Baraga, who traveled the Great Lakes for 37 years in the early 1800s opening missions for the Indians.

Village of Baraga photo

MNRTF Project TF09-120, total $50,000, went to develop the Village of Baraga Marina Boardwalk and Boat Launch.

With 904 square miles, Baraga County is 13th largest county and 78th largest in population with 8,860 residents.

As an Upper Peninsula county without significant sedimentary geological strata, the likelihood of the presence of oil and/or natural gas is precluded in Baraga County, so no holes have been drilled there to search for petroleum. Baraga County has received $1,346,600 in 9 Michigan Natural Resources Trust Fund grants, ranking 65th in number of grants received and 70th in grant dollars awarded.

BARAGA COUNTY active or closed MNRTF Projects

ARVON TOWNSHIP

Project	Type	Amount
TF14-0270 Waterfront Park Improvements	DEV	$45,000

BARAGA COUNTY

Project	Type	Amount
TF061 Point Abbaye	ACQ	$195,000

DNR - FOREST, MINERAL & FIRE MANAGEMENT

Project	Type	Amount
TF95-817 Point Abbaye	ACQ	$175,000

DNR - PARKS & RECREATION DIVISION

Project	Type	Amount
TF459 Big Huron River Mouth	ACQ	$115,000

L'ANSE

Project	Type	Amount
TF94-251 L'Anse Harbor Boat Launch	DEV	$91,600

L'ANSE AREA SCHOOLS

Project	Type	Amount
TF09-115 L'Anse Area Schools Village Park	DEV	$440,000

VILLAGE OF BARAGA

Project	Type	Amount
TF09-120 Marina Boardwalk and Boat Launch	DEV	$50,000
TF12-072 Marina Peninsula Boardwalk	DEV	$50,000
TF13-057 Baraga Lake Superior Shoreline	DEV	$185,000

BARAGA COUNTY TOTAL $ 1,346,600

Barry County

Michigan's eighth oldest County, Barry County was established in 1829 and named for Kentuckian William.T. Barry, Postmaster General 1829-1835, during Andrew Jackson's Administration.

With 556 square miles, Barry County is 38th largest county and 33rd largest in population with 59,173 residents.

Since oil was discovered there in 1939, 255 holes have been drilled in the search for oil and gas. Barry County has produced 937,635 barrels of oil and no natural gas, ranking 51st among the 64 oil producing Michigan counties.

Bridgefind.com photo

MNRTF grant TF08-107 $215,300, went to develop McKeown Bridge Park in Barry County.

Barry County has received $2,649,800 in 7 Michigan Natural Resources Trust Fund grants, ranking 73rd in number of grants received and 68th in grant dollars awarded.

BARRY COUNTY active or closed MNRTF Projects

Project	Type	Amount
BARRY COUNTY		
TF08-107 McKeown Bridge Park Development	DEV	$215,300
DNR – WILDLIFE DIVISION		
TF14-0233 Barry State Game Area	ACQ	$1,100,000
HASTINGS		
TF99-283 Hastings Riverwalk Development	DEV	$284,000
TF09-111 Hastings Riverwalk Development	DEV	$370,000
TF11-080 Tyden Park Hastings Riverwalk Extension	DEV	$244,900
TF13-080 Paul Henry Trail Extension Riverwalk Dev.	DEV	$300,000
MIDDLEVILLE		
TF14-0158 Middleville Waterfront Property	ACQ	$135,600

BARRY COUNTY TOTAL 2,649,800

Bay County

Bay County was named for the Saginaw Bay and where the mouth of the Saginaw River makes it a busy commercial and pleasure port. It is comprised of parts of Arenac, Midland and Saginaw counties, formally as Bay County in 1857.

With 444 square miles, Bay County is 79th largest county but 19th largest in population with 107,771 residents. Since oil was discovered there in 1935, 910 holes have been drilled in the search for oil and gas. Bay County has produced 32,917,076 barrels of oil and 71.712 billion cubic feet of natural gas, ranking 14th and 18th respectively among the 64 oil or gas producing Michigan counties.

Bay County has received $4,758,326 in 24 Michigan Natural Resources Trust Fund grants, ranking 22nd in number of grants received and 38th in grant dollars awarded.

BAY COUNTY active or closed MNRTF Projects

BAY CITY

TF06-022 Wenonah Park Renovation	DEV	$500,000
TF09-062 Birney Park Renovations	DEV	$325,000

Bay City's 27th Street Rail Trail was acquired and developed with MNRTF grants TF93-230 and TRF98-006, totaling $238,000.

TF87-128 Saginaw River Pier	DEV	$400,000
TF89-030 Wenonah Park Riverfront	DEV	$375,000
TF93-229 Riverwalk Land Acquisition	ACQ	$55,000
TF93-230 Railtrail-27th St. Land	ACQ	$60,000
TF98-006 27th Street Railtrail	DEV	$178,000
BAY COUNTY		
TF00-354 Bay County Wetlands Improvements	DEV	$88,226
TF01-087 Bay County Trail Improvements	DEV	$22,000
TF09-027 Pinconning Park Improvements	DEV	$325,000
TF88-110 Pinconning Park Improvements	DEV	$60,000
TF95-255 Keit Linear Park	ACQ	$375,000

Bay City's 27th Saginaw River Pier was developed with MNRTF grant TF87-128 in the amount of $400,000. Bay City has received $1,893,000 in seven Michigan Natural Resources Trust Fund grants.

DNR - FISHERIES DIVISION		
TF90-186 Saginaw Bay Shore Dev.	DEV	$150,000
DNR - PARKS & RECREATION DIVISION		
TF91-020 Saginaw River Boat Access	ACQ	$500,000
TF95-299 Mackinac Island Land Acquisition	ACQ	$250,000
DNR - WILDLIFE DIVISION		
TF381 Quanicassee SGA	ACQ	$135,000
ESSEXVILLE		
TF91-254 Smith Park Improvements	DEV	$69,000
FRANKENLUST TOWNSHIP		
TF11-089 Great Lakes Bay Reg. Trail Bridge	DEV	$300,000
TF14-234 Great Lakes Bay Reg. Trail Development	DEV	$280,000

FRASER TOWNSHIP		
TF95-253 Linwood Road Scenic Point	DEV	$53,000
HAMPTON TOWNSHIP		
TF00-063 Expansion of Finn Road Park	ACQ	$130,800
PINCONNING		
TF97-167 Pinconning Riverwalk Land Acquisition	ACQ	$18,000
PORTSMOUTH TOWNSHIP		
TF95-200 Township Railtrail	DEV	$102,300
WILLIAMS TOWNSHIP		
TF913 Williams Township Park Expansion	ACQ	$7,000

BAY COUNTY TOTAL $ 4,758,326

At September 13, 2004, ceremonies, the Michigan Oil And Gas Association and the Bay Area Convention and Visitors Bureau presented an Award of Excellence Award to the City of Bay City for outstanding use of Michigan Natural Resources Trust Fund grants in Wenonah Park. Present were, l. to r.: Michigan Sen. James Barcia - D-Bay City; Tom Nieman - Executive Director-Bay Arts Council; Frank L. Mortl – President, Michigan Oil And Gas Association; Tom Mall - Vice Chairman of the Board, Michigan Oil And Gas Association; Shirley Roberts - Executive Director, Bay Area Convention and Visitors Bureau; Bob Katt – Mayor of Bay City and Robert Bellman - City Manager- Bay City.

Benzie County

Benzie County's name came from an English interpretation of the name the French gave the areas primary river *Aux Bec Scies*, which was further corrupted from "Betsie". It was set off as a county from neighboring Leelanau County and formally established in 1863.

With 321 square miles, Benzie County is the smallest Michigan county and 65th largest in population with 17,525 residents. Since oil was discovered there in 1976, 178 holes have been drilled in the search for oil and gas. Benzie County has produced 6,913,645 barrels of oil and 15.352 billion cubic feet of natural gas, ranking 30th and 39th respectively among the 64 oil or gas producing Michigan counties. Benzie County has received $11,701,453 in 21 Michigan Natural Resources Trust Fund grants, ranking 27th in number of grants received and 17th in grant dollars awarded.

Grand Traverse Regional Land Conservancy photo

MNRTF grants TF97-082, 98-264 and 10-164, totaling $3,988,175, went to acquiring land for inclusion in the Railroad Point Natural area near Beulah on the shores of Crystal Lake, preserving the largest undeveloped parcel left on the lake.

BENZIE COUNTY active or closed MNRTF Projects

ALMIRA

TF08-015 Ann Lakefront Park Acquisition	ACQ	$478,100

ALMIRA TOWNSHIP

TF01-016 Ransom Lake Natural Area	ACQ	$859,920

TF05-118 Ransom Lake Natural Area	DEV	$81,400
BENZIE COUNTY		
TF10-164 Railroad Point Natural Area Expansion	ACQ	$1,387,100
TF97-082 Railroad Point-Crystal Lake	ACQ	$2,142,037
TF98-264 Railroad Point Natural Area Add., Crystal Lake	ACQ	$459,038
TF99-075 Betsie Valley Trail-Trailhead Facilities	DEV	$254,263
TF99-401 Betsie Valley Trail	DEV	$432,000

Benzie County photo

MNRTF grants TF01-016, and 05-118, Acquisition and Development grants totaling $941,320, went to Almira Township's Ransom Lake.

BEULAH		
TF10-073 Crystal Lake Waterfront Revitalization	DEV	$227,500
DNR - FISHERIES DIVISION		
TF93-433 Betsie River Access	DEV	$228,800
DNR - FOREST, MINERAL & FIRE MANAGEMENT		
TF774 Pearl Lake	ACQ	$180,000
TF92-860 Platte Rivermouth	ACQ	$140,000
TF94-293 Betsie Valley Trail Corridor	ACQ	$500,000
TF98-189 Pearl Lake Property	ACQ	$911,050
DNR – FOREST RESOURCES DIVISION		
TF13-124 Dair Creek Property	ACQ	$700,000
DNR - PARKS & RECREATION DIVISION		
TF95-808 Crystal Lake-Denton Property	ACQ	$850,000
ELBERTA		
TF08-034 South Elberta Dunes Natural Area Acquisition	ACQ	$1,158,800
TF98-033 A.A.RR Park/Betsie Valley Trail Head Dev.	DEV	$314,545
TF99-014 Historic Waterfront Trailhead Park-Ph. II	DEV	$258,000
FRANKFORT		
TF03-175 Lake Michigan Beach Park Restoration	DEV	$92,000
LONG LAKE TOWNSHIP		
TF14-223 Cedar Run Creek Parking	DEV	$46,900

BENZIE COUNTY TOTAL $ 11,701,453

Berrien County

Berrien County, home of the first U.S. Highway Travel Information, opened in 1935 on U.S. 12 near New Buffalo, was named in honor of Georgian John M. Berrien, who was President Andrew Jackson's Attorney General 1829-1831. It was set off and formally established in 1829.

With 571 square miles, Berrien County is 42nd largest county and 15th largest in population with 156,813 residents.

The Village of Berrien Springs used MNRTF grant TF-96-060, $43,350 to improve their Shamrock Park and Campground (only one we know of with an onsite charter fishing service) and will use grant TF10-109 $306,800, for more campsites in the inset area.

Since oil was discovered there in 1940, 96 holes have been drilled in the search for oil and gas. Berrien County has produced 35,501 barrels of oil and no natural gas, ranking 60th among the 64 oil or gas producing Michigan counties. Berrien County has received $15,424,163 in 38 Michigan Natural Resources Trust Fund grants, ranking 11h in number of grants received and 13th in grant dollars awarded.

BERRIEN COUNTY active or closed MNRTF Projects

BARODA TOWNSHIP		
TF10-071 Hess Lake Park Improvements	DEV	$256,000
BENTON HARBOR		
TF89-114 Jean Klock Park	DEV	$375,000
TF13-406 Union Field Park Improvements	DEV	$300,000
BERRIEN COUNTY		
TF00-081 Galien River County Park Preserve Acq.	ACQ	$832,500
TF10-011 Galien River County Park Development	DEV	$500,000
TF308 Manion Property	ACQ	$200,000

TF89-130 Silver Beach County Park-Phase I	ACQ	$1,500,000
TF90-030 Silver Beach County Park-Phase II	ACQ	$1,925,000
TF93-378 Silver Beach County Park	DEV	$375,000
TF12-108 Silver Beach County Park	DEV	$300,000
TF13-043 Love Creek County Park Expansion	ACQ	$114,500
TF14-143 Rocky Gap Improvements	DEV	$300,000
BERRIEN SPRINGS		
TF96-060 Shamrock Park Improvement	DEV	$43,350
BUCHANAN		
TF11-039 McCoy's Creek Trail Development	DEV	$288,000
CHIKAMING TOWNSHIP		
TF00-317 Chikaming Township Park & Preserve Acq.	ACQ	$1,499,788
TF03-137 Township Park and Preserve Development	DEV	$193,200
DNR - PARKS & RECREATION DIVISION		
TF671 Grand Mere Dunes	ACQ	$1,000,000
TF672 Grand Mere Dunes	ACQ	$225,000
TF848 Bridgman Dunes	ACQ	$2,250,000
DNR - WILDLIFE DIVISION		
TF95-810 Boyle Lake Property	ACQ	$500,000
LINCOLN TOWNSHIP		
TF90-129 Lincoln Twp. Beach/Nature	DEV	$81,000
NEW BUFFALO		
TF89-236 Transient Boat Mooring Facility	DEV	$266,300
NEW BUFFALO TOWNSHIP		
TF93-104 Memorial Park Addition-2	ACQ	$14,700
TF13-064 Kruger Road Park	ACQ	$150,000
NILES		
TF08-079 Riverfront and Plym Park Trail Dev.	DEV	$170,500
TF91-091 Riverfront Park Property	ACQ	$90,000
TF99-145 Riverfront Park Dock and Pier	DEV	$103,125
NILES TOWNSHIP		
TF09-082 Niles Community Park Expansion	ACQ	$90,000
TF12-111 Indiana-Michigan River Valle Trail	DEV	$286,000
ST. JOSEPH		
TF97-111 Lookout Park Expansion	ACQ	$145,000
TF11-095 Lions Park Beach Developments	DEV	$247,100
ST. JOSEPH TOWNSHIP		
TF09-017 Maiden Lane Community Park Imp.	DEV	$70,000
TF93-014 MDOT Property Development	ACQ	$102,000
VILLAGE OF BERRIEN SPRINGS		
TF10-109 Shamrock Park Campground Expansion	DEV	$306,800
WATERVLIET		
TF01-011 Hays Park Improvements	DEV	$70,000
TF04-057 Hays Park Project	DEV	$42,300
TF91-391 Mill Creek Park Development	DEV	$114,000
WEESAW TOWNSHIP		
TF07-082 Weesaw Township Park Acquisition	ACQ	$98,000

BERRIEN COUNTY TOTAL $ 15,424,163

Branch County

Branch County was named in honor of North Carolinian John Branch, who served as President Andrew Jackson's Secretary of War 1829-31. It was established as a county from an unorganized territory in 1829.

Branch County photo

MNRTF grants TF1044 and 10-033 $29,500, went the City of Coldwater for park acquisition and development.

With 507 square miles, Branch County is 71st largest county and 38th largest in population with 45,248 residents. Since oil was discovered there in the 1990s, 100 holes have been drilled in the search for oil and gas. Branch County has produced 4,207 barrels of oil and no natural gas, ranking 63rd among the 64 oil producing Michigan counties. Branch County has received $2,679,800 in 7 Michigan Natural Resources Trust Fund grants, ranking 71st in number of grants received and 52nd in grant dollars awarded.

BRANCH COUNTY active or closed MNRTF Projects

Project	Type	Amount
BRANCH COUNTY		
TF99-122 Quincy Park Improvements	DEV	$444,000
TF12-027 Memorial Park Improvements	DEV	$140,000
COLDWATER		
TF10-033 Optimist Park Playground Renovation	DEV	$15,000
TF1044 Coldwater Linear Park Exp	ACQ	$14,500
COLDWATER TOWNSHIP		
TF10-105 Coldwater Township Hall Park	DEV	$266,300
DNR - PARKS & RECREATION DIVISION		
TF86-126 Coldwater Lake Farms Ph. II	ACQ	$900,000
TF975 Coldwater Lake Farms	ACQ	$900,000
BRANCH COUNTY TOTAL $ 2,679,800		

Calhoun County

Calhoun County was named to honor John C. Calhoun 1782-1850, who served as U.S. Vice President for President Andrew Jackson from 1825-1832. It was set off as a county from unorganized territory in 1829 and formally established in 1833.

With 709 square miles, Calhoun

City of Battle Creek photo

MNRTF grant TF617, $995,000, went to help acquire land for Battle Creek's Lineal Park.

County is 27th largest county and 17th largest in population with 136,146 residents. Since oil was discovered there in 1941, 1,324 holes have been drilled in the search for oil and gas. Calhoun County has produced 21,622.614 barrels of oil and 40.547 billion cubic feet of natural gas, ranking 17th and 27th respectively among the 64 oil or gas producing Michigan counties. Calhoun County has received $4,241,876 in 16 Michigan Natural Resources Trust Fund grants, ranking 39th in number of grants received and 43rd in grant dollars awarded.

CALHOUN COUNTY active or closed MNRTF Projects

ALBION		
TF00-194 Stoffer Plaza Improvements	DEV	$55,500
TF01-070 Kalamazoo Riverfront Trail Acquisitions	ACQ	$56,250
TF07-004 Rieger Park Swimming and Beach Project	DEV	$127,500
TF86-242 Riverfront Development	ACQ	$45,500
BATTLE CREEK		
TF03-107 Bailey Park Improvements	DEV	$229,300
TF617 Lineal Park	ACQ	$995,000

TF89-095 Bailey Park Renovation	DEV	$375,000
TF99-187 Southside Park Land Purchase (Lakeview Woodland Park)	ACQ	$500,000
TF13-010 Willard Park Beach Relocation	DEV	300,000
CALHOUN COUNTY		
TF10-031 Calhoun County Trailway	DEV	$500,000
TF99-193 Ott Preserve Improvements	DEV	$231,962
HOMER		
TF99-070 Lakefront Park Improvements	DEV	$89,690

City of Marshall photo

Four MNRTF projects totaling $736,174 went to development of Marshall's Riverwalk.

MARSHALL		
TF00-139 Riverwalk Development	DEV	$191,444
TF94-078 Waterfront Trail Development	DEV	$157,500
TF98-027 Marshall Riverfront Trail-Stage III	ACQ	$29,230
TF98-040 Riverfront Trail-Stage II	DEV	$358,000

CALHOUN COUNTY TOTAL $ 4,241,876

Cass County

Cass County is among Michigan's oldest counties and is named for Lewis Cass 1782-1866, appointed Governor of the Michigan Territory by President Madison in 1813 and serving in that position until 1831, when he resigned to become Secretary of War for Andrew Jackson, then became U.S. Ambassador to France until 1842. From 1845 until 1848, Cass represented Michigan in the U.S. Senate and was again Secretary of War for President Buchanan. Cass County was organized in 1829 from an unorganized territory.

Cass County is 74th largest county with 492 square miles and 35th largest in population with 52,293 residents.

Since oil was discovered there in 1930, 365 holes have been drilled in the search for oil and gas. County has produced 687,507 barrels of oil and no natural gas, ranking 54th among the 64 oil producing Michigan counties.

MNRTF grants TF89-251, 96-087 and 99-226, a total $329,100, went to acquire lands for Cass County's 820 acre multi-use Dr. T. K. Lawless Park, open all year, proudly displaying signs for all 3 grants.

Cass County has received $2,539,447 in 12 Michigan Natural Resources Trust Fund grants, ranking 49th in number of grants received and 53rd in grant dollars awarded.

CASS COUNTY active or closed MNRTF Projects

CASS COUNTY		
TF89-251 Dr. T. K. Lawless Park	DEV	$81,400
TF96-087 Dr. T. K. Lawless Park East 80	ACQ	$96,000
TF99-226 Dr. T. K. Lawless Park North	ACQ	$151,700
DNR – FISHERIES DIVISION		
TF14-200 Dowagiac Creek Access	ACQ	$749,900

DOWAGIAC

TF08-021 Youth Sports Park Acquisition	ACQ	$100,000
TF89-126 Rudolphi Woods	ACQ	$115,100
TF94-100 Northwest Park	ACQ	$64,500
TF98-010 Heddon Park	DEV	$42,647

MNRTF grant TF98-010, $42,647, helped develop Dowagiac's James Heddon Park, alongside a millpond near the spot where Heddon tossed a small piece of wood he'd been carving into the water, where it was struck by a bass. The incident inspired Heddon to build a topwater fishing lure which he called the "Dowagiac." By the 1920s, Heddon's was the world's largest producer of quality fishing tackle.

TF11-016 Silver Creek Russom Park	DEV	$300,000
MICHIGAN STATE UNIVERSITY		
TF70-649 Newton Woods	ACQ	$440,000
SILVER CREEK TOWNSHIP		
TF08-151 Silver Creek Area Youth Sports Park	ACQ	$100,000
TF11-017 Silver Creek Russom Park	DEV	$298,200

CASS COUNTY TOTAL $ 2,539,447

Charlevoix County

Charlevoix County was named for Jesuit priest Pierre Francois Xavier de Charlevoix, 1682-1731, a New France historian. It was set off as a county from parts of Antrim, Emmet, and Otsego counties and formally established in 1869.

With 417 square miles, Charlevoix County is 80th largest county and 54th largest in population with 25,949 residents.

City of Charlevoix photo

The City of Charlevoix has received five Michigan Natural Resources Trust Fund grants totaling $1,341,955.

Since oil was discovered there in 1992, 245 holes have been drilled in the search for oil and gas. Charlevoix County has produced no oil and 24.523 billion cubic feet of natural gas, ranking 34th among the 64 oil and/or gas producing Michigan counties.

Charlevoix County has received $7,861,980 in 22 Michigan Natural Resources Trust Fund grants, ranking 25th in number of grants received and 27th in grant dollars awarded.

CHARLEVOIX COUNTY active or closed MNRTF Projects

BAY TOWNSHIP		
TF87-222 Eagle Island/Walloon Lake	ACQ	$90,000
BOYNE CITY		
TF99-180 Boyne River Walk Project	DEV	$187,925
TF13-107 Riverside Park Annex	ACQ	$48,600
CHARLEVOIX		
TF00-223 Wharfside Building Acquisition	ACQ	$500,000
TF875 Ferry Avenue Beach Expansion	ACQ	$132,000

TF89-123 Ferry Beach Park	DEV	$215,700
TF98-077 Depot Beach Park Land Acquisition	ACQ	$224,155
TF99-250 Michigan Beach Park Improvements	DEV	$270,100

Charlevoix Township photo

MNRTF grant TF07-112, $232,500, went to Charlevoix Township for Development of the Whiting Park Universal Access.

CHARLEVOIX COUNTY		
TF07-112 Whiting Park Universal Access Improvements	DEV	$232,500
TF89-667 Thumb Lake Beach Acq.	ACQ	$400,000
TF12-070 Butler Trust Property	ACQ	$214,200
TF13-052 Boyne City to Charlevoix Trail	DEV	$300,000
CHARLEVOIX SCHOOLS		
TF89-258 Beaver Island Lighthouse	ACQ	$33,800
CHARLEVOIX TOWNSHIP		
TF87-317 North Point Sand Dunes	ACQ	$400,000
TF11-073 Boyne City to US 31 Trail	DEV	$300,000
DNR - FOREST, MINERAL & FIRE MANAGEMENT		
TF05-142 Bear River Parcel Conservation Easement	ACQ	$280,000
TF98-190 Little Sand Bay, Beaver Island	ACQ	$400,000
EVELINE TOWNSHIP		
TF10-149 Eveline Township Lake Charlevoix Access	ACQ	$46,500
HAYES TOWNSHIP		
TF12-036 Camp Seagull – Lake Charlevoix	ACQ	$3,375,000
PEAINE TOWNSHIP		
TF13-089 Fox Point Acquisition	ACQ	$155,300
ST. JAMES TOWNSHIP		
TF92-319 Gull Harbor Park	ACQ	$30,000
WILSON TOWNSHIP		
TF86-337 Wilson Township Park	ACQ	$26,200

CHARLEVOIX COUNTY TOTAL $ 7,861,980

Cheboygan County

Cheboygan County was named for the river that runs through it, which in turn is believed to have been named for the Chippewa American Indians, *Cheboys* in Ojibwa and *gan* in the same language, meaning "water". It was set off as a county in 1840 and formally established in 1853.

The Mackinaw City Pier was developed with MNRTF grant TF88-181 for $257,700.

With 716 square miles, Cheboygan County is 25th largest county and 53rd largest in population with 26,152 residents.

Since oil was discovered there in 1976, 141 holes have been drilled in the search for oil and gas. Cheboygan County has produced 3,338,041 barrels of oil and 3.851 billion cubic feet of natural gas, ranking 38th and 47th respectively among the 64 oil or gas producing Michigan counties.

Cheboygan County has received $23,244,400 in 35 Michigan Natural Resources Trust Fund grants, ranking 14th in number of grants received and 8th in grant dollars awarded.

CHEBOYGAN COUNTY active or closed MNRTF Projects

BURT TOWNSHIP

TF10-047 Burt Lake Non-Motorized Trail Dev.	DEV	$398,500

CHEBOYGAN

TF02-002 Major City Park Riverfront Imp. Project II	DEV	$317,900
TF86-130 Major City Park Expansion	ACQ	$45,000
TF95-118 Gordon Turner Park Restroom	DEV	$45,800
TF99-055 Major City Park Riverfront Improvement	DEV	$266,200

DNR - FOREST, MINERAL & FIRE MANAGEMENT

TF04-133 Lee Grande Ranch Conservation Easement	ACQ	$2,750,000
TF05-141 Lee Grande Ranch Conservation Easement	ACQ	$2,750,000
TF06-135 Hackett Lake Conservation Easement	ACQ	$2,600,000
TF09-137 Little Pigeon River Property Acquisition	ACQ	$1,800,000
TF10-123 Pigeon River Property	ACQ	$1,000,000

TF470 Pigeon River-Ford	ACQ	$285,000
TF546 Pigeon River Moorhead	ACQ	$500,000
TF547 Pigeon River-Small Inhold.	ACQ	$100,000
TF679 Pigeon River Country S.F.-Inholding	ACQ	$100,000
TF894 Black Mountain Recreation Area	ACQ	$85,000
TF895 Pigeon River State Forest Inholdings	ACQ	$200,000
TF90-872 Mackinaw City/Hawks RR	ACQ	$1,800,000
TF97-184 Cheboygan-Gaylord Trail Corridor - Phase I	ACQ	$1,000,000
TF98-191 Cheboygan-Gaylord Trail-Phase II	ACQ	$1,500,000
TF98-303 Cheboygan-Gaylord Trail: Phase III	ACQ	$1,275,000
TF99-287 Cheboygan-Gaylord Trail-Phase V	ACQ	$1,275,000
TF99-442 Cheboygan-Gaylord Trail-Phase VI	ACQ	$1,250,000
DNR – PARKS & RECREATION DIVISION		
TF13-133 Cheboygan State Park	ACQ	$40,000
INVERNESS TOWNSHIP		
TF98-255 Polish Line Beach Expansion Project	ACQ	$75,000
MACKINAW CITY		
TF88-181 Mackinaw City Pier	DEV	$257,700
TF90-286 Deliyandes Property	ACQ	$94,500
MULLETT TOWNSHIP		
TF11-002 Topinabee Lakeside Park Improvements	DEV	$280,000
TUSCARORA TOWNSHIP		
TF00-040 Tuscarora Township Park Acquisition	ACQ	$1,184,000
TF09-072 Indian River Pathway Development	DEV	$393,400
TF10-063 Veterans Pier Development	DEV	$384,900
TF1033 DeVoe Park Burt Lake	ACQ	$135,000
TF11-084 Marina Park Trailhead Dev.	DEV	$250,900

MNRTF grant TF1033 for 135,000, went to acquire land that would become Tuscarora Township's DeVoe Park on Burt Lake.

VILLAGE OF MACKINAW CITY		
TF10-046 Conkling Heritage Park Improvements	DEV	$74,900
TF12-022 Gary R. Williams Park Extension	DEV	$241,200
WOLVERINE		
TF14-171 Renovations and Improvements of Lumberman's Park and Trailhead	DEV	$289,500

CHEBOYGAN COUNTY TOTAL $ 23,244,400

Chippewa County

Chippewa County was named for the Ojibwa Indian tribe also known as the Chippewas. It was set off as a county from Mackinac County in 1827 and formally established the same year.

Chippewa County's 1,561 square miles make it the 2nd largest Michigan county and 42nd largest in population with 38,520 residents.

An Upper Peninsula county, Chippewa is one of those with little significant sedimentary geological strata, precluding the likelihood of the presence of oil and/or natural gas. Regardless, 13 holes have been drilled there in the search for oil and natural gas with no result.

Chippewa County has received $6,093,800 in 18 Michigan Natural Resources Trust Fund grants, ranking 29th in number of grants received and 31st in grant dollars awarded.

CHIPPEWA COUNTY active or closed MNRTF Projects

DNR - FOREST, MINERAL & FIRE MANAGEMENT DIVISION

Project	Type	Amount
TF87-247 Island Explorer Trail	DEV	$300,000
TF92-847 Lake Superior Property	ACQ	$60,000
TF96-871 Whitefish Point	ACQ	$250,000
TF99-298 Biehl Property	ACQ	$250,000
TF10-157 Big Trout Lake Acquisition	ACQ	$1,000,000
TF14-272 Lake Superior Dune Swale Complex	ACQ	$530,000

DNR - PARKS & RECREATION DIVISION

Project	Type	Amount
TF96-269 Tahquamenon Falls River Frontage Acq.	ACQ	$600,000
TF13-132 Lime Island Recreation Area.	ACQ	$180,000

DNR - WILDLIFE DIVISION

Project	Type	Amount
TF00-254 Ten-Mile Marsh in East U.P. Acquisition	ACQ	$82,500
TF03-199 Upper Peninsula Deer Habitat Acquisitions	ACQ	$1,500,000

HULBERT TOWNSHIP

Project	Type	Amount
TF89-112 Rec. Trail Complex	ACQ	$37,600

KINROSS TOWNSHIP

TF87-014 Kincheloe Development	DEV	$80,000

Michigan Natural Resources Trust Fund grants TRF07-105, TRF07-174 and TRF97-234 totaling $683,500 were invested in Sault Ste. Marie's Ashmun Park.

SAULT STE MARIE

TF07-105 Ashmun Bay Park Trail Parcel Acquisition	ACQ	$36,000
TF07-174 Ashmun Bay Park Entrance Parcel Acq.	ACQ	$100,000
TF97-234 Ashmun Bay Park Acquisition	ACQ	$547,500
TF03-116 Sherman Park Beach Accessibility/Upgrade	DEV	$198,300
TF08-068 Rotary Park Development	DEV	$299,700
TF09-105 Sherman Park Picnic Shelter Development	DEV	$42,200

CHIPPEWA COUNTY TOTAL $6,093,800

Clare County

Called Kaykakee County when first set aside from part of Mackinac County in 1840, the area became Clare County in 1843, the name honoring Ireland's County Clare, homeland of many of the county's early settlers.

Lincoln Township's Shingle Lake Park at the 1880s lumbertown of Lake George received MNRTF grants TF07-035, $43,600 for park improvements. Newly-laid asphalt internal roads were curing in the park when this photo was taken.

Clare County's 567 square miles, make it 47th largest county and 48th largest in population with 30,926 residents.

Since oil was discovered there in 1938, 1,624 holes have been drilled in the search for oil and gas, making it 9th most drilled in the state. Clare County has produced 40,818,017 barrels of oil and 96.590 billion cubic feet of natural gas, ranking 11th and 14th respectively among the 64 oil or natural gas producing Michigan counties. Clare County has received $1,502,700 in 5 Michigan Natural Resources Trust Fund grants, ranking 77th in number of grants received and 68th in grant dollars awarded.

CLARE		
TF05-171 Pere Marquette Trail Extension	ACQ	$99,100
TF07-096 Pere Marquette Rail Trail Extension	DEV	$500,000
DNR - EXECUTIVE DIVISION		
TF12-132 Cranberry Lake Property	ACQ	$660,000
DNR - WILDLIFE DIVISION		
TF686 Deadman Swamp SGA	ACQ	$200,000
LINCOLN TOWNSHIP		
TF07-035 Shingle Lake Park Improvement	DEV	$43,600

CLARE COUNTY TOTAL $ 1,502,700

Clinton County

Clinton County is named for New York Governor DeWitt Clinton 1769-1828, who constructed the Erie Canal, opening "the West", including Michigan, to accelerated settlement. It was set off as a county in 1831 and formally established in 1839.

Francis Motz County Park is the largest MNRTF project in Clinton County.

With 572 square miles, Clinton County is 41st largest county and 26th largest in population with 75,382 residents. Since oil was discovered there in 1942, 90 holes have been drilled in the search for oil and gas. Clinton County has produced 4,121 barrels of oil and no natural gas, ranking 62nd among the 64 oil and/or gas producing Michigan counties. Clinton County has received $4,353,598 in 16 Michigan Natural Resources Trust Fund grants, ranking 41st in number of grants received and 38th in grant dollars awarded.

CLINTON COUNTY active or closed MNRTF Projects

Project	Type	Amount
BATH TOWNSHIP		
TF93-208 Park Lake Beach & Parking	ACQ	$42,800
TF11-050 Park Lake Preserve	ACQ	$40,000
CLINTON COUNTY		
TF04-047 Searles Property Acquisition	ACQ	$419,700
TF07-011 Motz County Park Development	DEV	$233,000
TF10-029 Motz County Park Addition	ACQ	$1,886,300
DEWITT		
TF89-139 Park Land Purchase	ACQ	$75,000
TF97-140 Dill and Riverside Parks	DEV	$317,298
TF12-101 Riverside Park Improvements	DEV	$64,400
DEWITT TOWNSHIP		
TF03-208 Water's Edge Park Acquisition	ACQ	$55,000
TF10-017 Valley Farms Park Miracle League Field	DEV	$394,200
TF12-099 Looking Glass River Park Improvements	DEV	$78,000
DNR - OFFICE OF COMMUNICATIONS		
TF09-129 Rose Lake Shooting Range Development	DEV	$75,000

Francis Motz County Park in Section 30 of Greenbush Township northwest of St. Johns, is Clinton County's first park, having been acquired with MNRTF grant TF04-047, developed with grant TF07-011 and will be expanded by Acquisition grant TF10-029, totaling $2,539,000. Amenities include a sand beach and swimming area, beach house with 7 unisex restrooms, paved walkways and parking lot, picnic tables, grills, fishing pier and a covered pavilion.

The park was one of 17 worldwide finalists for, and won, the Michigan Chapter of the National MS Society 2010 annual da Vinci Awards®. Nominations were received from across the U.S., Canada, United Kingdom, France and Denmark. U.S. entries from 17 states and the District of Columbia included six from Michigan.

DNR - WILDLIFE DIVISION

TF230 Maple River SGA	ACQ	$450,000
TF92-355 Rose Lake Shooting Range	DEV	$66,000

ST. JOHNS

TF09-169 St. Johns Trailside Parkway Acquisition	ACQ	$106,900
TF14-109 City Park Improvements	DEV	$50,000

CLINTON COUNTY TOTAL $ 4,353,598

Crawford County

Crawford County was set aside as an unpopulated territory from Mackinac County in 1818 and was first called *Shawano* after an Ojibwa Chief. In 1843 the name was changed to Crawford to honor Col. William Crawford, a friend of George Washington, who was killed fighting Indians in Ohio in 1782.

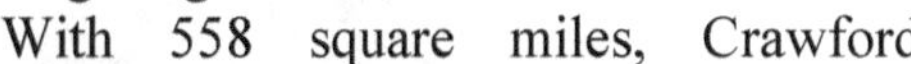

With 558 square miles, Crawford

MNRTF grant TF00-146, $327,796 went to Crawford County for development of the Grayling Fish Hatchery Interpretive Center.

County is 56th largest county and 70th largest in population with 14,074 residents. Since oil was discovered there in 1947, 327 holes have been drilled in the search for oil and gas. Crawford County has produced 36,906,696 barrels of oil and 163.116 billion cubic feet of natural gas, ranking 13th and 11th respectively among the 64 oil or gas producing Michigan counties. Crawford County has received $5,381,796 in 13 Michigan Natural Resources Trust Fund grants, ranking 47th in number of grants received and 37th in grant dollars awarded.

CRAWFORD COUNTY active or closed MNRTF Projects

CRAWFORD COUNTY

Project	Type	Amount
TF00-146 Grayling Fish Interpretive Center	DEV	$327,796

DNR - FOREST, MINERAL & FIRE MANAGEMENT DIVISION

Project	Type	Amount
TF00-244 Upper Manistee River Property	ACQ	$1,600,000
TF1017 George Mason River Retreat	ACQ	$200,000
TF339 George Mason River Retreat	ACQ	$55,000

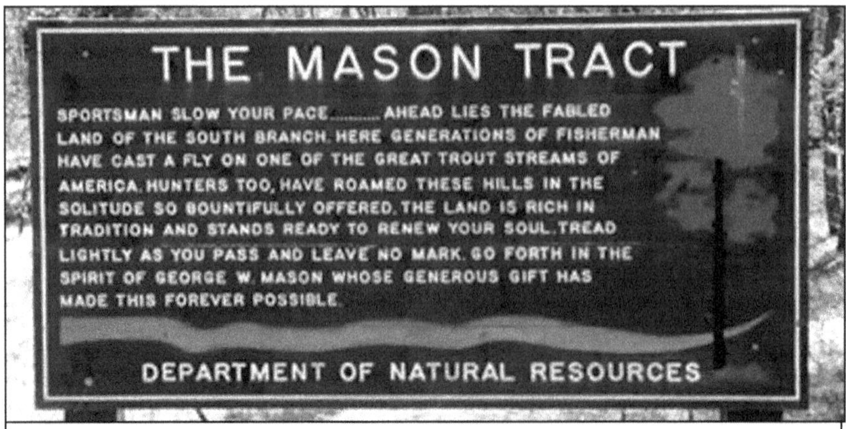

MNRTF grants TF339, 675, 1017 and 71-017, totaling $455,000, went to acquisition of the George Mason River Retreat, a 4,493 acre special management area along the South Branch of the AuSable River designed to protect the quality fishing waters of this area. The Mason Tract originated from acceptance of a 1,500 acre gift from the George Mason family in 1954. Over time, additional acreage has been acquired from the US Forest Service and private individuals through land exchanges. Curiously, when a deep directional well was proposed, targeted more than a mile under the Tract, with location outside the Tract, great hue and cry arose against drilling, which could have eventually augmented the fund that benefited the Tract.

TF675 George Mason River Retreat-Wessels Tract	ACQ	$100,000
TF71-017 George Mason River Retreat	ACQ	$100,000
TF92-352 Williams Tract Acquisition	ACQ	$520,000
TF943 AuSable River-MacArthur Property	ACQ	$900,000
DNR - OFFICE OF LAND & FACILITIES		
TF06-132 Ralph A. MacMullan Conference Center Imp.	DEV	$500,000
TF07-118 Ralph A. MacMullan Conference Center Imp.	DEV	$500,000
DNR – PARKS & RECREATION DIVISION		
TF14-137 RAM Center II	DEV	$300,000
GRAYLING		
TF03-064 Grayling River Park Development	DEV	$349,000
GRAYLING TOWNSHIP		
TF00-388 Nature Park by the Fish Hatchery	DEV	$230,000

CRAWFORD COUNTY TOTAL $ 5,681,796

Delta County

Delta County was named in reference to the Greek latter "Delta" because of the triangular shape of the original county which originally included parts of Menominee, Dickinson and Iron Counties. It was set off as a county in 1843 from Mackinac County and formally established in 1861.

With 1,170 square miles, Delta County is 5th largest county and 43rd largest in population with 37,069 residents.

Delta County is an Upper Peninsula county with little significant sedimentary geological strata, precluding the likelihood of the presence of oil and /or natural gas. Nonetheless, four holes have been drilled there to search for petroleum, making Delta the 72nd most drilled of 74 counties that have seen drilling for oil or natural gas. One of those holes was a prospect drilled in 1903 by a Cream City Development Company of Milwaukee, Wisconsin. All were dry holes.

Delta County has received $1,995,150 in 17 Michigan Natural Resources Trust Fund grants, ranking 37th in number of grants received and 60th in grant dollars awarded.

DELTA COUNTY active or closed MNRTF Projects

DELTA COUNTY

TF10-144 Sac Bay Land Acquisition	ACQ	$90,000

Delta Count photo *MNRTF grants TF86-149, TF89-083 Delta County's Fuller Park Expansion and Fuller Park Phase 1 total $292,500.*

TF86-149 Fuller Park Expansion	ACQ	$67,500
TF89-083 Fuller Park-Phase I	DEV	$225,000
TF12-115 Pioneer Trail Park Pavilion	DEV	$50,000
DNR - EDUCATION & OUTREACH		
TF98-304 DNR - UP State Fair Pocket Park	DEV	$250,000
DNR - FOREST, MINERAL & FIRE MANAGEMENT		
TF650 Thornton Parcel	ACQ	$20,000

TF983 Point Detour	ACQ	$160,000
DNR - OFFICE OF COMMUNICATIONS		
TF06-127 Upper Peninsula Pocket Park Renovation	DEV	$178,300
ESCANABA		
TF00-185 Ludington Park Beachhouse Renovation	DEV	$192,500
TF87-240 Escanaba Municipal Marina	DEV	$300,000
TF90-365 Walch Estate Property	ACQ	$22,500
TF97-088 Ludington Park Bike Path/Walkway Project	DEV	$17,500
TF99-384 Acquisition of Escanaba Riverfront Property	ACQ	$102,750

City of Escanaba photo

MNRTF Project TF99-384, an Acquisition grant for $102,750 for acquiring Escanaba Riverfront Property, was one of five Trust Fund grants for the City of Escanaba totaling $635,250.

GLADSTONE		
TF05-021 Gladstone 10th Street Pier	DEV	$155,000
TF08-014 Van Cleve Park Harbor Point Revitalization	DEV	$100,000
NAHMA TOWNSHIP		
TF92-004 Nahma Township Parkland	ACQ	$18,000
WELLS TOWNSHIP		
TF12-004 Sports Complex Concession Stand	DEV	$41,600

DELTA COUNTY TOTAL $ 1,995,100

Dickinson County

Michigan's newest county, Dickinson County is named in honor of Donald M. Dickinson 1876-1917, U. S. Postmaster General 1888-1889 under the Grover Cleveland administration. It was formally established in 1891, set off from parts of Iron, Marquette and Menominee counties.

City of Iron Mountain photo

MNRTF grant TF10-056 - $500,000 - Iron Mountain City Park, where deer, occasionally albino, abound.

With 766 square miles, Dickinson County is 22nd largest county and 52nd largest in population with 26,168 residents.

Because Dickinson is an Upper Peninsula county with no significant sedimentary geological strata, precluding the likelihood of the presence of oil and/or natural gas, no holes have been drilled there to search for petroleum.

Dickinson County has received $3,128,700 in 8 Michigan Natural Resources Trust Fund grants, ranking 67th in number of grants received and 48th in grant dollars awarded.

DICKINSON COUNTY active or closed MNRTF Projects

DICKINSON COUNTY		
TF03-126 Sewage Lagoon and Railroad Grade Property	ACQ	$20,700
TF718 Hanbury Lake Park	ACQ	$54,000
TF94-265 Fumee Lake Natural Area	ACQ	$396,200
DNRE - FOREST MANAGEMENT DIVISION		
TF10-122 Sturgeon River Corridor Acquisition	ACQ	$1,750,000
IRON MOUNTAIN		
TF08-024 Millie Mine Bat Viewing Site Trail	DEV	$158,400
TF10-056 City Park Improvements	DEV	$500,000
KINGSFORD		
TF90-355 Cowboy Lake Recr. Area	DEV	$136,900
NORWAY		
TF90-344 Strawberry Lake Project	DEV	$112,500

DICKINSON COUNTY TOTAL $ 3,128,700

Eaton County

Named in honor of another Jackson administration Secretary of War 1829-1831 John Henry Eaton, Eaton County was established from an unorganized territory in 1837.

With 576 square miles, Eaton County is 37th largest county and 20th largest in population with 107,759 residents. Since oil was discovered there in 1972, 333 holes have been drilled in the search for oil and gas. Eaton County has produced 6,109,667 barrels of oil and 54.600 billion cubic feet of natural gas, ranking 31st and 20th respectively among the 64 oil or gas producing Michigan counties. Eaton County has received $1,902,900 in 11 Michigan Natural Resources Trust Fund grants, ranking 49th in number of grants received and 54th in grant dollars awarded.

Eaton County's Lincoln Brick Park near Grand Ledge, received $60,000 for land acquisition in MNRTF grant TF94-152.

EATON COUNTY active or closed MNRTF Projects

DELTA TOWNSHIP		
TF00-052 Hunter's Orchard Park Development	DEV	$65,000
TF08-005 Sharp Park East-West Connector	DEV	$244,700
TF316 Anderson Nature Park	ACQ	$185,000
DIMONDALE		
TF11-005 Island Park	DEV	$169,900
DNR - WILDLIFE DIVISION		
TF537 Tamarack Lake Mini Game Area	ACQ	$150,000
EATON RAPIDS		
TF11-063 Mill Street Landing Improvements	DEV	$300,000
EATON COUNTY		
TF05-033 Fox Memorial Park Improvements	DEV	$298,000
TF94-152 Lincoln Brick Park-Phase IV	ACQ	$60,000
GRAND LEDGE		
TF06-118 Grand Ledge Riverwalk	DEV	$192,100
TF11-041 Jaycee Park Boat Launch	DEV	$138,800
HAMLIN TOWNSHIP		
TF10-022 Hamlin Township Park Acquisition	ACQ	$99,400

EATON COUNTY TOTAL $ 1,902,900

Emmet County

Emmet County is named for Irish nationalist and rebel leader Robert Emmet 1778-1803, It was set aside from part of Mackinac county in 1840 and called Tongadana County until 1843 when the name changed and Emmet County formally established in 1853.

With 468 square miles, Emmet County is 77th largest county and 47th largest in population with 32,694 residents. Emmet County has little sedimentary rock strata, making oil and/or natural gas presence unlikely. Nevertheless, 5 holes have been drilled in the search for oil and gas there, making Emmet 69th of Michigan's 74 counties that have seen petroleum exploratory holes drilled. Emmet County has received $16,868,050 in 26 Michigan Natural Resources Trust Fund grants, ranking 29th in number of grants and 12th in grant dollars awarded.

MyNorth.com photo

The Skyline Trail is part of the North Country Trail System and runs the length of Petoskey. It is an 11,000 year-old glacial moraine, left by retreating glaciers and now enjoyed by the public with the help of MNRTF Acquisition grant TF08-010, $99,000.

EMMET COUNTY active or closed MNRTF Projects

ALANSON		
TF06-201 Crooked River Access Project	ACQ	$99,000
BEAR CREEK TOWNSHIP		
TF05-063 Walloon Lake Access	ACQ	$2,018,400
TF08-092 Jones Landing Park	DEV	$487,600
TF86-254 Spring Lake Park	ACQ	$270,000
DNR - FISHERIES DIVISION		
TF12-130 Oden State Fish Hatchery	DEV	$300,000
DNR - PARKS & RECREATION DIVISION		
TF691 Sturgeon Bay Dunes	ACQ	$840,000
TF13-138 North Western State Trail Surfacing	DEV	$282,000
EMMET COUNTY		
TF01-029 Camp Pet-O-Se-Ga Campground Dev.	DEV	$107,600
TF02-026 Resort Bluffs	ACQ	$869,400
TF06-077 Camp Pet-o-se-ga Campground Facilities	DEV	$490,700

TF589 Cecil Bay	ACQ	$300,000
TF87-080 Cecil Bay	ACQ	$74,000
TF89-208 Camp Pet-o-se-ga	ACQ	$550,000
TF94-124 Headlands Property Acquisition	ACQ	$3,405,000

Little Traverse Land Conservancy photo

The Headlands property is a 600 acre property with 12,000 feet of rocky frontage on the Straits of Mackinac, acquired with the help of MNRTF grant TF94-124 for $3,405,000.

TF98-037 Little Traverse Bay View Park	ACQ	$345,600
TF11-051 Petoskey to Alanson Rail-Trail	DEV	$300,000
TF14-230 Camp Pet-o-se-ga Water Access & Dock	DEV	$49,000
PETOSKEY		
TF08-010 Skyline Trail Acquisition	ACQ	$99,000
TF11-009 Quarry Harbor Non-Motorized Trail	DEV	$59,700
TF11-030 Petoskey Downtown Greenway-North Segment	DEV	$300,000
READMOND TOWNSHIP		
TF93-049 Middle Village Church Beach	ACQ	$686,300
TF96-051 Middle Village Church Beach	ACQ	$67,500
RESORT TOWNSHIP		
TF94-165 Bay Harbor Lake Frontage	ACQ	$4,335,000
TF96-054 Resort Township Parks	DEV	$125,250
TF11-019 Sagimore Acquisition	DEV	$157,000
VILLAGE OF ALANSON		
TF09-114 Island Sanctuary Park Boardwalk	DEV	$250,000

EMMET COUNTY TOTAL $ 16,868,050

Genesee County

Genesee County was set off from parts of Lapeer, Saginaw and Shiawasee counties in 1835 and named with an adaptation of the Seneca Indian word *je-nis-hi-yeh*, meaning "beautiful valley" after an upstate New York valley where many of this area of southeastern Michigan's settlers had originated. Genesee was formally established in 1836.

With 640 square miles, Genesee County is 33rd largest county and 5th largest in population with 425,790 residents.

Genesee County photo

MNRTF grants TF00-170 and TF707, totaling $530,000, went to help acquire and develop Linden Genesee County Park.

Since oil was discovered there in 1941, 95 holes have been drilled in the search for oil and gas. Genesee County has produced 696,545 barrels of oil and 486.9 million cubic feet of natural gas, ranking 53rd and 51st respectively among the 64 oil or gas producing Michigan counties.

Genesee County has received $6,474,691 in 35 Michigan Natural Resources Trust Fund grants, ranking 13th in number of grants received and 34th in grant dollars awarded.

GENESEE COUNTY active or closed MNRTF Projects

BURTON

TF12-060 Kelly Lake Park Improvements	DEV	$171,000

CLIO

TF11-104 Pine Run Trail Improvements	DEV	$45,000

TF11-110 Pine Run Retaining Wall Stabilization	DEV	$79,800
TF12-124 Clio City Park Trolley Line Trail	DEV	$127,500
DAVISON		
TF02-139 Davison Regional Park Trailways	DEV	$307,700
DAVISON TOWNSHIP		
TF04-147 Davison Township Trail	DEV	$266,400
TF13-036 R. Williams Nature Park Improvements	DEV	$220,500
DNR - PARKS & RECREATION DIVISION		
TF91-018 ORV Park Expansion	ACQ	$635,000
TF990 Lake Fenton	ACQ	$149,000
FENTON		
TF88-160 Shiawassee River Walkway	ACQ	$18,750
FLINT		
TF00-163 Flint Park Lake Development	DEV	$151,787
TF08-075 Grand Traverse Greenway Property Acq.	ACQ	$525,000
TF87-118 Flint River Shoreline	DEV	$400,000
TF88-151 Flint River Shoreline	DEV	$375,000
TF12-109 Riverbank Park Development	DEV	$300,000
TF13-070 McKinley Park Improvements	DEV	$225,000
FLUSHING TOWNSHIP		
TF04-034 Flushing Township Nature Park Imp.	DEV	$131,600
TF92-141 Flint River Property Acquisition	ACQ	$168,750
TF95-248 Flushing Township Park	DEV	$151,000

Genesee County photo

MNRTF grant TF01-040, $152,529 went to develop Buell Lake County Park.

GENESEE COUNTY		
TF00-170 Linden Park Renovation	DEV	$330,000
TF01-040 Buell Lake Park Improvement	DEV	$152,529
TF621 Holloway Reservoir	ACQ	$135,000
TF707 Linden County Park Extension	ACQ	$200,000
TF90-225 Public Acc./Fishing Site	DEV	$86,250
TF93-122 Richfield Park Land Acq.	ACQ	$135,000

TF94-177 Stepping Stone Falls Walk	DEV	$75,000
TF97-045 Bluegill Bike Path Extension	DEV	$75,000
GRAND BLANC		
TF205 McFarlan Farm	ACQ	$185,000
TF88-249 Grand Blanc Commons	DEV	$19,125
LINDEN		
TF01-134 Shiawassee River District Trails	DEV	$125,000
MONTROSE TOWNSHIP		
TF09-025 Barber Memorial Park Improvements	DEV	$348,500
TF14-182 Montrose Township Property	DEV	$103, 400
MOUNT MORRIS TOWNSHIP		
TF02-064 Bicentennial Park Improvements	DEV	$36,600

Richfield Township photo

MNRTF grants TF10-147 and TF90-400, totaling $30,600, went to help acquire property for Genesee County's Richfield Township Park.

RICHFIELD TOWNSHIP		
TF90-400 Richfield Township Property Acq.	ACQ	$9,000
VIENNA TOWNSHIP		
TF91-126 Bike Path West Extension	ACQ	$10,500

GENESEE COUNTY TOTAL $6,474,691

Gladwin County

Gladwin County was named in honor of Major Henry Gladwin, who was commander of the fort at Detroit 1763-64, a period that included the siege by Ottawa American Indian Chief Pontiac. It was set off as a county in 1831 and formally established in 1855.

With 507 square miles, Gladwin County is 70th largest county and 56th largest in population with 25,692 residents. Since oil was discovered there in 1934, 855 holes have been drilled in the search for oil and gas.

MNRTF grant TF09-051, $200,000, was used to improve the Gladwin City Park and Campground. The fishing platform is in memory of "A True Conservation Hero", Gladwin resident Michael D. Turner "for his exceptional work and dedication to the Cedar River and many other Conservation Projects within Gladwin County."

Gladwin County has produced 41,726,872 barrels of crude oil and 18.687 billion cubic feet of natural gas, ranking 10th and 36th respectively among the 64 oil or gas producing Michigan counties. Gladwin County has received $496,389 in 4 Michigan Natural Resources Trust Fund grants, ranking 80th in number of grants received and 82nd in grant dollars awarded.

GLADWIN COUNTY active or closed MNRTF Projects

BEAVERTON

TF05-068 Beaverton Fishing Piers	DEV	$59,000

GLADWIN

TF00-329 North-South Park Riverwalk	DEV	$139,889
TF09-051 Gladwin City Park and Campground Imp.	DEV	$200,000
TF90-329 Riverfront Development	DEV	$97,500

GLADWIN COUNTY TOTAL $496,389

Gogebic County

Michigan's northwestern most county, Gogebic Count's name is believed to have been based on the Chippewa Indian word "*bic*", meaning rock. It was set off as a county in 1887 and formally established in 1889.

With 1,102 square miles, Gogebic County is 7th largest county and 67th largest in population with 16,427 residents. Gogebic County is an Upper Peninsula county with no significant sedimentary geological strata, precluding the likelihood of the presence of oil and/or natural gas. No holes have been drilled there to search for petroleum. Gogebic County has received $4,157,900 in 23 Michigan Natural Resources Trust Fund grants, ranking 23rd in number of grants received and 44th in grant dollars awarded.

Michigan Natural Resources Trust Fund grant TF93-267 - $86,300 – was used to rehabilitate the Lake Gogebic Dock, where perch fishermen, including the author, try their luck. The south end of Lake Gogebic is in Gogebic County in the Central Time Zone, while the north end is in Ontonagan County in the Eastern Time Zone.

GOGEBIC COUNTY active or closed MNRTF Projects

BESSEMER

TF11-065 Mary Street Ethnic Commons & Trailhead DEV $279,900

TF13-056 Bluff Valley Park Development.	DEV	$45,000
DNR - PARKS & RECREATION DIVISION		
TF98-306 Presque Isle River Acquisition	ACQ	$430,000
GOGEBIC COUNTY		
TF10-094 Little Girl's Point Improvements	DEV	$235,500
TF93-267 Lake Gogebic Dock Rehabilitation	DEV	$86,300
TF14-166 Ironwood to Bessemer Trail Project	DEV	$295,000
IRONWOOD		
TF03-210 Recreation Trail	ACQ	$6,900
TF08-035 Hiawatha Rotary Skate Park	DEV	$46,300
TF97-156 Norrie Park Riverside Improvements	DEV	$53,700
TF11-112 Depot Recreation Park & Trailhead Imp.	DEV	$295,900
TF12-123 Michigan's Western Gateway Trail	DEV	$225,000
TF14-136 Curry Park Improvements	DEV	$37,000
TF14-221 Depot Park Playground	DEV	$37,700

MNRTF grant TF98-306, $430,000, went to the Michigan DNR to acquire more Presque Isle River property.

IRONWOOD TOWNSHIP		
TF10-082 Airport Recreation Park Improvements	DEV	$291,400
TF698 Lost Lake Wilderness	ACQ	$270,000
TF91-376 Lost Lake Park	DEV	$40,000
WAKEFIELD		
TF00-016 Southwest Lakeshore Development	DEV	$136,000
TF08-042 Sunday Lake Trail and Eddy Park Imp.	DEV	$147,700
TF91-303 Sunday Lake Improvements	DEV	$69,000
TF13-034 Eddy Park Improvements	DEV	$112,500
WATERSMEET TOWNSHIP		
TF09-123 Central Agonikak Nat'l Rec. Trail Enhance	DEV	$240,000
TF10-179 North Agonikak Nat'l Rec. Trail Enhance	DEV	$500,000
TF11-113 South Agonikak Nat'l Rec. Trail Enhance.	DEV	$276,800

GOGEBIC COUNTY TOTAL $ 4,157,900

Grand Traverse County

Grand Traverse County was named by the French phrase *grande travers*, meaning "long crossing", the name given the area by French voyageurs. It was set off as a county from part of Omeena County, which was annexed to Grand Traverse in 1853, and formally established in 1851.

With 465 square miles, Grand Traverse County is 78th largest county

On September 27, 2000 the Michigan Oil and Gas Association (MOGA) Award of Excellence was presented to the City of Traverse City for outstanding use of MNRTF grant TF88-184, 280,000, which helped develop that city's West Bay Beach. The Presentation was made by MOGA Chairman of the Board Greg Fogle, second left, with Rotary Charities Marsha Smith, left, Shell Exploration & Production's Terry Brand – at the podium, Traverse City Mayor Linda Smyka, and Traverse City Convention and Visitors Bureaus Deborah Knudson.

and 23rd largest in population with 86,986 residents.

Since oil was discovered there in 1971, 1,578 holes have been drilled in the search for oil and gas. Grand Traverse County has produced 68,929,184 barrels of oil and 588.496 billion cubic feet of natural gas, ranking 5th in both outputs among the 64 oil or gas producing Michigan counties.

Grand Traverse County has received $42,042,013 in 48 Michigan Natural Resources Trust Fund grants, ranking 9th in number of grants received and 4th in grant dollars awarded.

GRAND TRAVERSE COUNTY active /closed MNRTF Projects

ACME TOWNSHIP		
TF00-162 Yuba Creek Natural Area Acquisition	ACQ	$1,576,021
TF08-095 Acme Waterfront Park Acquisition	ACQ	$3,006,200
TF09-171 Acme Waterfront Park - Phase II	ACQ	$2,266,500
TF96-110 Deepwater Point Natural Area	ACQ	$1,968,000
TF11-082 Acme Waterfront Park - Phase III	DEV	$862,500
DNR - FOREST, MINERAL & FIRE MANAGEMENT		
TF07-168 Jaxon Creek Corridor Acquisition	ACQ	$1,050,000
TF884 Ellis Lake	ACQ	$445,000
TF98-300 Henri and Sons Property	ACQ	$400,000
TF99-294 Frost Property	ACQ	$1,560,000
TF13-125 Strombolis Lake Property	ACQ	$1,000,000
DNR - PARKS & RECREATION DIVISION		
TF08-129 Mitchell Creek Land Acquisition	ACQ	$1,000,000
*TF269 Traverse City State Park	ACQ	$800,000
*TF361 Traverse City State Park	ACQ	$400,000
TF88-311 Murray Farms, Inc.	ACQ	$1,060,400
TF96-266 Old Mission Park Site	DEV	$275,000
TF13-131 Old Mooring Place Acquisition	ACQ	$2,500,000

Little Traverse Land Conservancy photo

Two MNRTF grants totaling $1,554,400, assisted by Little Traverse Land Conservancy, went to Long Lake Township's Cedar Run Creek Natural Area for land acquisition and preservation.

EAST BAY TOWNSHIP		
TF01-166 Gen's Park Improvement Project	DEV	$121,360
TF92-106 Bayfront Parkland Acquisition	ACQ	$202,500

TF14-076 Grace MacDonald Park Accessibility	DEV	$50,000
FIFE LAKE		
TF697 Fife Lake Access	ACQ	$55,000
GARFIELD CHARTER TOWNSHIP		
TF02-220 Boardman Nature Ed. Reserve Expansion	ACQ	$505,000
TF09-173 Boardman Lake Trail & Nature Reserve Expns.	ACQ	$1,231,800
TF11-109 Historic Barns Park & Garden	DEV	$300,000
TF12-141 Buffalo Ridge Trail Development	DEV	$199,000
TF13-118 Boardman Valley Nature Preserve	ACQ	$270,000
GRAND TRAVERSE COUNTY		
TF00-356 Meyer Addition to Nature Education Reserve	ACQ	$786,509
TF01-227 Maple Bay and Natural Area	ACQ	$6,816,920
TF05-104 Boardman Lake Trail West	DEV	$500,000
TF90-310 VASA Trail Project	DEV	$95,500
TF93-405 Boardman Property Acquisition	ACQ	$321,000
KINGSLEY		
TF03-079 Civic Center South	DEV	$125,000
LONG LAKE TOWNSHIP		
TF00-055 Taylor Park Development	DEV	$25,175
TF06-051 Cedar Run Creek Natural Area Acquisition	ACQ	$999,500
TF07-162 Cedar Run Creek Natural Area Addition	ACQ	$554,900
TF97-204 Bullhead Lake Natural Area	ACQ	$108,800
TF12-071 Timbers Recreation Area	ACQ	$2,073,000
PENINSULA TOWNSHIP		
TF87-273 Haserot Beach Park Expansion	ACQ	$28,000
TF95-149 PDR Easement Acquisition	ACQ	$1,000,000
TF13-086 Bowers Harbor Park Expansion	ACQ	$626,800
TRAVERSE CITY		
TF02-151 Boardman Lake Trail - East	DEV	$500,000
TF10-062 Clinch Park Bayfront Revitalization	DEV	$450,800
TF704 West Grand Traverse Bay Acquisition	ACQ	$300,000
TF88-184 West Bay Beach	DEV	$280,950
TF92-199 Riverfront Acquisition	ACQ	$228,500
TF99-160 Hull Park Waterfront	DEV	$365,730
TF11-060 Boardman Lake Trail West	DEV	$210,000
WHITEWATER TOWNSHIP		
TF00-319 Petobego Natural Area Acquisition	ACQ	$680,048
TF03-206 Battle Creek Natural Area	ACQ	$1,860,600

GRAND TRAVERSE COUNTY TOTAL $ 42,042,013

*At July 21, 2011 ceremonies, Traverse City State Park was renamed the Keith J. Charters Traverse City State Park, in honor of the longest serving member of the Michigan Natural Resources Commission and the Michigan Natural Resources Trust Fund Board, Traverse City resident Keith Charters. Charters retired from the Michigan Natural Resources Trust Fund Board in October, 2014.

Gratiot County

Gratiot County is named for Charles Gratiot, 1788-1855, West Point engineering graduate who rebuilt old Fort St. Joseph, renamed Fort Gratiot, during the war of 1812 at today's Port Huron, Michigan.

Gratiot County's Reed Park, near North Star, was a $495,000 MNRTF Development grant project.

Set aside in 1831 and formally established in 1855, Gratiot County has 570 square miles, and is 43rd largest county and has 42,476 residents to rank 41st in population. Since oil was discovered there in 1927, 57 holes have been drilled in the search for oil and gas. Gratiot County has produced 1,251,153 barrels of oil and 15.110 billion cubic feet of natural gas, ranking 48th and 41st respectively among the 64 oil or gas producing Michigan counties. Gratiot County has received $1,383,500 in 9 Michigan Natural Resources Trust Fund grants, ranking 64th in number of grants received and 70th in grant dollars awarded.

GRATIOT COUNTY active or closed MNRTF Projects

Project	Type	Amount
ALMA		
TF04-087 Riverwalk Extension Project	DEV	$288,800
TF91-258 Riverwalk Connector-Phase I	DEV	$25,500
TF11-103 Park Access Enhancement Project	DEV	$91,300
DNR - FISHERIES DIVISION		
TF773 Pine River Property	ACQ	$42,000
GRATIOT COUNTY		
TF06-006 Reed County Park Improvements	DEV	$495,000
ITHACA		
TF06-061 McNabb Park Land Acquisition	ACQ	$40,700
TF10-026 McNabb Park Site Development	DEV	$183,700
ST. LOUIS		
TF91-204 Westgate Park Development-Phase I	DEV	$55,500
TF13-093 Leppien Park Improvements	DEV	$161,000

GRATIOT COUNTY TOTAL $ 1,383,500

Hillsdale County

Hillsdale County is named to describe the area's landscape and terrain, with rolling hills and grassy valleys. It was set off as a county in 1829 and formally established in 1835.

MNRTF grant TF89-265 - $37,500 - went to help acquire the land for Moscow Township's Headwaters Park, which hosts the Moscow Township Hall in the old depot of the Michigan and Ohio Railroad.

With 599 square miles, Hillsdale County is 36th largest county and 37th largest in population with 46,688 residents. Since oil was discovered there in 1957, 1,130 holes have been drilled in the search for oil and gas. Hillsdale County is the largest oil producing Michigan county, having produced 124,760,516 barrels of oil and 230.003 billion cubic feet of natural gas to rank 1st and 8th respectively among the 64 oil or gas producing Michigan counties., producing 230,003,351 billion cubic feet of natural gas Hillsdale County has received $1,200,575 in 6 Michigan Natural Resources Trust Fund grants, ranking 74th in both number of grants received and in grant dollars awarded.

HILLSDALE COUNTY active or closed MNRTF Projects

DNR - WILDLIFE DIVISION		
TF418 Merkel Property	ACQ	$365,000
HILLSDALE		
TF98-051 Hillsdale's Project Preserve	ACQ	$354,375
LITCHFIELD		
TF91-369 Firemen's Park Development	DEV	$47,700
MOSCOW TOWNSHIP		
TF89-265 Headwaters Neighborhood Park	ACQ	$37,500
READING TOWNSHIP		
TF1026 Kimball YMCA Environmental Education	ACQ	$100,000
VILLAGE OF JONESVILLE		
TF13-037 Jonesville Rail-Trail	DEV	$296,000

HILLSDALE COUNTY TOTAL $ 1,200,575

Houghton County

Houghton County was named for Dr. Douglass Houghton 1809-1845, physician, surgeon, Mayor of Detroit 1842-1845, and first State Geologist. Houghton died after a fateful plunge into Lake Superior while gathering rock samples *(see Midland County)*. It was carved from parts of Marquette and Ontonagon counties and formally established in 1845.

With 1,012 square miles, Houghton County is 10th largest county and 44th largest in population with 36,628 residents. Because Houghton is an Upper Peninsula county with no significant sedimentary geological strata, precluding the likelihood of the presence of oil and/or natural gas, no holes have been drilled there to search for petroleum. Houghton County has received $2,112,500 in 29 Michigan Natural Resources Trust Fund grants, ranking 18th in number of grants received and 58th in grant dollars awarded.

Chassell Township photo

MNRTF Project TF89-267, $98,800, went to the Chassell Township Centennial Park. The park's features include: a Children's Garden; Playground; Park Pavilion; Boat Launch; Fishing Pier; and a Swimming Beach among others.

HOUGHTON COUNTY active or closed MNRTF Projects

CALUMET

TF08-004 Lions Club Park Nature Trail	DEV	$20,400

CALUMET TOWNSHIP

TF03-026 Lakeshore Park Restroom Facility	ACQ	$42,000
TF05-119 Swedetown Recreation Area Acquisition	ACQ	$105,200
TF1053 Lake Superior Park Expan.	ACQ	$14,000
TF96-183 Swedetown Trails Land Acquisition	ACQ	$209,475
TF97-096 Lakeshore Park Improvements	DEV	$27,225
TF11-074 Calumet Lions Park Trail Development	DEV	29,000
TF14-207 Railroad Depot Acquisition	ACQ	$80,000

CHASSELL TOWNSHIP		
TF89-267 Chassell Township Park	DEV	$98,800
DNR - FOREST, MINERAL & FIRE MANAGEMENT		
TF544 Hancock-Calumet Trail	ACQ	$78,000
TF677 Hungarian Falls	ACQ	$21,000
HANCOCK		
TF01-153 Portage Lake Waterfront Boardwalk Addition	DEV	$70,000
TF11-021 Navy Street Park Boat Launch	DEV	$262,500
HOUGHTON		
TF00-006 College Avenue Park	DEV	$16,800
TF02-141 Houghton Nara Nature Trail Phase II	DEV	$49,000
TF02-211 Waterfront Land Acquisition	ACQ	$390,000

Michigan Tech photo

MNRTF Project TF02-221, $390,000, went to the City of Houghton for Waterfront Land Acquisition. Houghton has received five MNRTF grants totaling $690,800.

TF86-205 Lakefront West Beach	DEV	$187,000
TF96-161 Nara Park	DEV	$48,000
TF14-090 Central Houghton Greenspace	ACQ	$80,500
LAKE LINDEN		
TF01-188 2001 Recreation Area Improvements	DEV	$26,000
TF97-016 Dock and Parking Improvement	DEV	$20,000
OSCEOLA TOWNSHIP		
TF02-172 Osceola Township Sandy Bottom Park	DEV	$46,000
TF03-158 Electric Park Land Acquisition	ACQ	$27,000
TF86-068A Dollar Bay Ball Field	ACQ	$25,500
TF86-068D Dollar Bay Ball Field	DEV	$38,000
SOUTH RANGE		
TF92-281 Vets Memorial Park Expansion	ACQ	$15,000
STANTON TOWNSHIP		
TF89-085 North Shore Park	DEV	$37,500
TF93-044 Oskar Bay Recreation Center	DEV	$26,100
TORCH LAKE TOWNSHIP		
TF88-188 Hubbell Launch Site	ACQ	$22,500

HOUGHTON COUNTY TOTAL $ 2,112,500

Huron County

The French word *hure,* for "head", was an influence on naming the lake and this county at the tip of the Lower Peninsula "Thumb". Early French travelers dubbed the lake *Lac des Hurons* when they noted the distinctive way local American Indians dressed their hair. The name from old maps stuck and the county was organized in 1840 from part of Sanilac County.

With 837 square miles, Huron County is 18th largest county and 45th largest in population with 33,118 residents. Since oil was discovered there in 1944, 101 holes have been drilled in the search for oil and gas, making Huron County Michigan's 57th most drilled county. Huron County has produced 95,771 barrels of oil and no natural gas, ranking 57th among the 64 oil or gas producing Michigan counties.

Huron County has received $8,949,480 in 21 Michigan Natural Resources Trust Fund grants, ranking 28th in number of grants received and 25th in grant dollars awarded.

PureMichigan.com photo

MNRTF grants TF08-056, and 10-093, totaling $560,000, went to the Village of Port Austin for Veteran's Waterfront Park improvements and Tower Park expansion property acquisition.

HURON COUNTY active or closed MNRTF Projects

CASEVILLE

TF87-121 Caseville Harbor Expan.	DEV	$400,000

TF90-212 Breakwall/Pointe Park	DEV	$74,300
DNR - WILDLIFE DIVISION		
TF370 Gagetown State Game Area	ACQ	$350,000
TF847 Detroit Edison Site	ACQ	$2,500,000
TF965 Detroit Edison/Huron County	ACQ	$2,500,000

HARBOR BEACH		
TF88-026 North Park Campground	DEV	$375,000
TF11-052 Waterfront Development	DEV	$281,000
TF12-084 Judge James H. Lincoln Mem. Bathing Beach	ACQ	$150,000
TF13-087 PFC Brian Backus Mem Nature Trail	DEV	$27,000
HURON COUNTY		
TF712 Sebewaing Park and Marina	ACQ	$225,000
TF769 Wagener Co. Park Addition	ACQ	$151,000
TF89-124 Sebewaing Park Dev.	DEV	$318,400
TF93-279 Wagener Park	DEV	$207,000
TF95-128 Lighthouse Park Development	DEV	$225,000
TF98-054 Stafford Park Acquisition	ACQ	$147,000
PIGEON		
TF91-182 Park Expansion	ACQ	$94,500
PORT AUSTIN		
TF08-056 Veterans Waterfront Park Improvements	DEV	$500,000
SEBEWAING		
TF03-001 Sebewaing Park Project	DEV	$36,480
TF89-009 Marina Project	ACQ	$215,300
TF92-289 Millerwise Park	DEV	$112,500
VILLAGE OF PORT AUSTIN		
TF10-093 Tower Park Acquisition	ACQ	$60,000
	HURON COUNTY TOTAL	**$ 8,949,480**

Ingham County

Ingham County was named for Samuel D. Ingham 1779-1860, U.S. Secretary of the Treasury, 1829-31, for President Andrew Jackson. It was set off as a county in 1829 from parts of Shiawassee and Washtenaw Counties and unorganized territory and formally established in 1838.

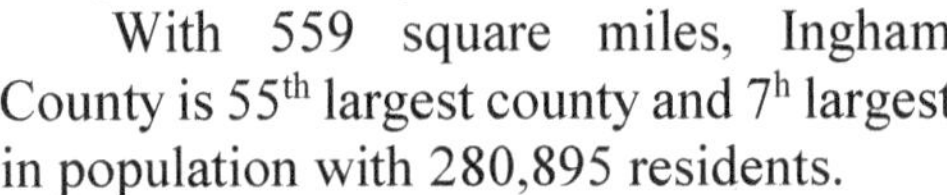

With 559 square miles, Ingham County is 55th largest county and 7^{h} largest in population with 280,895 residents.

Since oil was discovered there in 1970, 464 holes have been drilled in the search for oil and gas. Ingham County has produced 24,284,638 barrels of oil and 52.361 billion cubic feet of natural gas, ranking 16th and

On September 25, 2000, the Michigan Oil And Gas Association (MOGA) Award of Excellence was presented to the City of Lansing for outstanding use of Michigan Natural Resources Trust Fund grants for the Lansing River Trail. Left to right are: Lansing Mayor David Hollinger, MOGA President Frank L. Mortl, Greater Lansing Visitors and Convention Bureau Executive Director Tom Galton and MOGA Legal and Legislative Committee Chair, oil and gas attorney Gary Worman. The River Trail has received 8 MNRTF grants totaling $3,094,500.

22nd respectively among the 64 oil or gas producing Michigan counties.

Ingham County has received $17,864,525 in 50 Michigan Natural Resources Trust Fund grants, ranking 7th in number of grants received and 11th in grant dollars awarded.

INGHAM COUNTY active or closed MNRTF Projects

DELHI TOWNSHIP		
TF10-049 Valhalla Park Restroom/Pavilion	DEV	$283,100
TF11-064 North Trail Connector	DEV	$300,000
DNR - OFFICE OF COMMUNICATIONS		
TF06-133 Multi-Use Shooting Sports/Education Facility	DEV	$500,000
TF11-135 Dansville State Game	DEV	$300,000
EAST LANSING		
TF04-121 Northern Tier Trail	DEV	$92,400
TF07-087 White Park Improvements	DEV	$225,000
TF08-065 Hawk Nest Park Development	DEV	$262,500
TF08-140 White Park Expansion #2	ACQ	$68,500
TF08-141 White Park Expansion #1	ACQ	$429,000
TF95-010 Environmental Corridors	ACQ	$765,400
TF97-155 Northern Tier Bike/Hike Trail	DEV	$375,000
TF12-082 Patriarche Park Playground	DEV	$300,000

Ingham County's Lake Lansing Park has received 3 Michigan Natural Resources Trust fund Acquisition grants for park and beach expansion totaling 2,651,200.

INGHAM COUNTY		
TF08-073 Burchfield Park Fishing Dock	DEV	$60,000
TF08-138 Lake Lansing Park North Expansion	ACQ	$1,982,200
TF630 Burchfield Park formerly Grand River Park	ACQ	$30,000
TF800 Burchfield Park formerly Grand River Park	ACQ	$120,000
TF86-133 Lake Lansing Park Expansion	ACQ	$375,000
TF91-093 Burchfield Pk formerly Gr. River Pk-N. Bluff	DEV	$300,000
TF92-183 Lake Lansing Beach Expansion	ACQ	$294,300
TF93-165 Solomon Pit Acquisition Hawk Island Co. Pk	ACQ	$900,000
TF99-111 Hawk Island County Park	DEV	$493,000
LANSING		
TF02-127 Moores Park Improvements	DEV	$247,800
TF03-106 River Trail South Extension	DEV	$226,500
TF04-078 River Trail South Extension	DEV	$500,000
TF05-071 Lansing River Trail South Extension	DEV	$426,500
TF06-050 Hunter Pool Renovation	DEV	$500,000
TF08-147 Hunter's Ridge Land Acquisition	ACQ	$785,300
TF10-050 Crego Park Development	DEV	$500,000
TF86-229 Urban Recreation Trail	DEV	$262,500
TF87-244 Lansing Urban Rec. Trail	DEV	$250,000

TF88-138 River Trail	DEV	$375,000
TF89-187 Lansing River Trail '89	DEV	$375,000
TF90-261 Lansing River Trail '90	DEV	$316,500
TF95-122 River Trail West-Phase II	DEV	$375,000
TF95-125 Fenner Arboretum Inholding Acquisition	ACQ	$360,000
TF96-102 Frances Park Shoreline	DEV	$408,900
TF97-027 River Trail Moores Park - Elm Street	DEV	$500,000
TF12-019 Frances Park Trail Improvement	DEV	$300,000
LESLIE PUBLIC SCHOOLS		
TF07-085 Russell Miller "Wild 100" Nature Center Dev.	DEV	$400,000
MERIDIAN TOWNSHIP		
TF01-024 Hartrick Park Development	DEV	$488,125

MNRTF Acquisition grant TF93-337, $383,600, helped purchase land for Ingham County's Williamston Township Community Park.

TF1078 Red Cedar Riverfront Park	ACQ	$180,000
TF628 Riverfront Rec. Area	ACQ	$125,000
TF87-212 Central Park North (Nancy L. Moore Park)	ACQ	$90,000
TF94-194 Harris Nature Center-Phase I	DEV	$119,600
TF09-068 Central Park Fishing Dock	DEV	$30,000
TF12-024 Wonch Park Pathway	DEV	$45,000
WILLIAMSTON		
TF08-081 McCormick Park Improvements	DEV	$391,100
TF616 Williamston Rec. Corridor	ACQ	$105,000
TF95-121 Red Cedar River Rapids	DEV	$342,700
WILLIAMSTOWN TOWNSHIP		
TF93-337 Park Land Acquisition	ACQ	$383,600

INGHAM COUNTY TOTAL $17,864,525

Ionia County

Ionia County was named in honor of one of the early Greek peoples and a region in ancient Greece that included the Aegean Sea and Islands. It was set aside as a county in 1831 and formally established in 1837.

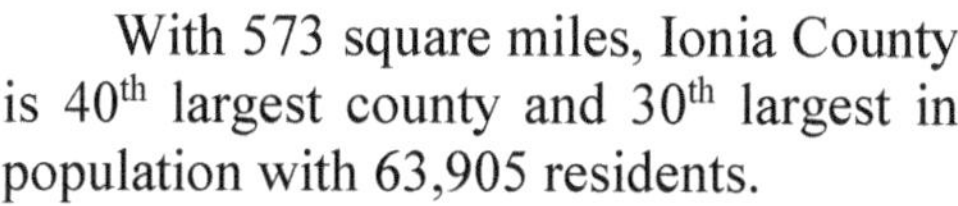

With 573 square miles, Ionia County is 40th largest county and 30th largest in population with 63,905 residents.

Since oil was discovered there in 1947, 107 holes have been drilled in the search for oil and gas. Ionia County has produced 48,633 barrels of oil and no natural gas, ranking 58th among the 64 oil and/or gas producing Michigan counties.

Ionia County has received $3,924,660 in 22 Michigan Natural Resources Trust Fund grants, ranking 25th in number of grants received and 45th in grant dollars awarded.

IONIA COUNTY active or closed MNRTF Projects

BELDING

Project	Type	Amount
TF01-139 Belding Pathway	DEV	$211,640
TF05-052 Silk City Nature Trail	DEV	$166,400
TF10-048 Lightning Bend Preserve Addition	ACQ	$226,700
TF12-073 Silk City Nature Trail	DEV	$274,800

MNRTF grant TF86-184, $320,000, was used by the Michigan Department of Natural Resources Parks and Recreation Division to build the beach house at the Ionia Recreation Area.

DNR - PARKS & RECREATION DIVISION

Project	Type	Amount
TF86-194 Ionia Recreation Area Beachhouse	DEV	$320,000

DNR - WILDLIFE DIVISION

Project	Type	Amount
TF538 Ionia County Mini Game Area	ACQ	$200,000

TF685 Ionia Co. Mini-Game Area	ACQ	$250,000
IONIA		
TF93-363 Rail Corridor and Trestle	ACQ	$37,500
TF97-026 Ionia Grand Rivertrail	DEV	$269,350
IONIA COUNTY		
TF04-007 Green View Point Park Improvements	DEV	$144,700
TF11-059 Rail-Trail Development	DEV	$300,000
LAKE ODESSA		
TF11-034 Lake Odessa Municipal Beach Development	DEV	$200,000
PEWAMO		
TF11-040 Pewamo Trailhead Development	DEV	$85,200
PORTLAND		
TF08-011 Portland Trail Connector Loop	DEV	$284,800
TF91-106 Rivertrail Park	DEV	$244,200

Four MNRTF grants, totaling $271,370, have gone to the town of Saranac for projects including the Riverwalk Park, shown above during the 2011 spring Grand River flood and the Boat/Canoe Launch on the other side of the bridge beyond the solitary visitor.

SARANAC		
TF01-092 Community Park Development	DEV	$165,470
TF04-059 Riverwalk Park	DEV	$59,500
TF89-024 Saranac Boat/Canoe Launch	ACQ	$10,400
TF98-074 Scheid Park Expansion	ACQ	$36,000
TF12-079 Boat Launch Park Landing	ACQ	$74,000
VILLAGE OF LYONS		
TF12-043 Hazel Devore Park Improvement	DEV	$164,000
VILLAGE OF MUIR		
TF13-015 CIS Trail Spur & Pedestrian Bridge	DEV	$200,000

IONIA COUNTY TOTAL $3,924,660

Iosco County

Iosco County was named by Henry Schoolcraft for a legendary Ottawa hero, when first set aside from an unorganized territory in 1840, the county was known as *Kanotin* County until 1843, then was formally established in 1857.

With 549 square miles, Iosco County is 61st largest county and 55th largest in population with 25,887 residents.

City of Tawas photo

MNRTF grant TF86-167, $65,000, went to expand Tawas City Park.

Since oil was discovered there in 1987, 50 holes have been drilled in the search for oil and gas. Iosco County has produced 1,909,281 barrels of oil and 11.410 billion cubic feet of natural gas, ranking 45th and 43rd respectively among the 64 oil or gas producing Michigan counties.

Iosco County has received $3,867,600 in 17 Michigan Natural Resources Trust Fund grants, ranking 35th in number of grants received and 46th in grant dollars awarded.

IOSCO COUNTY active or closed MNRTF Projects

DNR - PARKS & RECREATION DIVISION

TF92-330 Boating Expansion.-AuSable River	DEV	$127,000

EAST TAWAS

TF03-205 Holiday Inn Property Acquisition	ACQ	$96,500
TF397 Evans Parcel	ACQ	$50,000
TF88-245 East Tawas Waterfront	DEV	$24,900
TF97-199 Newman Street Waterfront Project	DEV	$302,600
TF13-020 East Tawas City Park	ACQ	$406,300

IOSCO TOWNSHIP

TF11-091 Aloe Property Acquisition	ACQ	$148,000
OSCODA TOWNSHIP		
TF06-090 Oscoda Beach Park Boardwalk Development	DEV	$44,800
TF08-016 Oscoda Beach Park Observation/Fishing Pier	DEV	$460,000
TF93-144 Riverbank Park	ACQ	$300,000

Oscoda Township photo

Oscoda Township's Oscoda Beach Park in Iosco County has received 4 MNRTF Acquisition and Development grants totaling $1,284,100.

TF94-162 Oscoda Beach Park Expansion	ACQ	$29,300
TF95-219 Oscoda Huron Sunrise Park	ACQ	$750,000
PLAINFIELD TOWNSHIP		
TF06-046 Plainfield Township Nature Park Imp.	DEV	$332,000
TF09-026 Plainfield Nature Park Expansion	ACQ	$428,400
TAWAS CITY		
TF08-038 Gateway Park Renovation	DEV	$134,000
TF86-167 Tawas City Park Expansion	ACQ	$65,000
TF91-319 Shoreline Park Expansion	ACQ	$168,800

IOSCO COUNTY TOTAL $ 3,867,600

Iron County

Iron County is named for the iron and mines located in the county, set off from Marquette and Menominee counties and established in 1885. With 1,166 square miles, Iron County is 6th largest county and 72nd largest in population with 11,817 residents. Because Houghton is an Upper Peninsula county with no significant sedimentary geological strata, precluding the likelihood of the presence of oil and/or natural gas, so no holes have been drilled there to search for petroleum. Iron County has received $1,941,890 in 17 Michigan Natural Resources Trust Fund grants, ranking 39th in number of grants received and 61st in grant dollars awarded.

Iron County photo

MNRTF Project TF05-128 - $90,000, went to Iron County's Pentoga Park Campground.

BATES TOWNSHIP		
TF11-105 Bates Township Park Improvements	DEV	$155,900
CASPIAN		
TF03-166 Iron River Frontage Acquisition	ACQ	$13,300
TF04-086 Apple Blossom Trail Extension	DEV	$134,900
TF05-122 Fishing Quarry Park Development	DEV	$48,800
TF92-077 Apple Blossom Trail	DEV	$84,000
CRYSTAL FALLS		
TF86-090 Crystella Ski Hill	ACQ	$16,800
TF99-266 Paint River Walk	DEV	$167,090
CRYSTAL FALLS TOWNSHIP		
TF08-058 Gibson Lake Park Improvements	DEV	$179,500
DNR - FOREST, MINERAL & FIRE MANAGEMENT		
TF997 Net River Wetlands	ACQ	$28,200
GAASTRA		
TF11-077 Rest Room Facilities Development	DEV	$64,200
TF14-247 Recreation Complex	DEV	$37,000
IRON COUNTY		
TF05-128 Pentoga Park Campground Improvements	DEV	$90,000
TF10-064 Iron County Heritage Trail	DEV	$500,000
TF87-093 Iron County Fairground	DEV	$58,000
IRON RIVER		
TF89-224 Iron River Waterfront	DEV	$227,600
TF05-077 Apple Blossom Trail River Walkway	DEV	$86,700
TF12-066 Nelson Field Accessibility	DEV	$49,900

IRON COUNTY TOTAL $ 1,941,890

Isabella County

Isabella County, traditional home of "The Oil Capital of Michigan" was named in honor of Spain's Queen Isabella 1451-1504, who financed Christopher Columbus' voyage that is commonly attributed with discovery of "the new world", North America. It was set off as a county in 1831 and formally established in 1859.

With 574 square miles, Isabella County is 38th largest county and 28th largest in population with 70,311 residents.

One of the last standing traditional oil derricks in the state with a sign declaring Mt. Pleasant – Oil Capital of Michigan" along US-127.

The discovery of the Mt. Pleasant Field in 1928 brought an influx of people and equipment to the county, sheltering the area from the worst financial stress of the Great Depression. Since then, 1,693 holes have been drilled in the search for oil and gas. Isabella County has produced 46,787,507 barrels of oil and 38.177 billion cubic feet of natural gas, ranking 9th and 31st respectively among the 64 oil or gas producing Michigan counties. Isabella County has received $1,854,862 in 6 Michigan Natural Resources Trust Fund grants, ranking 69th in number of grants received and 59h in grant dollars awarded.

ISABELLA COUNTY active or closed MNRTF Projects

ISABELLA COUNTY

Project	Type	Amount
TF03-068 Coldwater Lake Park Development	DEV	$211,500
TF95-085 Herrick Recreation Area	DEV	$155,100

MNRTF Projects TF607, 88-059, and 01-187, totaling $1,005,500, went to Mt. Pleasant's Chippewa River Restoration and Mill Pond Park, shown above before and after completion.

TF98-009 Pere Marquette Rail-Trail	DEV	$482,762
MOUNT PLEASANT		
TF01-187 Chippewa River Restoration Project	DEV	$500,000
TF607 Mill Pond Park	ACQ	$337,500
TF88-059 Mill Pond Park	DEV	$168,000

ISABELLA COUNTY TOTAL $ 1,854,862

Michigan Oil And Gas Association July 28, 2003 Award of Excellence ceremonies for the outstanding use of MNRTF grants for the Chippewa River Restoration Award of Excellence ceremonies for the outstanding use of MNRTF grants for the Chippewa River Restoration were attended by: Dave Maness; City Commissioners James Moreno and Cynthia Bradley; Mt. Pleasant City Manager Paul Preston; Mayor Adam Miller; Bob Butka; MOGA Chairman of the Board Jim Stark; Dan McGuire; Bob Long; Mt. Pleasant City Planner Tony Kulick; MOGA President Frank L. Mortl; Mt. Pleasant Area Convention and Visitors Bureau Mary Parfitt; and Mt. Pleasant Area Community Foundation's Michelle Gostomiski.

Jackson County

Jackson County was named in honor of Andrew Jackson 1767-1845, seventh President of the United States 1829-1837, who was President when Michigan became a state and was admitted to the Union in 1837. After several years of attempting to be granted statehood, the Michigan Territory agreed to abandon its dispute with Ohio over the Toledo Strip in exchange for accepting the northern peninsula of land, now known as Michigan's Upper Peninsula. Following an 1840 expedition to the Upper Peninsula by State Geologist Douglass Houghton and Henry Rowe Schoolcraft, who discovered rich deposits of copper, the United States first "mineral rush" began, nine years before the California Gold Rush. Jackson was set off as a county in 1829 and was formally established in 1832. Jackson named several Michigan Territory counties after his cabinet members.

With 701 square miles, Jackson County is 29th largest county and 14th

MNRTF Development grant TF99-209, $88,750, went to Jackson County's Swain's Lake Park improvement.

largest in population with 160,248 residents. Since oil was discovered there in 1953, 700 holes have been drilled in the search for oil and gas. Jackson County has produced 20,082,046 barrels of oil and 32.759 billion cubic feet of natural gas, ranking 21st and 32nd respectively among the 64 oil or gas producing Michigan counties. Jackson County has received $3,020,600 in 17 Michigan Natural Resources Trust Fund grants, ranking 36th in number of grants received and 49th in grant dollars awarded.

JACKSON COUNTY active or closed MNRTF Projects

CONCORD		
TF86-148 Gottschalk Park Expansion	ACQ	$39,700
DNR - PARKS & RECREATION DIVISION		
TF291 Waterloo Recreation Area	ACQ	$115,000
TF584 L. Pleasant Lake-Waterloo	ACQ	$560,000
DNR - WILDLIFE DIVISION		
TF93-420 Sharonville Shooting Range	DEV	$125,000
GRASS LAKE TOWNSHIP		
TF93-326 Park Land Acquisition	ACQ	$28,500
JACKSON		
TF96-056 Sharp Park Land Acquisition	ACQ	$101,250
TF97-113 Grand River Greenway/Trail	ACQ	$119,000
TF11-081 Bloomfield Park Courts Resurfacing	ACQ	$70,000
TF14-268 Riverwalk to Inter-City Trail	DEV	$300,000
JACKSON COUNTY		
TF05-117 Falling Waters Trail Project	DEV	$500,000
TF08-085 Sparks County Park Urban Fishing Project	DEV	$360,000
TF86-259 Non-Motorized Rec. Trail	DEV	$54,700
TF94-114 Grass Lake Park Improvements	DEV	$104,300
TF95-066 Vandercook Lake Park Improvements	DEV	$157,500
TF99-209 Swain's Lake Park Improvements	DEV	$88,750
TF11-085 Sparks County Park Trail Connector	ACQ	$187,500

Jason Atenberger of Parma, Michigan, leads bicyclists along the Falling Waters Trail toward the Village of Concord Trailhead Park, one of two interrelated MNRTF grant project totaling $609,400.

VILLAGE OF CONCORD		
TF09-050 Concord Mill Pond Trailhead Pk/ Fall. Waters	DEV	$109,400

JACKSON COUNTY TOTAL 3,020,600

Kalamazoo County

Kalamazoo County is named for the river that runs through the area. The American Indian origin of the name, is uncertain and has been translated a number of ways, including "it goes fast" and "bothered by smoke". It was set off as a county in 1829 and formally established in 1840.

The Michigan Oil And Gas Association (MOGA) Award of Excellence for outstanding use of Michigan Natural Resources Trust Fund grants was presented August 13, 2002 to the Parks Foundation of Kalamazoo County (PFKC) by Miller Energy's Jim Carl, representing MOGA. Accepting the award were: Al Slinks, PFKC President; and Betty Lee Ongley, PFKC Past President; and Jerry Albertson, Kalamazoo County Parks and Recreation Department.

With 562 square miles, Kalamazoo County is 58th largest county and 9th largest in population with 250,331 residents.

Since oil was discovered there in 1944, 158 holes have been drilled in the search for oil and gas. Kalamazoo County has produced 37,543 barrels of oil and no natural gas, ranking 59th among the 64 oil and/or gas producing Michigan counties. Kalamazoo County has received $6,685,600 in 31 Michigan Natural Resources Trust Fund grants, ranking 17th in number of grants received and 33rd in grant dollars awarded.

KALAMAZOO COUNTY active or closed MNRTF Projects

COMSTOCK TOWNSHIP

Project	Type	Amount
TF92-129 River Villa Preserve	ACQ	$82,500
TF11-003 Robert Morris Park	ACQ	$300,000

DNR - FISHERIES DIVISION

Project	Type	Amount
TF86-249 Augusta Creek	ACQ	$298,000

DNR - PARKS & RECREATION DIVISION

Project	Type	Amount
TF88-201 Kal-Haven Trail Phase II	DEV	$250,000

DNR - PARKS & RECREATION DIVISION

Project	Type	Amount
TF88-201 Kal-Haven Trail Phase II	DEV	$250,000

Michigan Oil & Gas News photo

Kalamazoo County's Markin Glen Park and Beach has received two Michigan Natural Resources Trust Fund grants for Acquisition and Development totaling $357,000.

GALESBURG

Project	Type	Amount
TF10-090 Ike Payne Park Improvements	DEV	$162,200
TF10-091 Community Park Improvements	DEV	$266,600

KALAMAZOO

Project	Type	Amount
TF10-039 Woods Lake Park Improvements	DEV	$363,200
TF87-200 Arcadia Creek	ACQ	$500,000
TF94-033 Vine Neighborhood Land	ACQ	$37,500
TF96-135 VerSluis/Dickinson Park Renovations	DEV	$500,000

KALAMAZOO COUNTY

Project	Type	Amount
TF96-142 Markin Glen Beach and Roads	DEV	$300,000
TF12-117 River Oaks County Park Improvements	DEV	$300,000
TF14-194 KRVT Portage Creek Trail	DEV	$300,000

KALAMAZOO TOWNSHIP

Project	Type	Amount
TF405 Grand Prairie Golf Course	ACQ	$45,000
TF99-082 Markin Glen River Access/KRVT	ACQ	$57,000

Oshtemo Township photo

The Oshtemo Township Park behind the Township Hall in the Village of Oshtemo boasts a baseball field, walking paths and a disc golf course. The township has received two Michigan Natural Resources Trust Fund grants for park property Acquisition and Development totaling $606,600.

OSHTEMO TOWNSHIP		
TF86-074 Oshtemo Township Park	ACQ	$117,600
TF10-113 Oshtemo Township Park Development	DEV	$489,000
TF12-046 Flesher Field Park Improvements	DEV	$300,000
TF13-069 Flesher Field Park Improvements	DEV	$300,000
TF14-170 Grange Hall Playground Improvements	DEV	$30,000
PARCHMENT		
TF91-343 Riverfront Park	DEV	$71,900
PORTAGE		
TF00-367 Lakeview Park Development	DEV	$200,000
TF87-289 West Lake Nature Preserve	DEV	$100,000
TF91-335 Ramona Park Improvements	DEV	$150,000
TF95-212 Bishop's Bog Preserve Trail	DEV	$150,000
TF98-145 Portage Creek Bicentennial Park Trail Dev.	DEV	$113,000
TEXAS TOWNSHIP		
TF10-025 Farmer's Market Trailhead/Mini-Park	DEV	$287,800
TF11-047 Texas Drive Non-Motorized Trail Extension	DEV	$300,000
VICKSBURG		
TF94-155 Vicksburg Recreational Park	ACQ	$131,300
TF96-155 Vicksburg Recreation Area	DEV	$183,000

KALAMAZOO COUNTY TOTAL $6,865,600

Kalkaska County

Kalkaska County was set aside as an unorganized county in 1840 from part of Mackinac County and was originally named *Wabassee* County after a Potawatomi Chieftain. In 1843, Henry Rowe Schoolcraft named it *Calkaska*, presumably a derivative of "calcraft", for Schoolcrafts's grandfather and "cass" for Michigan's Governor Lewis Cass. The county was formally established as Kalkaska in 1870.

MNRTF Project TF95-852, was a $450,000 Acquisition grant to the Michigan DNRE Forest, Mineral & Fire Management Department, in cooperation with the Grand Traverse Regional Land Conservancy to secure and preserve the Seven Bridges area of Kalkaska County.

With 561 square miles, Kalkaska County is 54th largest county and 66th largest in population with 17,153 residents.

Since oil was discovered there in 1971, 1,174 holes have been drilled in the search for oil and gas. Kalkaska County has produced 63,323,995 barrels of oil and 619.681 billion cubic feet of natural gas, ranking 6th and 4th respectively among the 64 oil or gas producing Michigan counties.

Kalkaska County has received $7.027.900 in 17 Michigan Natural Resources Trust Fund grants, ranking 35th in number of grants received and 32nd in grant dollars awarded.

KALKASKA COUNTY active or closed MNRTF Projects

Project	Type	Amount
COLD SPRINGS TOWNSHIP		
TF11-008 Sands Park Development	DEV	$47,000
TF12-011 Sands Park Playground	DEV	$30,900
DNR - FOREST, MINERAL & FIRE MANAGEMENT		
TF05-140 Flowing Well Conservation Easement	ACQ	$3,500,000
TF807 Big Manistee River	ACQ	$125,000
TF86-064 Bear Lake Acquisition	ACQ	$40,000
TF87-389 Manistee River Acq,	ACQ	$1,000,000
TF91-021 Skegemog Lake Wildlife Area	ACQ	$250,000
TF93-842 Manistee River-Livingstone	ACQ	$720,200
TF95-852 Seven Bridges	ACQ	$450,000
TF98-187 North Branch Manistee River	ACQ	300,000

Elk-Skegemog Lake Association photo

The 3,300 acre Skegemog Swamp Wildlife Area, located in Kalkaska County is another partnership with the Grand Traverse Regional Land Conservancy. Seven miles of shoreline on Skegemog Lake and Torch River provide critical habitat for many species of wildlife. Six Michigan Natural Trust Fund grants totaling $725,000 have gone to acquire and preserve lands in the Area.

Project	Type	Amount
DNR - PARKS & RECREATION DIVISION		
TF757 Kettle Lake	ACQ	$70,000
DNR - WILDLIFE DIVISION		
TF183 Skegemog Lake Wildlife Area	ACQ	$95,000
TF455 Skegemog Lake	ACQ	$35,000
TF531 Skegemog Lake	ACQ	$70,000
TF659 Skegemog Lake Area	ACQ	$120,000
TF835 Skegemog Lake	ACQ	$155,000
KALKASKA COUNTY		
TF729 Rugg Pond Rec. Project	ACQ	$19,800

KALKASKA COUNTY TOTAL $ 7,027,900

Kent County

Kent County was named in honor of James Kent 1763-1847, a New York jurist who represented the Michigan Territory during its dispute over the Toledo Strip with Ohio. It was set off as a county from Mackinac County in 1831, then formally established and named in 1836.

With 856 square miles, Kent County is 16th largest county and 4th largest in population with 602,622 residents.

On June 29, 2001, the Michigan Oil And Gas Association (MOGA) Award of Excellence for outstanding use of Michigan Natural Resources Trust Fund grants was presented to the City of Grand Rapids Riverside Trail Park, MNRTF grant TF96-091 - $500,000. Representing MOGA were Cook Energy's Jeff Cook, left, and Wolverine Gas & Oil's Richard Moritz, 2nd left, and MOGA President Frank L. Mortl, 2nd from right. Accepting the award for the city were Grand Rapids/Kent County Convention and Visitors Bureau President Steve Wilson and Grand Rapids Mayor Kurt Kimball.

Since oil was discovered there in 1938, 485 holes have been drilled in the search for oil and gas. Kent County has produced 19,112,843 barrels of oil and 5.360 billion cubic feet of natural gas, ranking 22nd and 47th respectively among the 64 oil or gas producing Michigan counties. Kent County has received $26,173,153 in 66 Michigan Natural Resources Trust

Fund grants, ranking 5th in number of grants received and 6th in grant dollars awarded.

KENT COUNTY active or closed MNRTF Projects

ADA TOWNSHIP		
TF05-106 Roselle Park Trail Improvements	DEV	$122,200
ALGOMA TOWNSHIP		
TF95-185 River's Edge Park	ACQ	$25,000
TF06-002 River's Edge Park Addition	ACQ	$49,000
TF10-099 Algoma RSC Archery Center Development	DEV	$500,000
CANNON TOWNSHIP		
TF05-076 Cannon Township Non-Motorized Trail	DEV	$500,000

The Cedar Springs Frederick Meijer White Pine Rail-Trail Staging Area was developed with MNRTF grant TF-09-003, $100,000.

CASCADE TOWNSHIP		
TF08-149 Cascade Natural Park Acquisition	ACQ	$1,200,000
CEDAR SPRINGS		
TF09-003 Frederick Meijer White Pine Trl. Staging Area	DEV	$100,000
DNR - FOREST, MINERAL & FIRE MANAGEMENT		
TF08-155 Grand River Edges Rail-Trail Acquisition	ACQ	$850,000
EAST GRAND RAPIDS		
TF08-054 Reeds Lake Waterfront Park	DEV	$490,000
TF91-177 Waterfront Park Expansion	ACQ	$800,300
GRAND RAPIDS		
TF618 Blandford Nature Center	ACQ	$35,000
TF87-201 Jaycee Family Park	DEV	$300,000
TF88-238 Sesquicentennial River	DEV	$375,000
TF91-089 Huff Park Renovation	DEV	$294,000
TF95-133 Butterworth Bridge and Trail	ACQ	$108,000
TF95-135 Plaster Creek Trail	DEV	$375,000
TF96-091 Riverside Park Trail	DEV	$500,000
TF98-124 6th Street Bridge Park Renovations	DEV	$493,284
TF11-023 Pleasant Park Development	DEV	$300,000
GRAND RAPIDS TOWNSHIP		
TF00-061 Acquisition of Doezema Farm	ACQ	$1,280,000
GRANDVILLE		

TF01-179 Kent Trails - Grandville Extension	DEV	$471,500
TF07-100 Grandville & Kent Trails Pathway Connection	DEV	$118,800
TF87-187 Japinga Park	ACQ	$50,000

Millennium Park, southwest of Grand Rapids, has received three MNRTF grants totaling $5,000,200. The park encompasses 1,500 acres of heavily-used land for public recreation with rolling terrain, extensive wetlands and lakes. Facilities within the park include a six-acre beach and splashpad, nearly 20 miles of trails, and other diverse opportunities for recreation. Touching Grand Rapids, Walker, Grandville and Wyoming, Millennium Park is one of our nation's largest urban parks. The park contains several working oil wells but, after accepting MNRTF monies rooted in Michigan oil and gas lease and royalty monies from state-owned mineral properties, ironically some elements tried to have those wells shut down rather than paying homage to the park's principal enabler.

GRATTAN TOWNSHIP

TF06-087 Satterlee Park Acquisition	ACQ	$30,000
TF10-060 Sealy Creek Park Expansion	ACQ	$48,100

KENT COUNTY

TF00-058 Millennium Park Facilities Development	DEV	$500,000
TF00-059 Pickerel Lake Trail Addition	DEV	$240,500
TF00-328 Millennium Park Land Acquisition	ACQ	$1,110,200
TF01-078 Millennium Park Acquisition II	ACQ	$3,390,000
TF02-126 Wahlfield Park Development	DEV	$236,500
TF05-055 Thornapple Coldwater Park Acquisition	ACQ	$962,000
TF06-205 Chief Hazy Cloud Park Expansion	ACQ	$1,110,000
TF87-177 Caledonia Park	ACQ	$37,500
TF90-104 Pickerel Lake Property	ACQ	$1,050,000
TF96-104 Wabasis Lake Park Upgrade	DEV	$320,000
TF96-105 Pickerel Lake Acquisition	ACQ	$490,000
TF97-121 Ruehs Park Addition	ACQ	$67,200
TF97-122 Palmer Park Renovation	DEV	$250,000
TF98-099 Rogue River Park Redevelopment	DEV	$482,762

TF98-271 Regional Parkland Purchase	ACQ	$443,800
TF99-176 Purchase Regional Parkland	ACQ	$1,572,500
TF13-071 Pickeral Lake Park Boardwalk Replacement	DEV	$250,000
TF14-229 Two Rivers Park Addition	ACQ	$810,000
KENTWOOD		
TF01-023 East Paris Nature Park Development	DEV	$82,618
TF05-026 Kenneth Stanaback Park	DEV	$99,400
TF08-062 North Stanaback Park Acquisition	ACQ	$85,000
TF09-029 Pinewood Park Splash Pad	DEV	$65,000
TF91-056 Heyboer/Keller Park	ACQ	$75,000
TF98-029 Bowen Property Acquisition	ACQ	$26,250
TF11-024 Northeast Park Boardwalk Expansion	DEV	$125,400
LOWELL		
TF11-066 Flat River Amphitheater Park Extension	DEV	$300,000
LOWELL AREA RECREATION AUTHORITY		
TF09-058 The Lowell Area Trailway	DEV	$398,000
LOWELL TOWNSHIP		
TF91-227 Grand River Riverfront Park	ACQ	$49,500
TF98-248 Lowell Charter Township Park	DEV	$142,335
PLAINFIELD TOWNSHIP		
TF09-166 Grand Isle Acquisition	ACQ	$520,000
TF97-241 Versluis Park Improvements	DEV	$154,900
ROCKFORD		
TF03-095 Rogue River Trail Network	DEV	$118,200
TF06-069 Rogue River Trail Network Ext./Peppler Pk.	DEV	$222,700
TF10-059 Rouge River Nature Trail Development	DEV	$86,500
TF903 Rogue River Frontage	ACQ	$20,000
TF97-098 Rogue River Overlook/Fishing Imp.	DEV	$92,554
SPARTA		
TF92-275 Rogue River Park Acquisition	ACQ	$33,750
WALKER		
TF91-230 Alpine Estates Park Expansion	ACQ	$60,000
WYOMING		
TF08-001 Oriole Park Site Development	DEV	$378,900
TF87-018 Buck Creek Nature Preserve	DEV	$120,000
TF98-063 Battjes Park Passive Recreation	DEV	$179,000

KENT COUNTY TOTAL $26,173,153

Keweenaw County

Keweenaw County's name comes from an Ojibwa word "*gakiiwewaning*", which means "portage". It was carved from Houghton County and formally organized in 1861.

With 541 square miles, Keweenaw County is 64th largest county and 83rd largest in population with 2,156 residents Keweenaw is an Upper Peninsula county with no significant sedimentary geological strata, precluding the likelihood of the presence of oil and/or natural gas, so no holes have been drilled there to search for petroleum. Keweenaw County has received $21,418.577 in 17 Michigan Natural Resources Trust Fund grants, ranking 32nd in terms number of grants received but 9th in grant dollars awarded.

Funds for the Future photo

MNRTF grants TF01-196, 02-187 and 863, all Acquisition grants, total $13,000,000, use to purchase and preserve the tip of the Keweenaw Peninsula for public recreation purposes. This is one of the Fund's largest undertakings and is the northernmost of Michigan Natural Resources Trust Fund projects.

KEWEENAW COUNTY active/closed MNRTF Projects

ALLOUEZ TOWNSHIP

TF03-125 Seneca Lake Township Park /Recreation Area ACQ $175,500

DNR - FOREST, MINERAL & FIRE MANAGEMENT

TF01-196 Tip of the Keweenaw	ACQ	$5,000,000
TF02-187 Tip of the Keweenaw Acquisition- Phase II	ACQ	$7,500,000
TF863 Keweenaw Tract	ACQ	$500,000

DNR - PARKS & RECREATION DIVISION

TF94-849 Fort Wilkins St. Park Addition	ACQ	$1,850,000
TF14-190 Fort Wilkins State Historical Park Trail	ACQ	$750,000

EAGLE HARBOR TOWNSHIP

TF99-267 Eagle Harbor Township Nature Conservatory	ACQ	$493,077
TF11-099 Keweenaw Coastal Wildlife Corridor	ACQ	$498,000

Grant Township photo

GRANT TOWNSHIP'S HUNTER'S POINT AREA saw a total of $2,049,100 MNRTF grants devoted buying and improving the area for public recreation.

GRANT TOWNSHIP

TF04-104 Hunter's Point Acquisition	ACQ	$562,900
TF06-123 Hunter's Point Public Access Enhancement	DEV	$47,100
TF07-099 Hunter's Point Park Acquisition - Phase I	ACQ	$720,000
TF08-023 Hunter's Point Park Phase II	ACQ	$720,000
TF93-186 6th Street Waterfront Project	DEV	$60,000
TF97-109 Sixth Street Waterfront	DEV	$120,000

HOUGHTON

TF08-148 East Houghton Greenspace Property	ACQ	$22,000

KEWEENAW COUNTY

TF05-078 Gratiot River County Park Addition	ACQ	$1,957,500
TF99-276 Gratiot River Mouth Land Acquisition	ACQ	$442,500

KEWEENAW COUNTY TOTAL $21,418,577

Lake County

Named for the multitude of small lakes in the area and its proximity to Lake Michigan, Lake County was set off as a county in 1840 and was known as *Aischum* in honor of a Potawatomi Chief until 1843, when it was named Lake, formally established in 1870.

With 568 square miles, Lake County is 45th largest county and 73rd largest in population with 11,539 residents.

Since oil was discovered there in 1942, 244 holes have been drilled in the search for oil and gas. Lake County has produced 2,870,483 barrels of oil and 2.931 billion cubic feet of natural gas, ranking 40th and 49th respectively among the 64 oil or gas producing Michigan counties.

Shrine of the Pines photo

MNRTF grants TF508, and 86-244, totaling $144,700, went to Shrine of the Pines land Acquisition and facility Development.

Lake County has received $653,900 in 5 Michigan Natural Resources Trust Fund grants, ranking 66th in number of grants received and 79th in grant dollars awarded.

LAKE COUNTY active or closed MNRTF Projects

DNR – FOREST RESOURCES DIVISION		
TF13-126 Little Manistee River Property	ACQ	$100,000
DNR - PARKS & RECREATION DIVISION		
TF07-130 Lake Idlewild Park Development	DEV	$324,900
LAKE COUNTY		
TF508 Shrine of the Pines	ACQ	$90,000
TF86-244 Shrine of the Pines	DEV	$54,700
LUTHER		
TF11-042 Luther Mill Pond Park Improvements	DEV	$84,100

LAKE COUNTY TOTAL $ 653,900

Lapeer County

Lapeer County is believed to have been named with a corruption of the French word *la pierre*, meaning "flint". It was set off as a county in 1822 and formally established in 1837.

Lapeer County's 654 square miles make it 32nd largest county and with 88,319 residents, 22nd largest in population

MNRTF grant TF90-251 - $19,050 - went to Lapeer County for Rails to Trails. Southern Links Trailway connects Columbiaville, Otter Lake and Millington, here at Columbiaville, adjacent to MNRTF grant site TF10-030, Veteran's Memorial Boardwalk.

Since oil was discovered there in 1955, 198 holes have been drilled in the search for oil and gas. Lapeer County has produced 5,890,806 barrels of oil and 10.037 billion cubic feet of natural gas, ranking 32nd and 44th respectively among the 64 oil or gas producing Michigan counties.

Lapeer County has received $1,602,150 in 7 Michigan Natural Resources Trust Fund grants, ranking 72nd in number of grants received and 67th in grant dollars awarded.

DNR - WILDLIFE DIVISION		
TF176 Flint River, Lapeer SGA	ACQ	$497,000
TF350 Lapeer State Game Area	ACQ	$650,000
LAPEER		
TF90-251 Rails to Trails Acq.	ACQ	$19,050
TF90-252 Rowden Park Improvements	DEV	$157,400
LAPEER COUNTY		
TF07-038 General Squier Memorial Park Addition	ACQ	$58,600
MARATHON TOWNSHIP		
TF13-028 Marathon Twp. Park Land	ACQ	$98,600
VILLAGE OF COLUMBIAVILLE		
TF10-030 Veterans Memorial Boardwalk	DEV	$121,500

LAPEER COUNTY TOTAL $ 1,602, 150

Leelanau County

Leelanau County's name comes from an American Indian love story called *Leelinau* told by Henry Rowe Schoolcraft, who it is theorized created the story himself. It was set off as a county from part of Mackinac County in 1840 and formally established in 1863.

Leelanau County's 348 square miles, make it 82nd largest, second smallest county in the state and 63rd largest in population with 21,708 residents.

Elmwood Township photo

MNRTF grant TF07-039, $910,000, went to Elmwood Township's DeYoung Natural Area Acquisition.

Leelanau County is one of four Michigan Lower Peninsula Counties that produce no oil or gas, although 20 holes have been drilled there in the search for petroleum natural resources.

Leelanau County has received $12,575,600 in 19 Michigan Natural Resources Trust Fund grants, ranking 29h in number of grants received and 15th in grant dollars awarded.

LEELANAU COUNTY active or closed MNRTF Projects

BINGHAM TOWNSHIP

Project	Type	Amount
TF00-365 Addition to Mebert Creek Natural Area Acq.	ACQ	$27,000
TF92-019 Mebert Creek Natural Area	ACQ	$75,000

DNR - PARKS & RECREATION DIVISION

Project	Type	Amount
TF04-181 Lighthouse West Property/Leelanau State Park	ACQ	$630,000
TF05-147 Lighthouse W. Property Conservation Easement	ACQ	$330,000
TF06-142 Leelanau State Park Conservation Easement	ACQ	$2,043,800

DNR - WILDLIFE DIVISION

Project	Type	Amount
TF97-289 North Fox Island	ACQ	$2,000,000

ELMWOOD TOWNSHIP

Project	Type	Amount
TF07-039 DeYoung Natural Area Acquisition	ACQ	$910,200
TF07-095 Greilickville Harbor Park Improvements	DEV	210,300

EMPIRE

Project	Type	Amount
TF05-124 Lake Michigan Beach Park Improvements	DEV	$356,600

TF90-233 Empire Public Beach	DEV	$60,000
LEELANAU COUNTY		
TF06-024 Veronica Valley Park	ACQ	$600,000
LEELANAU TOWNSHIP		
TF2-105 Christmas Cove Adjacent Property	ACQ	$375,000
LELAND TOWNSHIP		
TF94-066 Hall Beach Project	ACQ	$163,500
TF97-009 Bartholomew Pk. Add. at Nedow's Bay Beach	ACQ	$202,000
TF11-020 Clay Cliffs Natural Area	ACQ	$2,933,000
SUTTONS BAY		
TF93-305 Klumpp Property Purchase	ACQ	$525,000
TF11-097 Front Street Pathway Development	ACQ	$240,000
SUTTONS BAY TOWNSHIP		
TF06-110 Herman Park Acquisition	ACQ	$394,200
VILLAGE OF NORTHPORT		
TF10-053 Waterfront Improvement Project	DEV	$500,000

Michigan DNRE photo

The lighthouse West Property of the Leelanau State Park and accompanying easements has received three MNRTF grants totaling $3,003,800.

LEELANAU COUNTY TOTAL $ 12,575,600

Lenawee County

Lenawee County was named by Henry Schoolcraft, perhaps from an American Indian word for man, either the Delaware "*leno*" or "*lenno*" or the Shawneee "*lenawa*". It was set off as a county and formally established in 1822.

MNRTF grants TF07-018, and 88-069, totaling $347,100, went to Clinton's Tate Park Development.

With 751 square miles, Lenawee County is 21st largest county and 28th largest in population with 99,892 residents.

Since oil was discovered there in 1961, 352 holes have been drilled in the search for oil and gas. Lenawee County has produced 1,655,138 barrels of oil and 377.069 million cubic feet of natural gas, ranking 47th and 53rd, respectively among the 64 oil or gas producing Michigan counties. Lenawee County has received $858,760 in 8 Michigan Natural Resources Trust Fund grants, ranking 60th in number of grants received and 69th in grant dollars awarded.

LENAWEE COUNTY active or closed MNRTF Projects

ADRIAN		
TF87-059 Island Park Riverstrip	ACQ	$75,000
BLISSFIELD		
TF96-066 Ellis Park Boat Launch	DEV	$33,720
CLINTON		
TF07-018 Tate Park Pathway and Fishing Docks	DEV	$297,600
TF88-069 Tate Memorial Park	DEV	$49,500
LENAWEE COUNTY		
TF10-102 Gerber Hill Park Improvements	DEV	$69,000
TF86-178 Ramsdell Nature Center	DEV	$163,000
MORENCI		
TF01-096 Wakefield Park Expansion	ACQ	$86,940
TECUMSEH		
TF94-156 Indian Crossing Trails	ACQ	$84,000

LENAWEE COUNTY TOTAL $ 858,760

Livingston County

Livingston County was named for President Andrew Jackson's Secretary of State from 1831 to 1833 Edward Livingston 1764-1836. It's boundaries were defined in 1833 and Livingston formally established as a county in 1836.

Cohoctah Township photo

MNRTF grant TF94-164, $60,000, went to acquire land for the Cohoctah Township Park.

With 568 square miles, Livingston County is 44th largest county and 11th largest in population with 180,967 residents.

Since oil was discovered there in 1935, 451 holes have been drilled in the search for oil and gas. Livingston County has produced 4,733,060 barrels of oil and 41.936 billion cubic feet of natural gas, ranking 33rd and 27th respectively among the 64 oil or gas producing Michigan counties.

Livingston County has received $7,639,655 in 17 Michigan Natural Resources Trust Fund grants, ranking 31st in number of grants received and 29th in grant dollars awarded.

LIVINGSTON COUNTY active or closed MNRTF Projects

BRIGHTON		
TF94-095 Millpond Park	DEV	$165,000
TF97-063 Mill Pond Trail Extension	DEV	$294,695
COHOCTAH TOWNSHIP		
TF94-164 Cohoctah Township Park	ACQ	$60,000
DEERFIELD TOWNSHIP		
TF00-188 Deerfield Hills Development Project	DEV	$31,220
TF97-093 Deerfield Hills Natural Area	ACQ	$2,190,000
DNR - PARKS & RECREATION DIVISION		
TF87-007 Island Lake Recreation Area	DEV	$500,000
DNR – WILDLIFE DIVISION		
TF10-162 Gregory State Game Area Land Initiative	ACQ	$875,000
TF366 Oak Grove State Game Area	ACQ	$210,000
HAMBURG TOWNSHIP		
TF13-014 Lakeland Trails Access	DEV	$125,400

HARTLAND TOWNSHIP

TF90-018 Nature Preserve	ACQ	$17,250
TF98-007 Hartland Township Park	ACQ	$345,000

HCMA

TF01-041 Lake Erie Metropark Hike-Bike/Shoreline Trl.	DEV	$199,800
TF03-023 Hudson Mills Metropark Hike/Bike Trail	DEV	$361,000
TF07-028 Indian Springs Metropark Land Acquisition	ACQ	$1,426,000
TF99-118 Huron Meadow Maltby Lake Access Play Area	DEV	$180,000

PUTNAM TOWNSHIP

TF10-001 Lakeland Trail Development - Putnam Twp.	DEV	$500,000

MNRTF grant TF10-041, $159,300, went to renovate the Village of Fowlerville Community Park in the heart of the town.

VILLAGE OF FOWLERVILLE

TF10-041 Fowlerville Community Park Renovation	DEV	$159,300

LIVINGSTON COUNTY TOTAL $ 7,639,655

Luce County

Luce County is named for Michigan Governor Cyrus G. Luce whose 1887-1891 administration saw northern Michigan's population and development grow, as well as seeing the Grand Hotel on Mackinac Island built.

It was set off as a county from parts of Chippewa and Mackinac counties and formally established in 1887.

Luce County photo

MNRTF grant TF99-437, for $114,393, was used for the development of Luce County Park on the south shore of North Manistique

With 903 square miles, Luce County is 14th largest county and 82nd largest in population with 6,631 residents.

Luce is an Upper Peninsula county so not a great prospect for oil or natural gas production because little to no significant sedimentary geological strata are there. Only two holes, both dry, have been drilled in Luce to search for petroleum, making it 73rd most drilled county in the state.

Luce County has received $914,393 in 3 Michigan Natural Resources Trust Fund grant, ranking 80th in number of grants received and 76th in grant dollars awarded.

LUCE COUNTY active or closed MNRTF Projects

DNR – EXECUTIVE OFFICE		
TF12-125 Two Hearted River Property	ACQ	$500,000
LUCE COUNTY		
TF99-437 County Park Revitalization	DEV	$114,393
NEWBERRY		
TF11-068 Complex Development	DEV	$300,000

LUCE COUNTY TOTAL $ 914,393

Mackinac County

Mackinac County is one of Michigan's oldest territories, set aside from Wayne County (founded in 1796) in 1818 as "*Michilimackinac*", a French term derived from an American Indian term describing the straits area between Michigan's Upper and Lower Peninsulas. It's English interpretation is "Mackinaw", which is the way both names are pronounced. In 1837, the county name was changed to Mackinac and it was formally established that year.

The MNRTF $160,600 grant TF01-008 went to develop the St. Ignace American Legion Park.

With 1,022 square miles, Mackinac County is 9th largest county and 74th largest in population with 11,113 residents.

An Upper Peninsula county, Mackinac is one of those with little significant sedimentary geological strata, precluding the likelihood of the presence of oil and/or natural gas. But 4 holes have been drilled there in the search for oil and natural gas with no result.

Mackinac County has received $9,107,550 in 22 Michigan Natural Resources Trust Fund grants, ranking 24th both in number of grants received and in grant dollars awarded.

MACKINAC COUNTY active or closed MNRTF Projects

CLARK TOWNSHIP		
TF94-002 Clark Township Beach	ACQ	$95,300
TF96-180 Township Swimming/Beach Area	DEV	$40,500
DNR - FOREST, MINERAL & FIRE MANAGEMENT		
TF86-120 Seiners Point Wild Area	ACQ	$35,000
TF94-297 Bethlehem Steel Property	ACQ	$1,820,000
TF979 Point Patterson	ACQ	$500,000
TF980 Ryerse Lake Bog	ACQ	$45,000
DNR - WILDLIFE DIVISION		
TF93-424 Bethlehem Steel Property	ACQ	$2,829,900
DNRE - MACKINAC ISLAND STATE PARK COMISSION		
TF10-127 Spring Trail Upgrade	DEV	$50,000
MACKINAC ISLAND STATE PARK COMMISSION		
TF01-205 Mackinac Island State Park Land Acq.	ACQ	$500,000
TF02-204 Acquisition on Mackinac Island	ACQ	$200,000
TF05-111 Old Mackinac Point Light Station Imp.	DEV	$189,000

TF95-298 Mackinac Island Land Acquisition	ACQ	$1,000,000
TF99-299 Mackinac Island State Park Land Acq.	ACQ	$500,000

The MNRTF $94,250 grant TF97-011 went to develop the Kiwanis Beach in St. Ignace. All told through 2010, St. Ignace has received $1,302,850 in nine Michigan Natural Resources grant.

ST. IGNACE

TF01-008 American Legion Park	DEV	$160,600
TF05-018 Huron Boardwalk	DEV	$137,500
TF08-013 Chief Wawatam Park Development	DEV	$134,000
TF1028 Marquette Among the Huron	ACQ	$126,000
TF91-237 Waterfront Park Extension	ACQ	$273,000
TF92-121 Railroad Acquisition	ACQ	$217,500
TF92-156 American Legion Memorial Park Dev.	DEV	$67,000
TF97-011 Kiwanis Beach Development	DEV	$94,250
TF99-026 Dock #3 Park Development	DEV	$93,000

MACKINAC COUNTY TOTAL $ 9,107,550

Macomb County

Macomb County was named in honor of American General Alexander Macomb, a hero of the War of 1812. It was set off as a county in 1818 from Wayne County and formally established as a county in 1822.

With 480 square miles, Macomb County is 75th largest county but 3rd largest in population with 840,978 residents.

Shelby Township photo

MNRTF grant TF98-243, $302,680, went to the Shelby Township's River Bends Park, helping to develop the park's Nature Center Building.

Since oil was discovered there in 1959, 650 holes have been drilled in the search for oil and gas. Macomb County has produced 1,128,771 barrels of oil and 18.45 billion cubic feet of natural gas, ranking 50th and 38th respectively among the 64 oil or gas producing Michigan counties.

Macomb County has received $8,498,930 in 26 Michigan Natural Resources Trust Fund grants, ranking 20th in number of grants received and 25th in grant dollars awarded.

MACOMB COUNTY active or closed MNRTF Projects

CHESTERFIELD TOWNSHIP

TF94-283 Brandenburg Park Improvements DEV $112,500

CLINTON TOWNSHIP

TF90-274 Clinton River Park ACQ $16,500

DNR - PARKS & RECREATION DIVISION

TF90-100 Harley Ensign Memorial DEV $375,000

TF97-287 Prolow Estate Acquisition, Lake St. Clair ACQ $1,500,000

DNR - WILDLIFE DIVISION

TF394 Salt River Marsh ACQ $40,000

EASTPOINTE

TF1073 St. Basil Property ACQ $45,000

TF86-105 Memorial Pk Baseball Flds DEV $45,000

FRASER

TF12-021 McKinley Barrier-Free Park Improvements DEV $300,000

HURON-CLINTON METROPOLITAN AUTHORITY

TF87-085 Metro Beach Nature Center Building DEV $225,000

TF12-057 Lake St. Clair Metropark Land ACQ $229,000

TF14-127 Stony Creek Boat Launch Redevelopment DEV $50,000

MACOMB COUNTY

TF02-166 Macomb Orchard Trail Acquisition ACQ $1,718,300

TF10-085 Nicholson Nature Center DEV $205,000

MACOMB TOWNSHIP

TF97-229 Township Park #1 ACQ $712,500

MOUNT CLEMENS

TF89-205 Oxford Drive Nature Area ACQ $71,400

TF90-141 Shadyside Park DEV $206,250

NEW BALTIMORE

TF90-338 Waterfront Park DEV $75,000

TF12-118 County Line Rd. Non-Motorized Ped. Path DEV $116,000

ROSEVILLE

TF08-086 Huron Park Accessibility Upgrade DEV $320,800

SHELBY TOWNSHIP

TF98-243 River Bends Park Nature Center Building DEV $302,680

TF12-115 Riverbends Park/Macomb Orchard Trail Con. DEV $300,000

STERLING HEIGHTS

TF02-030 Bike Path Riverland Dr. to Van Dyke Ave. DEV $220,000

TF399 Clinton River Pk Add. ACQ $167,500

TF90-091 Section 6 Nature Preserve ACQ $675,000

UTICA

TF07-054 Clinton River Hike Bike Trail Development DEV $350,000

WARREN

TF01-017 Rentz Park Development DEV $120,500

MACOMB COUNTY TOTAL $ 8,498,930

Manistee County

Manistee County is supposedly named derivative of "*ministigweyaa*", meaning "crooked river". The county was officially organized in 1840.

Manistee County's 544 square miles rank it 63rd largest county and 24,733 citizens place it 57th largest in population. Since Niagaran geological formation oil was discovered in Manistee County in 1973 at a depth of 4,780 feet, 1,720 holes have been drilled in the search for oil and gas, making it the 5th most drilled county among the 75 Michigan counties that have seen drilling.

Manistee County has produced 114,958,554 barrels of oil and 743.183 billion cubic feet of natural gas, ranking the county 2nd and 3rd respectively of the 65 Michigan oil and/or gas producing counties.

Manistee County has received $14,085,259 in 16 Michigan Natural Resources Trust Fund grants, ranking 39th in number of grants received and 14th in grant dollars.

Michigan DNRE photo

MNRTF Projects TF1027, and TF99-127, the Arcadia Township Marina Expansion and Arcadia South Beach both Acquisition projects, totaled $929,759 in MNRTF grants for Manistee County's Arcadia Township.

The Orchard Beach State Park in Manistee County distributes a hiking trail guide acknowledging on the trails loop 3 through 6 explaining oil and gas drilling exploration beneath the ground concluding "Dependent as we are on fossil fuels, Manistee is providing her share".

MANISTEE COUNTY active or closed MNRTF Projects

ARCADIA TOWNSHIP		
TF1027 Arcadia Twp. Marina Expansion	ACQ	$95,000
TF99-127 Arcadia South Beach	ACQ	$834,759
TF14-201 Arcadia Lake MI Beach Development	DEV	$278,700
DNR - EXECUTIVE OFFICE		
TF03-209 CMS Arcadia/Green Point Dunes	ACQ	$4,000,000
TF04-125 CMS Arcadia/Green Point Dunes	ACQ	$4,500,000
DNR – FISHERIES DIVISION		
TF11-125 Little Manistee River Weir	DEV	$300,000
DNR - FOREST, MINERAL & FIRE MANAGEMENT		
TF665 Springdale Betsie Forest	ACQ	$345,000
FILER TOWNSHIP		
TF390 Magoon Creek	ACQ	$150,000
MANISTEE		
TF07-040 Man Made Lake Acquisition	ACQ	$2,015,000

City of Manistee photo

MNRTF Project TF91-147, a Development grant of $375,000, helped develop the City of Manistee's Riverwalk West.

TF91-147 Manistee Riverwalk West	DEV	$375,000
TF94-240 Manistee Riverfront Park	DEV	$375,000
TF11-026 Manistee First Street Beach House	DEV	$280,000
MANISTEE TOWNSHIP		
TF1050 Bar Lake Outlet	ACQ	$17,500
ONEKAMA TOWNSHIP		
TF14-180 Langland Park Dev. On Lake Michigan	DEV	$261,000
VILLAGE OF EAST LAKE		
TF12-090 Penny Park Renovation	DEV	$141,000
VILLAGE OF ONEKAMA		
TF12-088 Penny Park Renovation	DEV	$97,300

MANISTEE COUNTY TOTAL $ 14,085,259

Marquette County

Marquette County's 1,820 square miles make it the largest county in Michigan while it's population of 67,077 residents rank it 15th in population. Marquette County is named for French Jesuit missionary Pere Jacque Marquette 1637-1675 who ranged the northern Great Lakes area, establishing the first European settlement, Sault Ste. Marie, as well as establishing the village of St. Ignace.

Iron Ore Heritage Recreation Authority photo

THE IRON ORE HERITAGE TRAIL is a 48 mile multi-use year-round trail in Marquette County. In 2009, the Iron Ore Heritage Recreation Authority received MNRTF grant TF09-071- $15,000 – for interpretive signs along the trail and in 2010 grant TF10-074 - $400,000 – was approved for Trail Development.

Marquette County was set off from Chippewa and Mackinac Counties and formally established as an entity in 1843.

An Upper Peninsula County, Marquette County has no significant sedimentary geological strata, precluding the likelihood of the presence of oil and/or natural gas. So no holes have been drilled there in the search for petroleum. Marquette County has received $10,515,620 in 47 Michigan Natural Resources Trust Fund grants, 9th in number of grants received and 21st in grant dollars awarded.

MARQUETTE COUNTY active or closed MNRTF Projects

CHAMPION TOWNSHIP		
TF01-049 Wetlands and Mager's Creek Acquisition	ACQ	$6,795
TF89-264 Champion Parkland Acq.	ACQ	$15,000
CHOCOLAY TOWNSHIP		
TF04-102 Chocolay River Water Trail Access Site	DEV	$18,300
TF86-301 Beaver Grove Rec. Area	ACQ	$12,300
TF88-103 Beaver Grove Rec. Area	DEV	$29,175
TF14-219 Lions Field Trailhead Dev. & Park Imp.	DEV	$50,000
DEPARTMENT OF HISTORY, ARTS & LIBRARIES		
TF06-126 Iron Industry Museum Interpretive Trl. System	DEV	$261,600
DNR - FOREST, MINERAL & FIRE MANAGEMENT		
TF543 Lake Superior and Ishpeming Trail	ACQ	$491,000

TF86-278 Little Presque Isle Rec.	DEV	$360,000
TF99-290 Marquette-Munising Rail-Trail	ACQ	$550,000
DNR - WILDLIFE DIVISION		
TF09-157 Huron Mountains Deeryard Complex	ACQ	$750,000
TF14-132 UP Grouse Enhancement Man. Syst. Trail Init.	DEV	$40,000
DNR - WILDLIFE		
TF10-161 Huron Mts. Deeryard Complex Addition Acq.	ACQ	$1,300,000
ELY TOWNSHIP		
TF87-129 Gold Mine Lake Park	ACQ	$18,000
FORSYTH TOWNSHIP		
TF04-077 Peter Nordeen Park Improvements	DEV	$425,600
TF10-076 Farquar/Metsa Tourist Park Improvements	DEV	$268,600
IRON ORE HERITAGE RECREATION AUTHORITY		
TF09-071 Iron Ore Heritage Trl. Interpretative Signage	DEV	$15,000
TF10-074 Iron Ore Heritage Trail Development	DEV	$400,000
TF12-049 Iron Ore Heritage Trail –Tilden Twp. Sec.	DEV	$281,000
TF14-159 Interpretive Signage	DEV	$22,000

City of Ishpeming photo

THE AL QUAAL RECREATION AREA is a natural 300-acre Ishpeming city park overlooking Teal Lake. It has a 1,200-foot iced toboggan run, downhill ski runs and a slalom run The City of Ishpeming has received 3 grants totaling $275,250 for acquisition of the Al Quaal property and two more grants totaling $510,000 for acquisition and development of the Teal Lake property.

ISHPEMING		
TF01-074 Land Acq.- Five Mining Property Parcels	ACQ	$50,000
TF08-105 Iron Ore Heritage Trail	DEV	$354,800
TF90-242 Al Quaal Land Acq - Ph I	ACQ	$101,250
TF91-080 Al Quaal Land Acquisition	ACQ	$84,000
TF94-054 Teal Lake Development	DEV	$60,000

TF95-316 Al Quaal Land Acquisition	ACQ	$90,000
TF97-228 Ishpeming/Negaunee Teal Lake Land Acq.	ACQ	$450,000
TF14-265 Malton Road Non-Motorized Trail	DEV	$91,400
ISHPEMING TOWNSHIP		
TF86-280 Ishpeming Recreation Area	ACQ	$25,000
MARQUETTE		
TF89-255 Lower Harbor Park Marina	DEV	$375,000
TF12-030 McCarty's Cove Permanent Restrooms	DEV	$88,800
TF13-053 Presque Isle/Harlow/Williams Restroom Fac.	DEV	$296,000
TF13-032 Camp Lambros Beach Park Acq.	ACQ	$1,440,000
MARQUETTE COUNTY		
TF04-089 Sugar Loaf Mountain Enhancements	DEV	$59,200
TF08-028 Perkins Park Improvements	DEV	$198,400
TF87-043 Sugar Loaf Natural Area	DEV	$12,5000

Perkins Park is a county park on Independence Lake at the village of Big Bay. Two MNRTF grants, one in 1995 and the other in 2008 totaling $330,400 have helped develop the park.

TF95-189 Perkins Park Development	DEV	$132,000
MARQUETTE TOWNSHIP		
TF10-081 Iron Ore Heritage Trailhead Acquisition	ACQ	$156,900
TF14-133 Twps. 1st Iron Ore Heritage Trail	DEV	$36,600
NEGAUNEE		
TF09-113 Pennies for the Park at Miners Park	DEV	$75,000
TF95-246 Teal Lake Access Improvements	DEV	$74,300
NEGAUNEE TOWNSHIP		
TF719 Kivela Road Recreation Area	ACQ	$11,000
POWELL		
TF08-104 Thomas Rock Scenic Overlook	DEV	$319,100
POWELL TOWNSHIP		
TF10-075 Thomas Rock Nature Area Acquisition	ACQ	$404,500
REPUBLIC TOWNSHIP		
TF08-106 Republic Iron Ore Heritage Trailhead	ACQ	$32,300
TF95-284 Michigamme Rv Access Site	ACQ	$11,000
TF13-119 Munson Park Improvements	DEV	$172,200

MARQUETTE COUNTY TOTAL $ 10,515,620

Mason County

Mason County was named for Stevens T. Mason 1811-1843, who was elected Governor of the Michigan Territory in 1834, then elected Governor of the State of Michigan when the territory achieved statehood in 1837, serving in that office until 1843. It was set off as a county from Mackinac County in 1840, named *Notipekago* County until 1843 and was formally established in 1855.

City of Ludington photo

MNRTF grant TF96-237, $500,000, went to Ludington's Waterfront Park Development.

With 495 square miles, Mason County is 73rd largest county and 50th largest in population with 28,705 residents.

Since oil was discovered there in 1948, 560 holes have been drilled in the search for oil and gas. Mason County has produced 8,911,903 barrels of oil and 51.042 billion cubic feet of natural gas, ranking 27th and 24th respectively among the 64 oil or gas producing Michigan counties.

Mason County has received $7,990,028 in 14 Michigan Natural Resources Trust Fund grants, ranking 45th in number of grants received and 26th in grant dollars awarded.

MASON COUNTY active or closed MNRTF Projects

DNR - EXECUTIVE OFFICE

TF96-862 Nordhouse Dunes Settlement	ACQ	$2,323,000
TF97-182 Nordhouse Dunes Settlement - Parcel C	ACQ	$2,593,428

DNR - PARKS & RECREATION DIVISION

TF92-343 Sargent Sand Parcel	ACQ	$1,100,000

LUDINGTON

TF03-003 Cartier Park Fishing Pier Installation	DEV	$82,500
TF08-051 Streams Park Breakwall Improvements	DEV	$125,300
TF93-046 Waterfront Park Acquisition	ACQ	$359,000
TF94-036 Copeyon Park Shelter (formerly Pere Marquette Lake Park)	DEV	$24,000
TF96-237 Ludington Waterfront Park	DEV	$500,000

MASON COUNTY

TF10-061 Mason County Fairgrounds Development	DEV	$320,000
TF11-056 Mason Co. Campground Entrance Imp.	DEV	$129,600

MEADE TOWNSHIP

TF09-066 Meade Township Park Development	DEV	$34,000
TF12-009 Mead Twp. Park Dev. Riverside Park	DEV	$32,500

MNRTF grants TF05-009 and 05-008, totaling $366,700, were used to develop Scottville's Riverfront Park Development.

SCOTTVILLE

TF05-008 Riverside Park Boat Launch Site Imp.	DEV	$82,300
TF05-009 Riverside Pk. Campground Redevelop	DEV	$284,400

MASON COUNTY TOTAL $ 7,990,028

Mecosta County

Mecosta County was named in honor of a Potawatomi Chieftain who signed the Washington Treaty of 1836, whose name is thought to mean "*bear cub*". It was set off as a county in 1840 and formally established in 1859.

City of Big Rapids photo

MNRTF Projects TF01-165, 02-163 and 07-097, totaling $1,292,700, went to Big Rapids Riverwalk Development.

With 556 square miles, Mecosta is 57th largest county and 40th largest in population with 42,798 residents. Since the discoverey of oil there in 1934, 1,219 holes have been drilled in the search for oil and gas. The county has produced 11,932,371 barrels of oil and 66.776 billion cubic feet of natural gas, ranking 25th and 20th respectively among the 64 oil or gas producing Michigan counties. Mecosta County has received $2,477,300 in 11 Michigan Natural Resources Trust Fund grants, ranking 57th in number of grants received and 53rd in grant dollars awarded.

MECOSTA COUNTY active or closed MNRTF Projects

Project	Type	Amount
BIG RAPIDS		
TF01-165 Big Rapids Riverwalk	DEV	$493,300
TF02-163 Big Rapids Riverwalk Development	DEV	$490,000
TF07-046 Mitchell Creek Nature Area Acquisition	ACQ	$143,700
TF07-097 Riverwalk Development - River Street Park	DEV	$309,400
TF97-178 Waterfront Trailway	DEV	$100,000
TF99-247 Waterfront Trailway	DEV	$163,000
DNR - PARKS & RECREATION DIVISION		
TF97-193 White Pine Trl. S. P. Big Rapids to Reed City	DEV	$500,000
MECOSTA COUNTY		
TF03-033 Brower Park Marina Bathhouse	DEV	$90,000
MORTON TOWNSHIP		
TF12-029 Morton Township Park Acquisition	DEV	$45,000
VILLAGE OF BARRYTON		
TF10-152 Barryton Park Improvements	DEV	$92,900
WHEATLAND TOWNSHIP		
TF14-254 Wheatland Township Pavillion	DEV	$50,000

MECOSTA COUNTY TOTAL $ 2,477,300

Menominee County

Menominee County was originally named Bleeker County when established in 1861 from part of Delta County. In 1863 it was renamed Menominee in honor of the area tribe of American Indians. With 1,044 square miles, Menominee County is 8th largest county and 60th largest in population with 24,029 residents.

Menominee County has received $5,898,400 in 9 Michigan Natural Resources Trust Fund grants, ranking 60th in grants received and 36th in grant dollars awarded.

City of Menominee photo

MNRTF Project 627 – $55,000, helped the City of Menominee acquire their Memorial Park property.

Menominee County has no significant sedimentary geological strata, precluding the likelihood of the presence of oil and/or natural gas, no holes have been drilled there to search for petroleum.

MENOMINEE COUNTY active or closed MNRTF Projects

DNR - FOREST, MINERAL & FIRE MANAGEMENT		
TF92-897 Peterson Property	ACQ	$388,000
TF96-257 Menominee River Block	ACQ	$2,000,000
DNR - WILDLIFE DIVISION		
TF02-201 Acquisition of Deeryards	ACQ	$500,000
DNRE - RECREATION DIVISION		
TF10-129 Quiver Falls and Piers Gorge Acquisition	ACQ	$2,400,000
MENOMINEE		
TF627 Memorial Park	ACQ	$55,000
TF86-118 Menominee Breakwater Wall	DEV	$500,000
MENOMINEE COUNTY		
TF728 Stoney Point Public Access Site	ACQ	$18,000
TF12-121 River Park Development	DEV	$18,700
TF13-075 Stoney Point Rehabilitation	DEV	$18,700

MENOMINEE COUNTY TOTAL $ 5,898,400

Midland County

Midland County is so named because it is located near the geographical center of Michigan's Lower Peninsula. It was set off as a county in 1831 and formally established in 1850.

This photo combines venues, the Sanford Pere Marquette Rail Trail staging area, Michigan Historical marker honoring the drilling of Michigan's first salt well, and the Sanford Lake Park (picnic shelter in the background), two of the three were recipients of MNRTF grants.

Midland County is 67th largest county, 521 square miles, and is 24th largest in population with 83,629 residents.

Since oil was discovered there in 1928, 1,331 holes have been drilled in the search for oil and gas. As a petroleum producer, output from Midland County has been 84,991,262 barrels of oil and 15.487 billion cubic feet of natural gas, ranking 4th and 39^{h} respectively among the 64 oil or gas producing Michigan counties. Midland County has received $2,309,915 in 10 Michigan Natural Resources Trust Fund grants, ranking 58th in number of grants received and 55th in grant dollars awarded.

MIDLAND COUNTY active or closed MNRTF Projects

Project	Type	Amount
DNR - FOREST, MINERAL & FIRE MANAGEMENT		
TF91-010 Reicker Property	ACQ	$250,000
EDENVILLE TOWNSHIP		
TF11-102 Township Trail, Fishing Pier & Dock	ACQ	$191,500
LINCOLN TOWNSHIP		
TF11-102 Lincoln Township Park Development	DEV	$144,700
MIDLAND COUNTY		
TF05-074 Sanford Lake Park Improvements	DEV	$444,000
TF06-029 Sanford Lake Park	DEV	$235,900
TF830 Proposed Midland Co. Park	ACQ	$195,000
TF88-114 Sanford Lake County Park	ACQ	$56,775
TF92-125 Pere Marquette Rail-Trail	DEV	$375,000
TF96-138 Pere Marquette Rail-Trail	DEV	$117,040
TF13-038 Pere Marquette Rail-Trail Imp. & Trailhead	DEV	$300,000

MIDLAND COUNTY TOTAL $ 2,309,915

Missaukee County

Missaukee County was named in honor of an Ottawa American Indian Chieftain who signed land grant treaties in 1831 and 1833. It was set off as a county from part of Mackinac County in 1840 and formally established in 1871.

Missaukee County photo

MNRTF grant TF06-138, $975,000, went to help acquire Missaukee County's Trisch Trust property for preservation.

With 567 square miles, Missaukee County is 46th largest county and 69th largest in population with 14,849 residents.

Since oil was discovered there in 1931, 880 holes have been drilled in the search for oil and gas. Missaukee County has produced 38,577,354 barrels of oil and 42.261 billion cubic feet of natural gas, ranking 12th and 26th respectively among the 64 oil or gas producing Michigan counties.

Missaukee County has received $975,000 in one Michigan Natural Resources Trust Fund grant, ranking 83rd in number of grants received and 76th in grant dollars awarded.

MISSAUKEE COUNTY active or closed MNRTF Projects

DNR - FOREST, MINERAL & FIRE MANAGEMENT

TF06-138 Trisch Trust Property Acquisition	ACQ	$975,000

MISSAUKEE COUNTY TOTAL $975,000

Monroe County

Monroe County was named in honor of Virginian James Monroe 1758-1831, fifth president of the United States and the last President remaining from the original American Founding Fathers. Monroe is most noted for his proclamation of the Monroe Doctrine in 1823, which stated that the United States would not tolerate further European intervention in the Americas.

Monroe County was set off as a county in 1817 and formally established in 1840.

With 551 square miles, Monroe County is 59th largest county and 16th largest in population with 152,021 residents.

City of Monroe photo

MNRTF Project TF97-072, $290,125, went to the City of Monroe for expansion of the Downtown Riverwalk.

Monroe County was briefly a local-use oil producing county for five years before the discovery of the Saginaw Field put Michigan in the ranks of commercially producing petroleum states. Since oil was discovered there in 1920, 193, holes have been drilled in the search for oil and gas. Monroe County has produced 870,528 barrels of oil and no natural gas, ranking 52nd among the 64 oil or gas producing Michigan counties and one of 31 counties without natural gas production.

Monroe County has received $7,678,155 in 10 Michigan Natural Resources Trust Fund grants, ranking 54th in number of grants received and 28th in grant dollars awarded.

MONROE COUNTY active or closed MNRTF Projects

DNR - PARKS & RECREATION DIVISION		
TF07-131 Sterling State Park Acquisition	ACQ	$925,000
TF86-193 Sterling S.P. Beachhouse	DEV	$375,000
TF98-206 Sterling S. P. Access.Wetlands Interp. Trl.	DEV	$292,600
DNR - WILDLIFE DIVISION		
TF885 Brest Bay	ACQ	$40,000
DUNDEE		
TF92-257 Ford Mill Fishing Pier	DEV	$72,750
LUNA PIER		
TF10-065 Lake Erie Beach and Pier Access	DEV	$490,000
MONROE		
TF88-259 Hellenberg Field	ACQ	$190,200

Michigan DNRE photo

MNRTF Projects TF86-193, 98-206 and 07-131, totaling $1,592,600 went to Sterling State Park.

TF97-072 Riverwalk Extension Project	DEV	$290,125
TF14-208 River Raisin Corridor	ACQ	$4,986,200
SOUTH ROCKWOOD		
TF01-052 LaBo Park Addition	ACQ	$16,280

MONROE COUNTY TOTAL $ 7,678,155

Montcalm County

Montcalm County was named in honor Frenchman Marquis De Montcalm 1712-1759, who was commander of North American forces during the Seven years War (the French and Indian War was the title in the area that would become the United States). It was set off as a county in 1831 and formally established in 1835.

Lakeview's Lakeside Park was developed with MNRTF grant TF95-229 for $51,000.

With 708 square miles, Montcalm County is 28th largest county and 31st largest in population with 63,342 residents.

Since oil was discovered there in 1933, 1,577 holes have been drilled in the search for oil and gas. Montcalm County has produced 20,344,243 barrels of oil and 72.972 billion cubic feet of natural gas, ranking 20th and 16th respectively among the 64 oil or gas producing Michigan counties. County has received $2,029,189 in 15 Michigan Natural Resources Trust Fund grants, ranking 39th in number of grants received and 52nd in grant dollars awarded.

MONTCALM COUNTY active or closed MNRTF Projects

BELVIDERE TOWNSHIP

TF11-072 Belvidere Township Park Fishing Pier	DEV	$59,000

CARSON CITY

TF10-042 Grove/Haridine W.Pk. Non-Motor Trl. Dev.	DEV	$90,000
TF88-086 Carson City West Park	DEV	$375,000

DNR - FOREST, MINERAL & FIRE MANAGEMENT

TF416 Tamarack Creek	ACQ	$80,000

DNR - WILDLIFE DIVISION

TF438 Salt River Marsh	ACQ	$115,000

GREENVILLE

TF01-091 Flat River Trail Acquisition	ACQ	$56,344

TF02-133 Flat River Trail Acquisitions	ACQ	$35,100
TF04-081 Fred Meijer Flat River Trail	DEV	$168,500
TF08-066 Baldwin Lake Beach Improvements	DEV	$277,900
TF88-161 Greenville Scenic Pathway	ACQ	$37,500
TF97-123 Flat River Trail	DEV	$300,000
TF98-097 Flat River Trail	DEV	$177,545
LAKEVIEW		
TF95-229 Lakeside Park Enhancement	DEV	$51,000
SHERIDAN		
TF04-056 Pearl Lake Park	DEV	$74,000
VILLAGE OF MCBRIDE		
TF11-101 Robert Lee Davis Mem Park Improvements	DEV	$132,300

MONTCALM COUNTY TOTAL $ 2,029,189

On October 12, 2004, Michigan Oil And Gas Association Award of Excellence ceremonies to recognize the City of Greenville for outstanding use of five Michigan Natural Resources Trust Fund grants totaling $737,489 for acquisition and development of the Flat River Trail. Attending were, left to right: Greenville City Manager George Bosanic; Michigan Oil & Gas Producers Education Foundation Chairman Tom Mall; Greenville Mayor Lloyd Walker; Michigan Representative Judy Emmons; Greenville Chamber of Commerce Co-Directors Kathy Jo Vanderlaan and Candy Kerschen; Southwestern Michigan Oil/Cook Brothers Byron Cook – who, representing MOGA, made the presentation; and Southwestern Michigan Oil's Jeff Cook.

Montmorency County

Carved from Mackinac County, Montmorency was named Chenoquet County, meaning "*big cloud*" in Ojibwa when set aside as a county in 1840. The name was changed to honor Count Montmorency, a Revolutionary War hero Frenchman, in 1843. The county was formally established in 1881.

Briley Township received MNRTF grant TF91-009, totaling $63,800, for land acquisition for Briley Park in Atlanta.

With 548 square miles, Montmorency County is 62nd largest county and 76h largest in population with 9,765 residents. The 3rd most drilled county in the state, since oil was discovered in 1945, 2,668 holes have been drilled there in the search for oil and gas. Montmorency County has produced 2,242,743 barrels of oil and 1,036.654 billion cubic feet of natural gas, ranking 44th and 2nd respectively among the 64 oil or gas producing Michigan counties. County has received $521,478 in 6 Michigan Natural Resources Trust Fund grants, ranking 75th in number of grants received and 80th in grant dollars awarded.

MONTMORENCY COUNTY active/closed MNRTF Projects

ALBERT TOWNSHIP		
TF01-142 E. Twin Lake Beach/Park/Boat Ramp Imp.	DEV	$50,718
BRILEY TOWNSHIP		
TF91-270 Briley Park Expansion	ACQ	$63,800
DNR - FOREST, MINERAL & FIRE MANAGEMENT		
TF91-009 O.K. Bet Club Purchase	ACQ	$170,000
HILLMAN		
TF06-053 Brush Creek Dam and Millpond Acquisition	ACQ	$37,000
TF97-048 Emerick Park Project	DEV	$104,860
HILLMAN TOWNSHIP		
TF94-115 Williams Tournament Park	ACQ	$95,100

MONTMORENCY COUNTY TOTAL $ 521,478

Multi-County Grants

The category of Michigan Natural Resources Trust Fund grants designated "Multi-County" are grants awarded to various divisions of the Michigan Department of Natural Resources for projects that exceed county boundaries or are generically awarded for dealing with a specific need in a number of counties. These can be projects too massive for a host local government entity to embrace or projects that come at the urging of land conservancies at the vanguard of preserving precious properties from commercial development. Such a project was the Kamehameha lands in the Upper Peninsula, which became a multiple-year MNRTF project more than $16,000,000 in grants. Or the monies can go to projects as mundane upgrading lake access properties and fixing fishing piers. Much has been done with this category of grants with rail-trails and Eco-Districts throughout the state. All told, this category is the grand champion of number of grants and total grant dollars, having seen 188 grants totaling $197,966,691 in grant monies find its way into all 83 Michigan counties.

MULTI-COUNTY active or closed MNRTF Projects

DNR - EXECUTIVE OFFICE

Project	Description	Type	Amount
TF02-219	Kamehameha Trust Land Acquisition - Phase I	ACQ	$4,000,000
TF04-124	Kamehameha Schools Land Project-Phase III	ACQ	$3,000,000
TF05-132	CMS Arcadia/Green Pt. Dunes Conserv. Ease.	ACQ	$2,675,000
TF05-133	Kamehameha Schools Dev. Rights Purchase	ACQ	$5,000,000
TF06-128	Kamehameha Schools Development Rights	DEV	$1,100,000
TF07-116	Building Demolition Initiative	DEV	$250,000
TF07-117	S.E. Michigan Eco-Region Land Consolidation	ACQ	$900,000
TF07-119	Northern Low. Pen. Eco-Region Consolidation	ACQ	$900,000
TF07-123	Upper Pen.Eco-Regions Land Consolidation	ACQ	$900,000
TF07-135	SW Lower Pen. Eco-Reg. Land Consolidation	ACQ	$900,000
TF07-167	Wisconsin Electric Energies Land Acq.	ACQ	$1,900,000
TF08-118	Building Demolition Initiative 2008	DEV	$250,000
TF08-119	Upper Pen. Eco-Regional Land Consolid.	ACQ	$500,000
TF08-126	SE Michigan Eco-Regional Land Consolid.	ACQ	$4,000,000
TF08-134	Northern Low. Pen. Eco-Reg. Land Consolid.	ACQ	$1,000,000
TF09-130	SW Low. Pen. Eco-Reg. Land Consolid.	ACQ	$500,000
TF09-131	Upper Peninsula Eco-Regional Land Con.	ACQ	$500,000
TF09-132	Southeast Michigan Eco-Region Acq.	ACQ	$3,800,000
TF09-133	Northern Low. Pen. Eco-Reg. Land Consolid.	ACQ	$500,000
TF09-155	Building Demolition Initiative	DEV	$175,000

A bicycle trail bridge over I-96 in Ottawa County.

TF89-133 Saginaw Bay Recreation Trail	DEV	$200,000
TF92-329 Handicap Accessibility	DEV	$1,000,000
TF93-426 Barrier-Free Accessibility	DEV	$500,000
TF94-286 Barrier-Free Access	DEV	$483,000
TF11-126 SW Upper Penin. Eco-Region Acq.	ACQ	$1,000,000
TF11-127 SW U.P. Eco-Region Acq. Land Consol	ACQ	$100
TF11-137 SE Michigan. Eco-Region	ACQ	$1,475,000
TF11-140 Northern L.P. Eco-Region Land Consolidation	ACQ	$100
DNR - FISHERIES DIVISION		
TF00-239 Fisheries Lump Sum	ACQ	$500,000
TF03-177 Fisheries Division Lump Sum	ACQ	$250,000
TF06-131 Inland Waters Access Initiative	ACQ	$750,000
TF1014 Various Fisheries	ACQ	$500,000
TF383 Fisheries Access Sites-R. 3	ACQ	$500,000
TF462 Various Rivers	ACQ	$500,000
TF541 Various Rivers-Fisheries	ACQ	$500,000
TF681 Fisheries-Various Rivers	ACQ	$500,000
TF86-150 Various Rivers	ACQ	$500,000
TF87-009 Various Fishing Access Sites	ACQ	$500,000
TF88-014 Various Fishing Access Sites	ACQ	$600,000
TF89-074 Various Rivers, Streams, Lakes	ACQ	$100,000
TF90-124 Recreation/Fish Lump Sum	ACQ	$1,200,000
TF900 Fisheries-Various Rivers	ACQ	$2,000,000
TF91-001 Lump Sum Acquisition Water Access	ACQ	$500,000
TF92-334 Water Access Lump Sum	ACQ	$1,000,000
TF93-432 Fisheries Lump Sum	ACQ	$500,000

TF94-290 Fisheries Lump Sum	ACQ	$500,000
TF95-307 Fisheries Lump Sum	ACQ	$500,000
TF96-255 Fisheries Lump Sum	ACQ	$500,000
TF97-274 Fisheries Lump Sum	ACQ	$250,000

DNR - FOREST, MINERAL & FIRE MANAGEMENT

TF00-240 Trail Acquisition Lump Sum	ACQ	$350,000
TF00-246 State Forest Lump Sum	ACQ	$700,000
TF01-204 State Forest Campground Access Imp.	DEV	$500,000
TF02-181 Alpena-Hawks-Rogers City Trail Acq.	ACQ	$850,000
TF03-184 Kamehameha Schools Land Project-Phase II	ACQ	$3,000,000
TF03-186 State Forest Lump Sum	ACQ	$300,000
TF11-131 Fred Meijer Ionia to Owosso Rail-Trail	DEV	$300,000
TF11-132 Rail-Trail Acquisitions	ACQ	$1,000,000
TF11-133 Statewide Equestrian Initiative	DEV	$300 ,000

DNR - FOREST, MINERAL & FIRE MANAGEMENT

TF04-134 State Forest Campground Improvements	DEV	$250,000
TF05-136 State Trailways Initiative	ACQ	$1,900,000
TF05-143 Campground Access Improvements	DEV	$500,000
TF055 Manistee-AuSable River: Phases I-II-III	ACQ	$8,000,000
TF06-134 State Trailways Acquisition Initiative	ACQ	$1,500,000
TF06-137 State Forest Land Consolidation Initiative	ACQ	$800,000
TF06-140 Campground Utility Improvements	DEV	$500,000
TF07-120 Betsie River Consolidation	ACQ	$1,300,000
TF07-121 Chippewa Landing Acquisition	ACQ	$400,000
TF07-122 State Trailways Initiative-Corridor Acq.	ACQ	$1,500,000
TF08-120 Alpena to Cheboygan State Rail-Trail Surface Improvements	DEV	$500,000

TF1016 Pigeon River Small Inholdings	ACQ	$200,000
TF549 AuSable-Manistee Lease	ACQ	$3,700,000
TF678 Abandoned RR ROW-Statewide	ACQ	$300,000
TF86-281 Pigeon River Small Inhold	ACQ	$200,000
TF87-384 Pigeon River S. Forest	ACQ	$200,000
TF87-386 Various State Forest Acquisitions	ACQ	$200,000
TF88-100 Manistee River Acquisition	ACQ	$1,000,000
TF88-101 Pigeon River S. Forest	ACQ	$1,000,000
TF89-150 Black Mtn Forest Rec.	DEV	$133,000
TF896 Abandoned Railroads	ACQ	$200,000
TF90-191 Railroad ROW Lump Sum	ACQ	$1,000,000
TF91-003 Abandoned RR ROW Trails	ACQ	$500,000
TF91-005 Lump Sum Pigeon River Inholdings	ACQ	$300,000
TF92-336 CSX Right-of-Way Acquisition	ACQ	$500,000
TF92-337 Trailway Acquisition Lump Sum	ACQ	$500,000
TF93-418 State Forest Sys Lump Sum	ACQ	$500,000
TF93-436 Trailway Acq. Lump Sum	ACQ	$500,000
TF94-303 State Trail Lump Sum	ACQ	$750,000
TF95-312 Trail Corridor Lump Sum	ACQ	$250,000
TF95-315 Removal/Disposal of Buildings	DEV	$200,000
TF96-256 State Forest System Lump Sum	ACQ	$500,000
TF96-258 Trail Corridor Lump Sum	ACQ	$500,000
TF97-276 Trail Corridor Lump Sum	ACQ	$500,000
TF98-188 State Forest Lump Sum	ACQ	$500,000
TF98-192 Trail Corridor Lump Sum	ACQ	$500,000
TF99-288 Trail Corridor Lump Sum	ACQ	$300,000
TF99-296 State Forest Lump Sum	ACQ	$500,000
DNR - GRANTS ADMINISTRATION		
TF00-401 MNRTF Board Small Acq. Grants Initiative	ACQ	$350,000
TF96-254 Local Unit Acquisition Lump Sum	ACQ	$250,000
DNR - PARKS & RECREATION DIVISION		
TF00-250 Fishing Piers in Southern Michigan S.P.	DEV	$456,500
TF00-252 State Park/Recreation Areas Lump Sum Acq.	ACQ	$700,000
TF01-210 White Pine, VanBuren & Lakelands Trail DeV.	DEV	$394,000
TF01-213 Southern Michigan Fishing Piers	DEV	$330,000
TF03-194 Various State Park Acquisitions	ACQ	$500,000
TF04-141 Various Park Acquisitions	ACQ	$2,000,000
TF05-151 State Park Camper Cabins	DEV	$375,600
TF06-141 State Park and Recreation Area Consolid.	ACQ	$1,200,000
TF08-128 Waterloo Recreation Land Initiative	ACQ	$2,500,000
TF08-130 State Park Infrastructure Repairs	DEV	$350,000
TF08-133 Inland Fishing Piers in S.P. and Rec. Areas	DEV	$250,000
TF09-148 State Park Infrastructure Development	DEV	$489,000
TF09-154 Pinckney State Rec. Area Land Consolid.	ACQ	$415,391
TF1013 Various State Parks	ACQ	$3,000,000
TF384 Waterways Acc. Sites-R.3	ACQ	$300,000
TF392 St. Pk & Rec. Areas-R.3	ACQ	$2,000,000
TF461 Var. St. Parks & Rec. Areas	ACQ	$2,000,000
TF532 Waterways PAS-Region III	ACQ	$300,000

TF534 Various St. Park & Rec.	ACQ	$3,000,000
TF680 Waterways Various P.A.S.	ACQ	$500,000
TF682 Various State Parks & Recreation Areas	ACQ	$3,000,000
TF86-062 Lump Sum Access Site	ACQ	$500,000
TF86-085 Various State Parks	ACQ	$3,000,000
TF86-284 Abandoned Railroad ROW	ACQ	$200,000
TF87-001 Var. State Park & Recreation Areas	ACQ	$2,000,000
TF87-203 Various Waterways Public Access Sites	ACQ	$500,000
TF88-029 Various Waterways Public Access Sites	ACQ	$500,000
TF88-199 Various State Park & Recreation Areas	ACQ	$4,000,000
TF89-077 Various State Parks/Recreation Areas	ACQ	$3,550,000
TF89-174 Lump Sum Public Access Site Acquisitions	ACQ	$700,000
TF89-175 Lump Sum Abandoned R-O-Ws	ACQ	250,000
TF899 Various State Park & Recreation	ACQ	$3,000,000
TF901 Waterways Various PAS	ACQ	$300,000
TF91-004 Various State Parks	ACQ	$1,000,000
TF92-342 Various State Parks	ACQ	$1,000,000
TF93-414 Boating Access Lump Sum	ACQ	$500,000
TF93-430 Various State Parks	ACQ	$1,000,000
TF94-310 State Park Lump Sum	ACQ	$500,000
TF94-311 Boating Lump Sum	ACQ	$500,000
TF95-305 Boating Lump Sum	ACQ	$500,000
TF95-306 Parks Lump Sum	ACQ	500,000
TF96-267 Various Boating Access Site Acquisition	ACQ	$1,000,000

TF96-268 State Park and Recreation Areas Lump Sum ACQ $1,000.000
TF98-198 Various S.P. and Recreation Areas Acq. ACQ $1,000,000
TF11-136 River Raisin Recreation Acq. ACQ $3,000,000
TF12 -133 Rail-Trail Acquisitions ACQ $300,000
TF12 -134 Fred Meijer Ionia/ Owosso Trail (Surf Imp.) DEV $300,000
TF12 -136 Pere Marquette State Trail Improvements DEV $300,000
TF13 -136 Statewide Showcase Tail Initiative DEV $300,000
TF13 -139 Fred Meijer White Pine Trail Surf/Bridge Imp. DEV $300,000

DNR - WILDLIFE DIVISION

TF00-255 State Wildlife Area Lump Sum ACQ $950,000
TF03-197 Southern Michigan Wetland Initiative ACQ $600,000
TF03-198 Wildlife Area Lump Sum Acquisitions ACQ $450,000
TF04-131 Winter Deeryard Consolidation Initiative ACQ $2,000,000
TF04-143 Wildlife Area Lump Sum ACQ $1,000,000
TF05-154 Wildlife Area Consolidation Lump Sum ACQ $1,250,000
TF05-155 Winter Deer Habitat Initiative ACQ $1,350,000
TF06-145 Winter Deer Habitat Initiative ACQ $875,000
TF06-146 Wildlife Land Consolidation Initiative ACQ $800,000
TF09-156 Grassland/Bird Habitat Initiative ACQ $1,000,000
TF1012 Southern Michigan Game Areas ACQ $2,000,000
TF376 So. MI State Game Areas ACQ $1,000,000
TF463 S. MI St. Game& Wild. Ar. ACQ $335,000
TF535 So. MI State Game & Wildlife Area ACQ $1,000,000
TF683 So. Michigan State Game & Wildlife Areas ACQ $1,125,000
TF86-080 Southern Mich. Game Areas ACQ $2,000,000
TF87-079 So. Mich. SGA's ACQ $4,000,000
TF88-064 Southern MI State Game and Wildlife Areas ACQ $5,500,000
TF89-073 Southern Michigan State Game Areas ACQ $3,550,000
TF891 So. MI State Game Area ACQ $2,000,000
TF90-002 Lump Sum ACQ $1,200,000
TF90-164 Great Lakes Marshes ACQ $500,000
TF91-002 State Wildlife Lump Sum ACQ $500,000
TF92-354 State Wildlife Lump Sum ACQ $1,000,000
TF93-422 State Wildlife Lump Sum ACQ $1,000,000
TF94-288 Wildlife Lump Sum ACQ 2,000,000
TF95-309 Wildlife Lump Sum/Munuscong Bay ACQ $1,500,000
TF96-272 State Wildlife Area Lump Sum ACQ $1,500,000
TF97-288 State Wildlife Area Lump Sum ACQ $500,000
TF98-308 State Wildlife Area Lump Sum ACQ $500,000
TF99-307 State Wildlife Area Lump Sum ACQ $580,000
TF99-444 State Wildlife Area Lump Sum ACQ $500,000
TF12 -139 Hunting Accessibility Initiative DEV $50,000
TF13 -136 Statewide Showcase Tail Initiative DEV $300,000

DNRE - FOREST MANAGEMENT DIVISION

TF10-120 State Trails Initiative ACQ $1,500,000

DNRE - STEWARDSHIP OFFICE

TF10-116 Southwest Lower Peninsula Eco-Region ACQ $1,000,000
TF10-121 Upper Pen. Eco-Regional Land Consolid. ACQ $1,000,000
TF10-131 Southeast Michigan Eco-Region Acq. ACQ $ 1,500,000

TF10-136 Urban Acres Upland Game Habitat	ACQ	$1,250,000
TF10-137 N. Lower Pen. Eco-Regional Land Con.	ACQ	$1,000,000

S.W. LOWER PENINSULA ECO-REGIONAL CONSOLIDATION

TF08-116 SW Lower Peninsula Eco-Regional Con.	ACQ	$500,000

MULTI-COUNTY TOTALS $ 197,966,691

Muskegon County

Muskegon County is named, like the river that meets Lake Michigan there, from the Ojibwa /Chippewa American Indian word *mashkig*, meaning "marsh" or "swamp". It was set off as a county from parts of Oceana and Ottawa counties formally established in 1859.

With 509 square miles, Muskegon County is 69h largest county and 12th largest in population with 172,188 residents.

Heritage Landing photo

MNRTF grant TF90-214, $375,000, went to Muskegon County's Heritage Landing Development.

Since oil was discovered there in 1927, Michigan's second commercially producing oil county, 979 holes have been drilled in the search for oil and gas. Muskegon County has produced 8,838,004 barrels of oil and

9.810 billion cubic feet of natural gas, ranking 28th and 45th respectively among the 64 oil or gas producing Michigan counties. Muskegon County has received $10,966,645 in 46 Michigan Natural Resources Trust Fund grants, ranking 10th in number of grants received and 20th in grant dollars awarded.

MUSKEGON COUNTY active or closed MNRTF Projects

Project	Type	Amount
DALTON TOWNSHIP		
TF03-207 Beegle Field Acquisition	ACQ	$30,000
DNR - FOREST, MINERAL & FIRE MANAGEMENT		
TF94-299 Ottawa-Muskegon Trail	DEV	$250,000
F98-197 Musketawa Trail: Muskegon-Ravenna	DEV	$150,000
DNR - PARKS & RECREATION DIVISION		
TF96-263 Hoffmaster S. P.Visitor Center Expansion	DEV	$499,360
DNR - WILDLIFE DIVISION		
TF86-070 Herman Properties-Ph. II	ACQ	$550,000
TF967 Herm Property Co's Farm	ACQ	$550,000
TF968 Arends Farm	ACQ $	$550,000
EGELSTON TOWNSHIP		
TF10-077 Sunset Beach Recreational Improvements	DEV	$82,100
TF96-169 Wolf Lake Park	DEV	$48,000

Muskegon County photo

MNRTF grants TF94-235 and 96-061, totaling $415,000, went to Muskegon County's Twin Lake Park Development.

TF96-169 Wolf Lake Park DEV $48,000

Project	Type	Amount
FRUITPORT TOWNSHIP		
TF10-014 Sheringer Soccer Park Improvements	DEV	$213,900
HOLTON TOWNSHIP		
TF98-084 Holton Recreation and Nature Center	ACQ	$49,600
LAKETON TOWNSHIP		
TF11-736 Bear Lake Road Non-Motorized Trail	DEV	$300,000
LAKEWOOD		
TF11-0728 Fox Lake Park Improvements	DEV	$45,000
LAKEWOOD CLUB		
TF07-073 Fox Lake Park Improvements	DEV	$49,100
MONTAGUE		
TF97-129 Maple Beach Park	DEV	$135,060
MONTAGUE TOWNSHIP		
TF99-210 Harvey Property Purchase	ACQ	$703,000

MUSKEGON

TF04-025 Muskegon Lakeshore Trail	DEV	$500,000
TF07-060 Smith-Ryerson Park Improvements	DEV	$433,400
TF90-035 Bronson Park Development	DEV	$375,000
TF93-020 Lakeshore Trail-Phase I	DEV	$375,000

MUSKEGON COUNTY

TF01-192 Blue Lake Park Renovations	DEV	$115,200
TF02-062 Pioneer County Park	DEV	$224,000
TF08-029 Meinert County Park Property Acquisition	ACQ	$428,300
TF86-326 Muskegon Lakefront Redev.	DEV	$400,000
TF90-214 Heritage Landing Waterfront	DEV	$375,000
TF94-235 Twin Lake Park Development	DEV	$187,500
TF96-061 Twin Lake Park	DEV	$227,500
TF11-088 Rotary Park	DEV	$150,800

MNRTF grants TF89-010 and 10-103, totaling $565,000, went to Muskegon Heights Mona Lake Park.

TF11-086 Rotary Park Development	DEV	$150,800
TF12-062 Pioneer Park Playground Equipment	DEV	$37,500

MUSKEGON HEIGHTS

TF10-103 Mona Lake Park Renovations	DEV	$500,000
TF89-010 Mona Lake Park	DEV	$65,000

MUSKEGON TOWNSHIP

TF88-175 Muskegon Softball World	ACQ	$300,000
TF13-077 Fred Meijer Berry Junction Trail	DEV	$300,000

NORTH MUSKEGON

TF03-014 Block 58 Lakeshore Park Imp.	DEV	$208,000
TF91-072 West End Park Playground Dev.	DEV	$120,000

NORTON SHORES

TF06-206 Black Lake Park Expansion	ACQ	$38,200
TF1020 Lake Harbor Park Expansion	ACQ	$50,000
TF98-114 Lake Harbor Park Expansion	ACQ	$190,125
TF13-084 Hines Property	ACQ	$146,800

ROOSEVELT PARK

TF11-054 Community Center Park Renovations	DEV	$48,000
TF12-059 Delmar Playfield Renovation	DEV	$28,300

WHITE RIVER TOWNSHIP

TF1032 Barrier Dunes Sanctuary	ACQ	$126,000

WHITEHALL

TF01-081 White Lake Pathway	DEV	$426,600
TF05-086 Goodrich Park Renovations	DEV	$90,500
TF07-037 White Lake Pathway South End Completion	DEV	$254,700
TF90-009 Svensson Park Dev.	DEV	$43,100

MUSKEGON COUNTY TOTAL $ 10,966.645

Newaygo County

Newaygo County was named in honor of a Chippewa Indian leader who signed the Saginaw Treaty of 1819. It was set aside as a county in 1840 from parts of Mackinac and Oceana counties and formally established in 1855.

With 842 square miles, Newaygo County is 17th largest county and 36th largest in population with 48,460 residents.

MNRTF grants TF1043, and 08-113, totaling $297,500, went to acquire more land and develop Newaygo County's Sandy Beach Park.

Since oil was discovered there in 1944, 938 holes have been drilled in the search for oil and gas. Newaygo County has produced 11,531,345 barrels of oil and 107.094 billion cubic feet of natural gas, ranking 26th and 13th respectively among the 64 oil or gas producing Michigan counties.

Newaygo County has received $2,947,400 in 10 Michigan Natural Resources Trust Fund grants, ranking 56th in number of grants and 50th in grant dollars awarded.

NEWAYGO COUNTY active or closed MNRTF Projects

BRIDGETON TOWNSHIP

TF06-202 Township Boat Launch Expansion	ACQ	$96,500

TF10-058 Muskegon River Waterways Trail	DEV	$146,500
BROOKS TOWNSHIP		
TF99-183 Cold Creek Forest Area	ACQ	$675,000
FREMONT		
TF05-107 Fremont Town and Country Path	DEV	$130,600
TF10-114 Fremont Lake Park Development	DEV	$180,300

MNRTF grant TF90-094 $84,000, went to develop the Village of Hesperia's Sports Park.

HESPERIA		
TF90-094 Village Park	DEV	$84,000
NEWAYGO		
TF95-065 Newaygo Riverfront Park	DEV	$375,000
NEWAYGO COUNTY		
TF06-204 Camp Swampy Acq.Diamond Lk. C.P.	ACQ	$962,000
TF08-113 Sandy Beach County Park Improvement	DEV	$267,500
TF1043 Sandy Beach County Park	ACQ	$30,000

NEWAYGO COUNTY TOTAL $ 2,947,400

Oakland County

Dr. Bela Hubbard, surveyor of Michigan described this area as a place of numerous "oak openings" meaning "majestic orchards of oaks and hickories varied by small prairies, grassy lawns and clear lakes", thus Oakland County was named. It was set off as a county in 1819 from part of Macomb County and formally established the following year, in 1820.

With 873 square miles, Oakland County is 15th largest county and 2nd largest in population with 1,202,362 residents.

Michigan DNR photo

MNRTF grant TF287, $5,000,000 went to the Michigan DNR Parks and Recreation Department to help acquire property for the Bald Mountain Recreation Area in Oakland County.

Since oil was discovered there in 1960, 265 holes have been drilled in the search for oil and gas. Oakland County has produced 7,488,086 barrels of oil and 52.515 billion cubic feet of natural gas, ranking 29th and 22nd respectively among the 64 oil or gas producing Michigan counties.

Oakland County received $70,338,969 in 122 Michigan Natural Resources Trust Fund grants, ranking first in both number of grants received and in grant dollars awarded among the state's individual counties.

OAKLAND COUNTY active or closed MNRTF Projects

ADDISON TOWNSHIP

Project	Type	Amount
TF09-033 Lake George Nature Park Acquisition	ACQ	$428,000
TF96-215 Watershed Township Park	ACQ	$840,000
TF97-136 Watershed Park (Fore Lakes Twp. Park)	ACQ	$1,260,000

AUBURN HILLS

Project	Type	Amount
TF00-092 New City Park Development	DEV	$235,000
TF93-117 Riverside Acquisition	ACQ	$525,000
TF94-035 Fisk Hawk Woods Nature Center	DEV	$43,600
TF95-090 Hawk Woods Nature Center	DEV	$90,000

Oakland County photo

MNRTF grant TF01-022, $163,200 was used to improve Oakland County's Independence Oaks Youth Camp.

TF96-078 Civic Center Park Expansion ACQ $1,108,700

BLOOMFIELD HILLS SCHOOLS

TF03-092 E.L. Johnson Nature Center Visitors' Center DEV $475,000

CLAWSON

TF13-151 Grant Park Restroom DEV $50,000

COMMERCE TOWNSHIP

TF878 Mill Race Park Extension ACQ $17,000

TF91-045 Section 36 Lake Acq. ACQ $375,000

TF91-196 Section 36 Lake Project DEV $332,900

COMMERCE, WALLED LAKE, WIXOM TRAILWAY MANAGEMENT COUNCIL

11-123 CW2 Airline Trailway ACQ $3,755,400

DNR - FOREST, MINERAL & FIRE MANAGEMENT

TF93-439 Polly-Ann Trail Acquisition ACQ $600,000

DNR - OFFICE OF COMMUNICATIONS

TF08-124 Bald Mountain Shooting Range DEV $500,000

DNR - PARKS & RECREATION DIVISION

TF00-251 Pontiac Lake Rec. Area Shoot Range Upgrade DEV $250,000

TF07-129 Proud Lake Electrical System Upgrades DEV $500,000

TF09-143 Dodge No. 4 S.P.Water System Replacement DEV $400,000

TF287 Bald Mountain Recreation Area ACQ $5,000,000

TF14-191 Oakland Park Adventure Park Partnership ACQ $2,900,000

DNR - WILDLIFE DIVISION

TF684 Horseshoe Lake SGA ACQ $500,000

TF13-129 Holly Recreation Area Land Initiative ACQ $3,030,000

FARMINGTON HILLS		
TF701 Spicer Property Acq.	ACQ	$1,200,000
TF87-234 Heritage Park	DEV	$195,000
TF88-254 Heritage Park	DEV	$300,000
TF89-100 Central Land Acquisition	ACQ	$661,200
TF91-297 Sod Farm Acquisition	ACQ	$1,000,000
TF92-049 Sod Farm Acquisition-Phase II	ACQ	$1,000,000
HAZEL PARK		
TF98-078 Orin McPherson/Scout Park Development	DEV	$38,826
HIGHLAND TOWNSHIP		
TF88-068 Township Community Park	ACQ	$164,250
TF98-135 Highland Township Park	ACQ	$425,000
TF14-124 Hickory Ridge Pines Park Expansion	ACQ	$127,800
HOLLY TOWNSHIP		
TF96-036 Holly Nature Center	DEV	$180,950
HURON CLINTON METROPOLITAN AUTHORITY		
TF08-033 Kensington Metropark-Milford Trl. Connector	DEV	$315,000
TF11-018 Kensington Metropark-Milford Trl. Connector	DEV	$94,000
INDEPENDENCE TOWNSHIP		
TF86-312 Bay Court Camp	ACQ	$375,000
TF92-101 Bay Court Park Beachfront	DEV	$308,400

Oakland County photo

MNRTF grants TF93-037 and 96-026, totaling $804,000 were used to help acquire property for Oakland County's Lyon Oaks Park.

LARTHRUP VILLAGE

TF11-012 Golden Gate Park Playground Equipment	DEV	$50,000

LYON TOWNSHIP

TF86-182 Lyon Comm. Park/I-96	DEV	$150,000
TF91-043 Community Park-Phase II	DEV	$375,000

MADISON HEIGHTS

TF492 Simonds Woods Natural Area	ACQ	$460,000
TF97-032 Suarez Woods Park Expansion	ACQ	$78,000

MILFORD

TF06-079 Hubbell Pond Park Non-Motorized Trail	DEV	$297,000

MILFORD TOWNSHIP

TF06-074 Milford to Kensington Metropark Trail	DEV	$400,000

NOVI

TF05-165 Village Wood Lake/Orchard Hills West Acq.	ACQ	$846,400
TF07-017 Novi Core Habitat Reserve Property Acq.	ACQ	$281,300
TF10-043 Landings Park Trailhead/Waterfront Develop.	DEV	$437,500
TF14-235 Novi NW Neighborhood Park	ACQ	$385,000

OAKLAND COUNTY

TF01-022 Independence Oaks Youth Camp	DEV	$163,200
TF04-003 Organizational Youth Camp-Connector Trail	DEV	$219,000
TF05-032 Highland Township Property Acquisition	ACQ	$1,440,000
TF06-199 Upper Bushman Lake Acquisition	ACQ	$1,900,000
TF07-030 Addison Oaks Trail Connector	ACQ	$228,800
TF10-098 Natural Areas Accessibility Improvements	DEV	$308,000
TF1048 Groveland Oaks Simpson Lake Thread Creek	ACQ	$344,900
TF603 Independence Oaks	ACQ	$387,000
TF89-002 Addison Oaks Acquisition	ACQ	$307,500
TF89-003 Lyon Rookery Acquisition	ACQ	$1,000,000
TF91-024 Rose Twp. Property Acq.	ACQ	$542,500
TF91-026 Lyon Rookery	ACQ	$837,500
TF93-037 Lyon Oaks Acquisition	ACQ	$630,000
TF95-052 Independence Oaks Restroom	DEV	$24,500
TF96-026 Lyon Oaks Acquisition	ACQ	$174,000
TF13-033 Independence Oaks Co. Park Univ. Ac. Boat Launch	DEV	$37,700
TF14-066 Univ. Acc. Fishing Pier Groveland Oaks Park	DEV	$36,300

OAKLAND TOWNSHIP

TF00-311 Bear Creek Park Development	DEV	$313,302
TF02-013 Oakland Township Lost Lake Park Acq.	ACQ	$1,762,800
TF05-102 Stony Creek Corridor Park Acquisition	ACQ	$893,700
TF07-057 Marsh View Park Development	DEV	$293,300
TF10-069 Lost Lake Nature Park Development	DEV	$154,900
TF99-128 Oakland Township Park Acquisition	ACQ	$2,010,101

ORCHARD LAKE

TF91-140 Cranbrook Nature Preserve	ACQ	$1,000,000
TF92-006 Nature Preserve Acquisition-Phase II	ACQ	$1,000,000

OXFORD CHARTER TOWNSHIP

TF92-163 Oxford Township Park #3	ACQ	$155,400

OXFORD TOWNSHIP

TF97-044 Township Park #3 Development	DEV	$93,930
TF98-013 Oakwood Road Land Acquisition	ACQ	$825,000
PAINT CREEK TRAILWAYS COMMISSION		
TF02-125 Paint Creek Trail Enhancement Project	DEV	$58,900
TF493 Paint Creek Trail Acquisition	ACQ	$240,000
PONTIAC		
TF01-115 Clinton River Trail Acquisition	ACQ	$412,160
TF08-040 Clinton River Trail Pedestrian Bridge	DEV	$485,000
TF97-232 Hawthorne Park Renovations	DEV	$168.750
TF13-065 Clinton River Trail Acquisition - Pontiac	DEV	$370,000
ROCHESTER		
TF00-312 Rochester Rails-to-Trails	ACQ	$1,608,786
TF02-043 Clinton River Trail Development	DEV	$175,000
ROCHESTER HILLS		
TF01-068 Clinton River Trail Acquisition	ACQ	$1,900,000
TF396 Ulbrich Tract	ACQ	$880,000
TF90-256 Avondale Park	DEV	$200,000
ROYAL OAK TOWNSHIP		
TF86-152 Mack Rowe Memorial Park	DEV	$22,000
SOUTHFIELD		
TF02-148 Berberian Property Acquisition	ACQ	$1,753,500
TF04-112 Carpenter Lake Park Develop & Restoration	DEV	$500,000
TF86-191 Meyer Leib Property	ACQ	$108,000
TF89-237 Section 24 Wetlands	ACQ	$218,800
TF90-393 Valley Woods Trail	DEV	$120,000
TF91-833 Evergreen Woods Park	ACQ	$950,000
TF14-275 Iglewood Park Renovation Project	DEV	$280,000
TF14-288 Horsetail Woods Acquisition	ACQ	$98,800
SPRINGFIELD TOWNSHIP		
TF1077 Shiawassee Basin Preserve	ACQ	$527,000
TF90-050 Shiawassee Basin Preserve	DEV	$129,000
TF13-100 Shiawassee Lake Property	ACQ	$99,900
SYLVAN LAKE		
TF01-046 Sylvan Lake Rail to Trail	ACQ	$162,000
TROY		
TF98-157 New Interpretive Center	DEV	$466,000
VILLAGE OF LEONARD		
TF10-051 Leonard Mill Park Acquisition	ACQ	$22,500
WALLED LAKE		
TF97-089 Mercer Beach	DEV	$97,170
WATERFORD TOWNSHIP		
TF05-097 Elizabeth Lake Woods Park Expansion	ACQ	$87,000
TF88-037 Walter Findley Property	ACQ	$281,250
TF91-263 Elizabeth Lake Woods	ACQ	$74,300
TF94-181 Fish Hatchery Park Development	DEV	$141,000
TF98-121 Maceday Lake Waterfront Park Acquisition	ACQ	$405,000
WEST BLOOMFIELD TOWNSHIP		
TF00-056 Karner Farm Expansion Project	ACQ	$352,594
TF07-013 Marshbank Park Improvement Project	DEV	$500,000

TF08-142 Michigan Air-Line Railway Acquisition	ACQ	$1,452,500
TF10-038 West Bloomfield Trail Development	DEV	$500,000
TF86-230 Acq. of Railroad R.O.W.	ACQ	$108,000
TF87-269 Acq. of Woods	ACQ	$500,000
TF88-172 Acquisition of Glieberman Woods—Phase II	ACQ	$500,000
TF89-235 Acquisition of Glieberman Woods-Phase III	ACQ	$500,000
TF92-204 Drake Road Park Acquisition	ACQ	$1,250,000

WESTERN OAKLAND COUNTY TRAILWAY MANAGEMENT COUNCIL

TF98-096 Huron Valley Trail Construction	DEV	$490,000

White Lake Township photo

MNRTF grant TF09-103, $350,000 went to the White Lake Township to develop Bloomer Park

WHITE LAKE TOWNSHIP

TF09-103 Bloomer Park Development	DEV	$350,000

WIXOM

TF88-007 West Maple Park Expansion	ACQ	$150,000
TF98-079 Wixom Habitat Development	DEV	$198,500

OAKLAND COUNTY TOTAL $ 70,338,969

Oceana County

Because of it's location on the shores of Lake Michigan, considered a fresh water "ocean", Oceana County was carved from part of Mackinac County as an unorganized territory in 1831 and formally organized as a county in 1855.

549 square miles make Oceana County 60th largest county and 26,570 residents 51st largest in population. Since oil was discovered there in 1945, 1,083 holes have been drilled in the search for oil and gas. Oceana County has produced 3,031,565 barrels of oil and 26.002 billion cubic feet of natural gas, ranking 39th and 47th respectively among the 64 oil or gas producing Michigan counties. Oceana County has received $2,145,682 in 11 Michigan Natural Resources Trust Fund grants, ranking 51st in number of grants received and 56th in grant dollars.

Rothbury's Glen M. Squires Park erected a picnic shelter and bathrooms with MNRTF grant TF91-067, a $27,000 Development grant.

OCEANA COUNTY active or closed MNRTF Projects

Project	Type	Amount
DNR - PARKS & RECREATION DIVISION		
TF86-314 Oceana Rec. Trail. (Hart-Montague Trail SP)	DEV	$506,800
TF13-137 Hart-Montague Trail State Park	DEV	$300,000
GOLDEN TOWNSHIP		
TF10-095 Gold 'N Silver Park Acquisition	ACQ	$400,600
NEWFIELD TOWNSHIP		
TF95-259 Oxbow-Scout Camp	DEV	$120,000
OCEANA COUNTY		
TF00-082 Gales Pond Boardwalk Extension	DEV	$17,282
TF03-034 Crystal Valley Park	DEV	$99,900
TF10-026 Mill Pond Park Development	DEV	$54,000
TF13-026 Hart-Montague Trail State Park Segment B	DEV	$300,000
PENTWATER TOWNSHIP		
T12-048 Long Bridge Road Fishing Deck	DEV	$287,400
ROTHBURY		
TF91-067 Picnic Shelter/Bathrooms	DEV	$27,000
SHELBY		
TF92-035 Rail Trail Enhancements	DEV	$32,700

OCEANA COUNTY TOTAL $ 2,145,682

Ogemaw County

Ogemaw County is named in honor of Saginaw Chippewa American Indian Chief *Ogemaw-kegato* 1794-1840. It was set off as a county in 1840, annexed to Iosco County in 1867, and formally established in 1873.

With 564 square miles, Ogemaw County is 52nd largest county and 64th largest in population with 21,699 residents.

Since oil was discovered there in 1933, 999 holes have been drilled in the search for oil and gas. Ogemaw County has produced 31,882,431 barrels of oil and 74.947 billion cubic feet of natural gas, ranking 15th and 16th respectively among the 64 oil or gas producing Michigan counties.

The 4,500 acre Rifle River Recreation Area, with ten streams and rivers in addition to 10 lakes and ponds, was developed in part with a $300,000 MNRTF grant to the Department of Natural Resources.

Ogemaw County has received $1,274,000 in 9 Michigan Natural Resources Trust Fund grants, ranking 66th in number of grants received and 73rd in grant dollars awarded.

Skidway Lake's Mike Spence bicycles along the Skidway Lake Boardwalk along Ogemaw County Road F-18, the Boardwalk was Mills Township's $251,000 MNRTF Development grant TF07-051.

OGEMAW COUNTY active or closed MNRTF Projects

DNR - PARKS & RECREATION DIVISION		
TF02-197 Rifle River Recreation Area	DEV	$300,000
MILLS TOWNSHIP		
TF07-051 Skidway Lake Boardwalk Development	DEV	$251,000
TF12-033 Elbow Lake Park Improvements	ACQ	$270,000
OGEMAW COUNTY		
TF92-320 Ogemaw Hills Recreation Complex	ACQ	$68,000
RICHLAND TOWNSHIP		
TF04-040 Hardwood Lake Campground Improvements	DEV	$32,600
ROSE CITY		
TF88-135 Houghton Creek Park	DEV	$33,000
WEST BRANCH		
TF10-089 North River Trail Development	DEV	$171,600
TF94-185 Irons Park Rivertrail	DEV	$40,000
TF97-069 Rivertrail Construction	DEV	$107,800

OGEMAW COUNTY TOTAL $ 1,274,000

Ontonagon County

Ontonagon County is named for the Ontonagon River, believed to have originated with the Ojibwa Indian word "*on-agon*", meaning "bowl. It was set off from parts of Chippewa and Mackinac County and formally established as a county in 1843.

Michigan DNR photo

MNRTF Project TF06-032, $87,000, went to Village of Ontonagon Marinat.

With 1,312 square miles, Ontonagon County is 3rd largest county and 81tst largest in population with 6,780 residents. Ontonagon is an Upper Peninsula county with no significant sedimentary geological strata, reducing the likelihood of oil and/or natural gas. Only one hole, dry, has been drilled there to search for petroleum, making it 74th most drilled county in the state.

Ontonagon County has received $1,487,000 in 9 Michigan Natural Resources Trust Fund grants, ranking 63rd in number of grants received and 694h in grant dollars awarded.

ONTONAGON COUNTY active or closed MNRTF Projects

Project	Type	Amount
DNR - FOREST, MINERAL & FIRE MANAGEMENT		
TF542 Bergland-Nestoria Trail	ACQ	$402,000
DNR - PARKS & RECREATION DIVISION		
TF90-808 Agate Falls	ACQ	$100,000
TF99-301 Bond Falls State Park-Initial Development	DEV	$290,000
INTERIOR TOWNSHIP		
TF11-001 Abbot Fox Community Park Handicap Access	DEV	$43,500
ONTONAGON		
TF06-032 Ontonagon Marina Acquisition	ACQ	$87,000
TF91-236 Island Shoreline Improvement	DEV	$75,000
TF14-078 Rose Island Paddlecraft Landing	DEV	$46,300
ONTONAGON COUNTY		
TF14-274 Improvements on Ontonogon County Park	DEV	$210,400
ONTONAGON TOWNSHIP		
TF06-075 Ontonagon Township Park Improvements	DEV	$232,800

ONTONAGON COUNTY TOTAL $ 1,487,000

Osceola County

Osceola County was named for an Ottawa Chieftain mentioned in the Washington Treaty of 1836. It was set off from part of Mackinac County in 1840, named *Unwattin* until 1843, and formally established in 1869.

Osceola County's 556 square miles and 23,568 residents, rank 49th largest in size and 62nd largest population. Since oil was discovered there in 1941, 1,218 holes have been drilled. Osceola County has produced 63,249,311 barrels of oil and 121,228, billion cubic feet of natural gas, ranking 7th and 12th respectively of Michigan oil or gas producing counties. Osceola County has received $1,922,900 in 11 Michigan Natural Resources Trust Fund grants, ranking 52nd in number of grants received and 63th in grant dollars.

City of Evart photo

MNRTF grants TF02-028, and 06-015, totaling $388,400, went to Evart's Riverside Park.

OSCEOLA COUNTY active or closed MNRTF Projects

DNR - FOREST, MINERAL & FIRE MANAGEMENT		
TF00-242 Hersey-Evart Trail Surfacing	DEV	$350,000
TF94-300 Clare-Baldwin Trail	DEV	$118,000
DNR - PARKS & RECREATION DIVISION		
TF94-306 White Pine Trail River Access	DEV	$250,000
EVART		
TF02-028 Riverside Park Acquisition	ACQ	$288,400
TF06-015 Riverside Park Improvements	DEV	$100,000
HERSEY		
TF01-128 Hersey Multi-use Park	DEV	$163,800
MARION		
TF07-102 Veterans Memorial Park Improvements	DEV	$105,000
OSCEOLA COUNTY		
TF12-002 Rose City Park Restroom/Campsite Imp.	DEV	$37,600
REED CITY		
TF02-063 Recreation Park Improvements	DEV	$256,800
TF98-109 Rambadt Park Restrooms/ Linear Pk. Improve.	DEV	$225,000
TUSTIN		
TF14-177 Little Creek Gazebo/Clinton Twp. Nature Prsve.	DEV	$28,300

OSCEOLA COUNTY TOTAL $ 1,922,900

Oscoda County

Indians called it *Os-Ka-Do-Yang*, meaning "where the plains begin", but Henry Rowe Schoolcraft is credited with naming the county by combining the American Indian words *mushcoda* "parairie/meadow" and *ossin* "pebble" to come up with *oscoda* to indicate a "pebbly prairie" to describe the area. Oscoda was set off as a county in 1840 and not settled by whites until 1863, then formally established in 1881.

With 565 square miles, Oscoda County is 51st largest county and 79th largest in population with 8,640 residents.

Since oil was discovered there in 1946, 432 holes have been drilled in the search for oil and gas. Oscoda County has produced 1,786,803 barrels of crude oil and 171.704 billion cubic feet of natural gas, ranking 46th and 10th respectively among the 64 oil or gas producing Michigan counties.

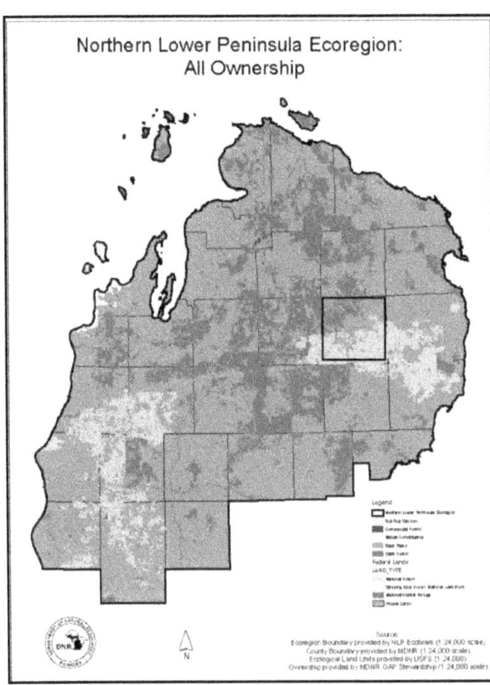

Oscoda County the last individual county of Michigan's 83 to directly receive any Michigan Natural Resources Trust Fund grants in 2013. The county received $134,800 in 1 grant to rank 83rd in grants and 82nd in grant dollars received.

Oscoda County is a part of the Northern Lower Peninsula DNR Eco-Region, which has received $2,400,000 in MNRTF grants TF07-119, TF08-134 and 09-132.

OSCODA COUNTY active or closed MNRTF Projects

CLINTON TOWNSHIP

TF13-050 Clinton Township Nature Preseserve/ Campground Acquisition ACQ $134,800

OSCODA COUNTY TOTAL $ 134,800

Otsego County

Otsego County was named an upper New York state county of the same name, homeplace of a number of the area's early settlers. It was set off as a county from part of Mackinac County in 1840, called Okkudo County until 1843 and formally established in 1875.

With 515 square miles, Otsego County is 68th largest county and 59th largest in population with 24,164 residents.

Since oil was discovered there in 1940, 4,518 holes have been drilled in the search for oil and gas. Otsego County has produced 109,607,137 barrels of oil and 1.602 trillion cubic feet of natural gas, ranking 3rd and 1st respectively among the 64 oil or gas producing Michigan counties.

Otsego County Fair photo
MNRTF grant TF86-115, $30,000, went to Otsego County for the acquisition of property to expand their fairgrounds.

Otsego County has received $6,910,060 in 10 Michigan Natural Resources Trust Fund grants, ranking 32nd in number of grants received and 16th in grant dollars awarded.

OTSEGO COUNTY active or closed MNRTF Projects

DNR - FOREST, MINERAL & FIRE MANAGEMENT		
TF08-153 Pigeon River Country Acquisition Initiative	ACQ	$1,000,000
TF473 Pigeon River TNC	ACQ	$50,000
TF520 Green Timbers	ACQ	$2,500,000
DNR - FOREST RESOURCES DIVISION		
TF14-259 Pigeon River County-Upper Black River Acq.	ACQ	$150,000
TF13-123 Pigeon River Property	ACQ	$500,000
DNRE - FOREST MANAGEMENT DIVISION		
TF10-119 Pigeon River Country Visitor Center Renov.	DEV	$50,000
TF10-124 Pigeon River County-Upper Black River Acq.	ACQ	$2,200,000

GAYLORD		
TF02-083 Elk View Acquisition	ACQ	$112,000
TF03-065 Freel/Doumas Park Renovation	DEV	$318,060
OTSEGO COUNTY		
TF86-115 Fairgrounds Expansion	ACQ	$30,000
OTSEGO COUNTY TOTAL		**$ 6,910,060**

MNRTF grant TF02-083, $112,000, went for the acquisition of property for Gaylord's Elk View Park, above. In September, 2005, Ray Barnhart (left below), on behalf of the Michigan Oil And Gas Association and Michigan Oil & Gas Producers Education Foundation, addressed Gaylord's Joe Duff - City Manager, Paul Beachnau - Executive Director, Gaylord Area Convention and Tourism Bureau, Joe Wambold - City Council member, Jerry Cambell - City Council member, Mayor Gladys Soloski and Stan Soloski, presenting the MOGA Award of Excellence to the City of Gaylord for outstanding use of MNRTF grants.

Ottawa County

Set off as a county area in 1831, and officially organized in 1837. The year Michigan became a state, Ottawa County was named the Ottawa Indian Tribe and the name is believed to derive from "*Ot-tah-way*", meaning "trader" for that tribe's commercial interaction with European settlers.

MNRTF Project TF88-112, $128,000, Spring Lake Bikeway, Spring Lake.

With 566 square miles, Ottawa County is 48th largest county and 8th largest in population with 263,801 residents. Since oil was discovered there in 1939, in the Berea geological formation at 1,320 feet, 1,008 holes have been drilled in the search for oil and gas. Ottawa County has produced 2,249,927 barrels of oil and 5.742 billion cubic feet of natural gas, ranking 43rd and 46th respectively among the 64 oil or gas producing Michigan counties. Ottawa County has received $30,693,215 in 74 Michigan Natural Resources Trust Fund grants, ranking 3rd in number of grants received and 5th in grant dollars awarded.

OTTAWA COUNTY active or closed MNRTF Projects

Project	Type	Amount
ALLENDALE TOWNSHIP		
TF07-041 Allendale Community Park Addition	ACQ	$88,200
TF86-094 Allendale Twp. Rec. Area	ACQ	$26,200
CROCKERY TOWNSHIP		
TF12-092 North Bank Trail	ACQ	$120,000
DNR - FOREST, MINERAL & FIRE MANAGEMENT		
TF92-335 Ottawa-Muskegon Trail-Phase I	DEV	$100,000
DNR - PARKS & RECREATION DIVISION		
TF09-145 Holland State Park Campground Restroom	DEV	$450,000
TF86-321 Bass River Recreation Area-Ph I	ACQ	$700,000
TF87-321 Bass River Rec. Area	ACQ	$900,000
TF89-233 Rosy Mound Acquisition	ACQ	$1,500,000
TF90-029 Rosy Mound Ph II Acquisition	ACQ	$1,500,000
TF996 Lake Macatawa Pub. Acc.	ACQ	$185,000
DNR - WILDLIFE DIVISION		
TF01-222 Bass River Rec. Area Acq - Bakale Property	ACQ	$3,215,000

FERRYSBURG		
TF717 North Shore Dune	ACQ	$301,000
GEORGETOWN TOWNSHIP		
TF10-054 Maplewood Park Improvements	DEV	$333,300
GRAND HAVEN		
TF08-076 East Grand River Park Improvements	DEV	$300,000
TF09-099 City Beach Improvements	DEV	$115,200
GRAND HAVEN CHARTER TOWNSHIP		
TF14-117 Hofma Park & Preserve Land	ACQ	$276,500

MNRTF Projects TF 90-254 and TF94-258, totaling $400,000, Pottawattomie Park, Ottawa Township.

GRAND HAVEN TOWNSHIP		
TF90-254 Pottawattomie Park Project	DEV	$300,000
TF94-258 Pottawattomie Park	DEV	$100,000
TF97-112 144th Avenue Land Acquisition	ACQ	$123,500
TF99-048 144th Avenue Boat Launch	DEV	$275,000
HOLLAND		
TF00-172 Kollen Park Renovation	DEV	$500,000
TF04-171 Heinz Waterfront Walkway	DEV	$500,000
TF93-389 Paw Paw Reserve Acquisition	ACQ	$60,000
TF94-282 Van Raalte Farm Improvements	DEV	$277,500
TF96-113 Paw Paw Reserve Development	DEV	$210,000
TF14-092 Windmill Park Garden Bridge & Regional Trail Connections	ACQ	$300,000
HOLLAND CHARTER TOWNSHIP		
TF14-121 Quincy Picnic Shelter Improvements	DEV	$50,000
TF13-040 Hawthorn Pond Natural Area	ACQ	$50,000
HOLLAND TOWNSHIP		
TF09-090 Helder Park Improvements	DEV	$275,000
TF306 Dunton Park	ACQ	$65,000
TF708 Howard B. Dunton Park	ACQ	$115,000

TF87-217 Dunton Park Expansion	ACQ	$243,000
TF91-339 H. B. Dunton Park Improvements	DEV	$225,000
TF92-294 H. B. Dunton Park Acquisition	ACQ	$937,500
TF95-137 Helder Park Expansion	ACQ	$243,800
TF97-132 Howard B. Dunton Park Expansion	DEV	$446,530
HUDSONVILLE		
TF89-226 New Holland Nature Park	ACQ	$90,000
OTTAWA COUNTY		
TF01-158 Rosy Mound Improvements	DEV	$500,000
TF01-159 Pigeon River Greenway Improvements	DEV	$471,000
TF03-146 Connor Bayou Acquisition	ACQ	$823,000
TF04-108 North Ottawa Dune Acquisition	ACQ	$3,900,000
TF06-067 Mount Pisgah Dune Protection Project	DEV	$280,000
TF06-208 Bur Oak Land Acquisition	ACQ	$773,000
TF07-090 Olive Shores Acquisition	ACQ	$2,000,000
TF09-075 Grand River Ravines Acquisition	ACQ	$720,000
TF710 Grand River Park	ACQ	$140,000
TF87-229 Grand River Park	DEV	$120,000

***MNRTF Project** TF94-282 Van Raalte Farm Improvement, $277,500. Preserves the farm of one of Holland's founders, Albertus Van Raalte, who platted a 60 acre village along the Black River in 1847 along with 700 settlers from the Netherlands. They named it Holland, meaning "wooded place", after their homeland.*

TF89-232 Pigeon Creek Expansion	ACQ	$107,300
TF91-051 Riverside Park Expansion	ACQ	$114,000
TF93-106 Pigeon Creek-Phase I	DEV	$315,000

TF95-208 North Beach Improvements	DEV	$150,000
TF97-242 Pigeon River Greenway Acquisition	ACQ	$397,500
TF98-052 Grose Park Improvements	DEV	$410,000
TF98-285 Pigeon River Greenway II	ACQ	$390,000
TF99-235 Crockery Creek Site Acquisition	ACQ	$805,000
TF10-101 Olive Shores Park Improvements	DEV	$365,000
TF11-106 Ottawa Beach Waterfront Walkway	DEV	$300,000
TF12-280 Grand River Accessible Kayak Launches	DEV	$47,500
TF12-078 Grand River Opens Space Expansion	ACQ	$130,000
PARK TOWNSHIP		
TF00-113 Pine Creek Trail Development	DEV	$335,775
TF89-245 Winstrom Park	DEV	$142,500
ROBINSON TOWNSHIP		
TF86-323 Robinson Twp. Central Pk.	ACQ	$49,000
SPRING LAKE		
TF00-136 Lakeside Beach Acquisition	ACQ	$122,550
TF88-112 Spring Lake Bikeway	DEV	$128,000
TF97-267 Community Boardwalk	DEV	$64,360
SPRING LAKE TOWNSHIP		
TF09-112 North Bank Trail Development	DEV	$231,500
TF10-165 Glafcke Family Public Preserve	ACQ	$61,200
TF11-048 Pellegrom Property Acquisition	ACQ	$30,000
TF12-064 Rycenga Park Picnic Shelter	DEV	$46,500
TF13-104 Hines Property Acquisition	ACQ	$94,900
TALLMADGE TOWNSHIP		
TF86-327 Tallmadge Township Park	ACQ	$36,000
VILLAGE OF SPRING LAKE		
TF09-015 Grand River Greenway Non-Motorized Trail	DEV	$465,000
ZEELAND TOWNSHIP		
TF03-070 Drenthe Grove Park Expansion	ACQ	$80,400
TF13-041 Drenthe Grove Park Improvements	DEV	$50,000

OTTAWA COUNTY TOTAL $ 30,693,215

Collette Wilson photo

MNRTF Project TF04-108, $3,900,000, North Ottawa Dunes Acqu-isition by Ottawa County.

Presque Isle County

Presque Isle County derives its name from a French phrase for peninsula, meaning "*almost an island*". It was set off as a county from part of Mackinac County in 1840 and formally established in 1871.

With 660 square miles, Presque Isle County is 31st largest county and 71st largest in population with 13,376 residents.

MNRTF grants TF89-061 and 87-109, totaling $284,000, helped acquire and develop the Black Mountain Forest Recreation area.

Since oil was discovered there in 1969, 465 holes have been drilled in the search for oil and gas, making it the 34th most drilled county in the state. Presque Isle County has produced 12,014,717 barrels of oil and 38.408 billion cubic feet of natural gas, ranking 24th and 30th respectively among the 64 oil or gas producing Michigan counties. Presque Isle County has received $4,581,700 in 14 Michigan Natural Resources Trust Fund grants, ranking 46th in number of grants received and 40th in grant dollars awarded.

PRESQUE ISLE active or closed MNRTF Projects

DNR - FISHERIES DIVISION

TF643 Trout River Pond	ACQ	$150,000

DNR - FOREST, MINERAL & FIRE MANAGEMENT		
TF08-121 Ocqueoc Falls Trlhd./Scenic Overlook Imp.	DEV	$500,000
TF89-152 Black Mountain Forest Inholding	ACQ	$142,000
TF90-109 Black Mountain Forest Recreation	DEV	$142,000
TF978 Thompson's Harbor	ACQ	$100,000
DNR - PARKS & RECREATION DIVISION		
TF442 Presque Isle Harbor	ACQ	$240,000
TF86-061 Presque Isle Harbor	DEV	$400,000
TF87-362 Lake Huron Shoreline	ACQ	$1,000,000
METZ TOWNSHIP		
TF12-013 Metz Trailside Park	DEV	$111,600
PRESQUE ISLE COUNTY		
TF10-035 Millersburg Hist. Depot Reg. Trailhead Dev.	DEV	$492,100

Presque Isle Township photo

MNRTF grants TF93-018, and 96-018, totaling $429,000, were used to acquire and develop the Old Presque Isle Lighthouse and Old Presque Isle Lighthouse Park.

PRESQUE ISLE TOWNSHIP		
TF93-018 Old Presque Isle Lighthouse	ACQ	$345,000
TF96-029 Old Presque Isle Lighthouse Park	DEV	$84,000
ROGERS CITY		
TF92-131 Harbor Expansion	DEV	$375,000
TF98-140 Rogers City Linkage Plan	DEV	$500,000

PRESQUE ISLE COUNTY TOTAL $ 4,581,700

Roscommon County

Roscommon County is named for the Irish County Roscommon. It was set off as a county in 1840 and formally established in 1875.

Roscommon County's 521 square miles make it 66th largest county and 58th largest in population with 24,449 residents. Since oil was discovered there in 1941, 417 holes have been drilled seeking oil and gas. Roscommon County has produced 3,588,199 barrels of oil and 2.149 billion cubic feet of natural gas, ranking 37th and 50th respectively among the 64 oil or gas producing Michigan counties. Roscommon County has received $11,149,300 in 14 Michigan Natural Resources Trust Fund grants, 44th in number of grants received and 19th in dollars awarded.

Two MNRTF grants totaling $2,800,000, went to Gerrish Township Park.

ROSCOMMON COUNTY active or closed MNRTF Projects

DENTON TOWNSHIP		
TF06-005 Houghton Lake Shore Property Acquisition	ACQ	$450,000
TF10-019 Trestle Park Development Project	DEV	$372,700
DNR - FOREST, MINERAL & FIRE MANAGEMENT		
TF08-122 Wolf Creek Corridor Flooding Complex Acq.	ACQ	$3,300,000
TF96-261 Houghton Lake State Forest Campground	DEV	$498,400
DNR - OFFICE OF LAND & FACILITIES		
TF08-125 Ralph A. MacMullan Conference Center Imp.	DEV	$500,000
DNR - PARKS & RECREATION DIVISION		
TF282 Houghton Lake Access	ACQ	$200,000
TF587 Marl Lake-S. Higgins Lake	ACQ	$740,000
DNR - WILDLIFE DIVISION		
TF05-156 Russell Lake Winter Deer Habitat Acquisition	ACQ	$1,820,000
GERRISH TOWNSHIP		
TF06-036 Gerrish Township Public Park	ACQ	$1,400,000
TF07-002 Gerrish Township Community Park-Phase II	ACQ	$1,400,000
LYON TOWNSHIP		
TF14-093 Park 27 Renovation	DEV	$40,000
ROSCOMMON TOWNSHIP		
TF07-049 Lakeview Park Improvement Project	DEV	$189,900
TF14-169 Lakeview Park UA Beach Park & Family Style Restrooms	DEV	$40,000
RICHFIELD TOWNSHIP		
TF11-027 Lake St. Helen Universal Access	DEV	$55,800

ROSCOMMON COUNTY TOTAL $ 11,149,300

Saginaw County

Saginaw County was the location of Michigan's first commercial oil field discovery in August of 1925. The county is believed to have been named for the Sauk American Indian Tribe, who lived near the mouth of the river which would be given the same name. It was set off as a county from Oakland County in 1822 and formally established in 1835.

The Saginaw County Rail Trail has received three MNRTF grants totaling $1,076,000.

With 809 square miles, Saginaw County is 21th largest county and 10th largest in population with 200,169 residents.

Since oil was discovered there in 1925, 609 holes have been drilled in the search for oil and gas. Saginaw County has produced 3,725,822 barrels of oil and only 6,000 cubic feet of natural gas, ranking 36th and 54th respectively among the 64 oil or gas producing Michigan counties. Saginaw County has received $7,037,603 in 33 Michigan Natural Resources Trust Fund grants, ranking 15th in number of grants received and 30th in grant dollars awarded.

SAGINAW COUNTY active or closed MNRTF Projects

Project	Type	Amount
BRIDGEPORT TOWNSHIP		
TF09-092 Liberty Park Improvements	DEV	$500,000
TF14-217 Cass River Water Trail Davis Park 27	DEV	$121,100
CHESANING		
TF90-222 Chesaning Showboat Park	DEV	$38,600
TF11-092 Cole Park Improvements	DEV	$300,000
TF14-220 Riverbank Improvements	DEV	$50,000
DNR - WILDLIFE DIVISION		
TF14-131 Shiawassee River SGA Dev. Initiative	DEV	$300,000
FRANKENMUTH		
TF09-101 Cass River Greenway Water Trail Dev.	DEV	$35,300
TF13-097 Cass River Greenway Water Trail Park Land	ACQ	$721,800
KOCHVILLE TOWNSHIP		
TF02-019 Township Park Expansion	ACQ	$63,800

SAGINAW		
TF00-106 Westside Riverfront Park Development	DEV	$256,153
TF07-072 Andersen Park Development	DEV	$51,800
TF08-039 Andersen Water Park Project	DEV	$480,000
TF410 Green Point Nature Center	ACQ	$22,000
TF90-343 Ojibway Island Renovation	DEV	$165,000
TF91-222 Rust Avenue Boat Launch	DEV	$375,000
TF12-086 Boulder Climbing Garden & Connector Path	DEV	$67,000
SAGINAW COUNTY		
TF01-082 Saginaw Valley Rail Trail	DEV	$493,000
TF03-119 Saginaw Valley Rail Trail	DEV	$493,000
TF1075 S & H Lake	ACQ	$247,500
TF503 Price Nature Center	ACQ	$25,000
TF716 Price Nature Center	ACQ	$12,000
TF87-271 S & H Lake	DEV	$400,000
TF88-095 Haithco Rec. Area-Phase II	DEV	$335,250
TF94-213 Saginaw Valley Rail Trail	ACQ	$90,000
TF11-090 Saginaw Valley Rail-Trail	DEV	$251,500
TF13-092 Great Lakes Bay Regional Trail	DEV	$280,000
SAGINAW INTERMEDIATE SCHOOL DISTRICT		
TF94-085 HOEC Renovation	DEV	$75,000
TF95-029 HOEC-Renovation, Phase III	DEV	$140,400
ST. CHARLES		
TF05-010 St. Charles Area Park Land Acquisition	ACQ	$45,700
TF87-164 Bad River Acquisition	ACQ	$45,000
THOMAS TOWNSHIP		
TF10-087 Roberts Park Improvements	DEV	$262,900
TF13-0007 Rothke Park Land Acquisition	ACQ	$39,700
ZILWAUKEE		
TF12-095 Riverfront Prk Imp. Lions Field Park Pool Hse.	DEV	$254,100

SAGINAW COUNTY TOTAL $ 7,037,603

The very first Michigan Oil And Gas Association (MOGA) Award of Excellence for outstanding use of Michigan Natural Resources Trust Fund grants was presented October 1, 2000 to the Saginaw Intermediate School District for Harley Outdoor Education Center HOEC. Representing MOGA were William C. Myler, Jr. and Jack R. Westbrook (left). Accepting for the HOEC was Director James Blaschka, with Michigan Representative James Howell and Michigan Representative Mike Goschka.

Saint Clair County

Saint Clair County, named for Scotsman Arthur Saint Clair, the first Governor of the Northwest Territory (north of the Ohio River including five Great Lakes States) from 1787 to 1802. It was set off as a county in 1820 and formally established in 1821.

With 724 square miles, Saint Clair County is 24th largest county and 13th largest in population with 163,040 residents. Saint Clair County was a local use oil county 39 years before Michigan became a commercially producing oil state in 1925 with the discovery of the Saginaw Field. Since oil was discovered there in 1886, 1,635 holes have been drilled in the search for oil and gas. Saint Clair County has produced 21,281,321 barrels of oil and 191.938 billion cubic feet of natural gas, ranking 20th and 10th respectively among the 64 oil or gas producing Michigan counties. Saint Clair County has received $12,543,949 in 35 Michigan Natural Resources Trust Fund grants, ranking 12th in number of grants received and 16th in grant dollars awarded.

SAINT CLAIR COUNTY active or closed MNRTF Projects

ALGONAC		
TF08-110 Lions Field Park Pool House Improvements	DEV	$255,100
BROCKWAY TOWNSHIP		
TF96-089 Brockway Township Park	ACQ	$104,834
TF13-001 Skate Park	DEV	$36,700
CLAY TOWNSHIP		
TF95-287 Non-Motorized Trail	DEV	$102,000
COTTRELLVILLE TOWNSHIP		
TF11-011 Cottrellville Twp. Riverfront Park Acquisition	ACQ	$347,700
DNR - PARKS & RECREATION DIVISION		
TF89-574 North Channel Site	ACQ	$960,000
TF91-016 Lake St. Clair Boat Access	DEV	$500,000
TF97-195 Algonac S.P. "Bridge to Bay" Rail-Trail	DEV	$148,750
DNR - WILDLIFE DIVISION		
TF042 St. Johns Marsh	ACQ	$1,065,000
TF377 St. Clair Flats	ACQ	$250,000
EAST CHINA TOWNSHIP		
TF94-092 East China Bike Trail	DEV	$160,700
GREENWOOD TOWNSHIP		
TF00-154 Township Park Expansion	ACQ	$63,360
MARINE CITY		
TF00-322 St. Clair River Beach Acquisition	ACQ	$487,105
TF98-110 Bridge to Bay Trail	ACQ	$15,400
MARYSVILLE		
TF87-038 Marysville City Park Exp	ACQ	$59,000
TF94-084 Riverfront Land Acquisition	ACQ	$48,000
TF13-115 Marysville City Park		

– Chrysler Beach Recreation Improvement	DEV	$239,900
PORT HURON		
TF95-120 Pine Grove Park	DEV	$158,900
TF96-049 16th and Dove Softball Lighting	DEV	$84,000
TF14-138 Lakeside Park Universal Redevelopment	DEV	$295,000
PORT HURON TOWNSHIP		
TF00-065 Purchase of Bakers Field	ACQ	$375,000
TF08-043 Bakers Field Park Development	DEV	$282,200

Sarah Davidson-Nelson Pine River Nature Center photo

Three MNRTF grants totaling $937,300, went to the Saint Clair RESA to help acquire and develop the Pine River Nature Center. (See Multi-County chapter for a picture of the Center's treehouse).

ST. CLAIR COUNTY		
TF03-129 Lake Huron Shoreline Acquisition	ACQ	$2,312,500
TF06-099 Belle River Property Acquisition	ACQ	$1,408,000
TF07-171 Camp Woodsong Fee Simple Acquisition	ACQ	$291,800
TF96-195 Wadhams to Avoca Rail Trail	ACQ	$161,000
TF11-116 Blue Water River Walk Expansion	ACQ	$150,000
TF13-106 North Channel Waterfront Acquisition	ACQ	$296,000
TF14-093 Blue Water River Walk Expansion Phase 2	ACQ	$118,400
TF14-094 Bouvier Bay Waterfront Acquisition	ACQ	$666,000
ST. CLAIR COUNTY RESA		
TF00-024 Pine River Nature Center Visitor Facilities	DEV	$370,000
TF04-115 Pine River Nature Center Trail Dev.	DEV	$360,500
TF96-024 Pine River Nature Center	ACQ	$206,800
ST. CLAIR TOWNSHIP		
TF04-168 Greig Park Expansion	ACQ	$100,000
WALES TOWNSHIP		
TF03-143 Wales Township Park Land Acquisition	ACQ	$74,300

SAINT CLAIR COUNTY TOTAL $ 12,543,949

Saint Joseph County

Saint Joseph County is one of Michigan's oldest and is named for the river that rambles through it, bringing the first settlers to southwestern Michigan. It was set off and organized in 1829.

With 504 square miles, Saint Joseph County is 72nd largest county and 32nd largest in population with 61,295 residents.

MNRTF grants TF348, 02-174 and 87-106, totaling $153,500, went to Three Rivers Scidmore Park.

Although 27 holes have been drilled in the search for oil and gas, making Saint Joseph the 67th most drilled of the 75 Michigan counties drilled, none has been discovered. Saint Joseph County has received $1,172,000 in 11 grants, ranking 53rd in number of grants and 75th in grant dollars awarded.

SAINT JOSEPH COUNTY active or closed MNRTF Projects

BURR OAK		
TF89-136 Boyer Field Expansion	ACQ	$15,000
MENDON		
TF89-079 Reed River Park Expan.	ACQ	$40,000
ST. JOSEPH COUNTY		
TF08-139 Cade Lake County Park Expansion	ACQ	$79,500
TF14-065 Stewart Lake Conservation Acquisition	ACQ	$504,800
THREE RIVERS		
TF02-174 Scidmore Park Riverwalk and Renovations	DEV	$101,500
TF348 Scidmore Park	ACQ	$20,000
TF87-106 Scidmore Park Int. Center	ACQ	$32,000
TF91-163 Marina Park	DEV	$52,200
VILLAGE OF COLON		
TF09-049 Colon Community Park Development	DEV	$200,000
VILLAGE OF CONSTANTINE		
TF10-020 Riverview Park Development	DEV	$91,000
TF10-146 Riverview Park Acquisition	ACQ	$36,000

SAINT JOSEPH COUNTY TOTAL $ 1,172,000

Sanilac County

Sanilac County was named in honor of a Wyandotte American Indian Chieftain. It was set off as a county in 1822 and formally established in 1848.

With 964 square miles, Sanilac County is 11th largest county and 39th largest in population with 43,114 residents.

Sanilac County photo

MNRTF grant TF08-012, $79,600, helped acquire additional land for Sanilac's Evergreen County Park.

Sanilac is one of four Michigan Lower Peninsula counties that has produced no oil or natural gas, although 80 holes have been drilled there in attempts to discover this valuable natural mineral resource.

Sanilac County has received $1,650,940 in 9 Michigan Natural Resources Trust Fund grants, ranking 62nd in terms of grants received and 65th in grant dollars awarded.

SANILAC COUNTY active or closed MNRTF Projects

BROWN CITY		
TF10-006 Pond and Nature Trail Enhancement	DEV	$35,000
CROSWELL		
TF00-155 River Bend Park Improvements	DEV	$82,240
FLYNN TOWNSHIP		
TF06-093 Hyponex Wetlands Property Acquisition	ACQ	$785,900
LEXINGTON		
TF90-229 Village Habor Pk Imprv.	DEV	$123,000
SANILAC COUNTY		
TF08-012 Evergreen Park Addition	ACQ	$79,600
TF96-069 Forester Park Restroom/Shower Project	DEV	$60,000
TF11-057 Evergreen Park Development	DEV	$300,000
TF12-069 Forester Park Accessible Playground Eqip.	DEV	$19,000
VILLAGE OF PORT SANILAC		
TF10-072 Fire Hall Park Improvements	DEV	$166,200

SANILAC COUNTY TOTAL $ 1,650.940

Schoolcraft County

Schoolcraft County, like Houghton County, is named for another giant in Michigan state history. Henry Rowe Schoolcraft, was a historian whose journals tell us much about the early days of Michigan's Upper Peninsula since he accompanied geologist Douglass Houghton on expeditions to evaluate the mineral potential of the area. Schoolcraft, 1793-1864 was also a geographer and was Superintendent of Indian Affairs for Michigan, living with his Chippewa Indian wife along the banks of the St. Mary's River at Sault Ste. Marie.

MNRTF Project TF99-300, $150,000 went to develop Palms Book State Park.

With 1,178 square miles, Schoolcraft is 4th largest county and 80th largest in population with 8,485 residents. It was set off and organized as a county from parts of Chippewa and Mackinac Counties in 1843.

Schoolcraft County is an Upper Peninsula county with little to no significant sedimentary geological strata, almost precluding the likelihood of the presence of oil and/or natural gas. Five holes been drilled there to search for petroleum, one with a non-commercial show of oil.

Schoolcraft County has received $1,849,000 in 9 Michigan Natural Resources Trust Fund grants, ranking 61st in number of grants received and 64th in grant dollars awarded.

SCHOOLCRAFT COUNTY active or closed MNRTF Projects

DNR - PARKS & RECREATION DIVISION		
TF99-300 Palms Book S.P.-Interpretive Facilities Ren.	DEV	$150,000
MANISTIQUE		
TF05-109 Manistique Central Park Improvements	DEV	$424,000
TF93-199 Waterfront Park Development	DEV	$90,000
TF12-074 Traders Point Lot 7	ACQ	$78,800
TF12-119 Lake Michigan & Manistique River Waterfront	ACQ	$779,400
TF13-111 Manistique Waterfront North Lot Acquisition	ACQ	$26,400
TF13-112 Manistique Waterfront Lot US-2 Acquisition	ACQ	$125,000
TF13-113 Manistique Riv. Waterfront Elk St. Acquisition	ACQ	$102,300
MANISTIQUE TOWNSHIP		
TF11-111 Township Park Barrier-Free Beach Access	DEV	$73,100

SCHOOLCRAFT COUNTY TOTAL $1,849,000

Shiawassee County

One of Michigan's oldest counties, Shiawassee County was named in honor of the river that transects the area. It was set off as a county in 1822 and formally established in 1837.

MNRTF grant TF89-046, $80,000, went to Owosso's Heritage Park to acquired adjacent lands to the famous James Oliver Curwood castle. Curwood, an early 20th Century author and zealous conservationist, was appointed to the Michigan Conservation Commission, forerunner of today's DNRE, administrator of the Michigan Natural Resources Trust Fund.

With 539 square miles, Shiawassee County is 65th largest county and 27th largest in population with 70,648 residents.

Since oil was discovered there in 1967, 76 holes have been drilled in the search for oil and gas. Shiawassee County has produced 322,513 barrels of oil and no natural gas, ranking the county 57th largest oil producers among the 64 oil and/or gas producing Michigan counties.

Shiawassee County has received $130,800 in 3 Michigan Natural Resources Trust Fund grants, ranking 82nd in number of grants received and 84th in grant dollars awarded.

SHIAWASSEE COUNTY active or closed MNRTF Projects

CORUNNA

Project	Type	Amount
TF89-045 McCurdy Park Acquisition	ACQ	$18,800

OWOSSO

Project	Type	Amount
TF89-046 Heritage Park/Curwood	ACQ	$80,000
TF96-242 Hopkins Lake Park Expansion	ACQ	$32,000

SHIAWASSEE COUNTY TOTAL $ 130,800

Tuscola County

Tuscola County is a made-up erstz Indian name roughly meaning "*prairie warrior*" created by Henry Schoolcraft. It was set aside in 1840 and formally established in 1850.

With 813 square miles, Tuscola County is 20th largest county and 34th largest in population with 55,729 residents. Oil was discovered there in 1936, and 348 holes have been drilled in the search for oil and gas. Tuscola County has produced 4,315,445 barrels of oil and 2.404 billion cubic feet of natural gas, ranking 36th and 50th respectively among the 64 oil or gas producing Michigan counties. Tuscola County has received $1,314,200 in 8 Michigan Natural Resources Trust Fund grants, ranking 68th in number of grants received and 72nd in grant dollars awarded.

MNRTF grants TF90-237, 90-238 and 07-097, totaling $210,000, helped acquire and develop Vassar's Riverside Park, where Ben and Gabrielle Cleveland enjoyed the playscape on an early May afternoon.

TUSCOLA COUNTY active or closed MNRTF Projects

Project	Type	Amount
CARO		
TF02-165 Chippewa Landing Park /Trl. Imp.	DEV	$369,400
DNR - WILDLIFE DIVISION		
TF573 Murphy Lake State Game Area	ACQ	$30,000
SOUTHERN LINKS TRAILWAY MANAGEMENT COUNCIL		
TF04-020 South. Links Trailway Management Council	ACQ	$500,000
TUSCOLA TOWNSHIP		
TF09-102 Cass River Greenway Water Trail Dev.	DEV	$32,700
VASSAR		
TF90-237 Vassar Riverside Park	ACQ	$84,000
TF90-238 Vassar Riverside Park	DEV	$126,000
TF97-084 Bikeway/Walkway Rail Trail	DEV	$129,500
TF14-070 Cass River Greenway Water Trail	DEV	$42,600

TUSCOLA COUNTY TOTAL $ 1,314,200

Van Buren County

Van Buren County was named in honor of Martin Van Buren 1782-1862, who was Secretary of State during the Andrew Jackson Administration 1829-1831, then Vice President of the United States 1833-1837 and finally eighth President of the United States 1837-1841. Van Buren County was set off from an unorganized territory in 1829 and formally established in 1837

With 611 square miles, Van Buren County is 35^{h} largest county and 25th largest in population with 76,258 residents.

Michigan Oil & Gas News photo

The Michigan Oil And Gas Association (MOGA) and Michigan Oil and Gas Producers Education Foundation (MOGPEF) presented their Award of Excellence for outstanding use of Michigan Natural Resources Trust Fund grants TF822 and TF86-006 totaling $963,000 for acquisition and development of the Van Buren County segment of the Kal-Haven Trail to the Friends of the Kal-Haven Trail. August 26, 2008, ceremonies took place at Bloomingdale. Right to left are: Pat Goodale – representing MOGA; Mike Coy – representing MOGPEF; Jeff Mitchell – Van Buren County; Carl Christensen and Ron Stalk – Friends of the Kal-Haven Trail; Sam Ewbank – Village of Bloomingdale; and State Representative Tonya Schuitmaker of Lawton. Not pictured but present at the ceremony was Michigan Natural Resources Commissioner Mary Brown of Kalamazoo.

Oil was discovered in July, 1938, in the tiny Van Buren County village of Bloomingdale, sparking an intense flurry of drilling of many wells very close together, prompting the passage of Michigan Act 61 of 1939, the Oil and Gas Law, considered classic oil and gas regulations. Among other things, Act 61 established minimum spacing between wells. Honoring its oil and gas past, which sheltered the town from the financial devastation of the last days of the Great Depression, the Village of Bloomingdale is establishing a Michigan Oil and Gas Exploration and Production Museum as part of their Depot Museum along the Kal-Haven Trail. Since oil was discovered there in 1938, 1,797 holes have been drilled in the search for oil and gas. Van Buren County has produced 12,269,564 barrels of oil and no natural gas, ranking 23rd among the 64 oil or gas producing Michigan counties.

Van Buren County has received $9,681,800 in 19 Michigan Natural Resources Trust Fund grants, ranking 31st in number of grants received and 22nd in grant dollars awarded.

VAN BUREN COUNTY active or closed MNRTF Projects

Project	Type	Amount
BANGOR		
TF04-170 Black River Heritage Trail / Boardwalk Project	DEV	$252,800
TF08-102 Veterans Park and Kiwanis Park Additions	ACQ	$37,800
TF86-146 Bangor Park	ACQ	$61,500
DNR - PARKS & RECREATION DIVISION		
TF822 Kal-Haven Trail State Park	ACQ	$700,000
TF86-006 Kal-Haven Trail Development	DEV	$263,000
TF90-175 Amicus Corp.-Van Buren SP	ACQ	$2,200,000
TF13-127 Wolf Lake Fish Hatchery	DEV	$295,000
TF14-189 Paw Paw/ Hartford Multi-Use Trail Partnership	ACQ	$750,000
DNR - WILDLIFE DIVISION		
TF13-128 Porter Township SGA Land Initiative	ACQ	$1,800,000
HARTFORD		
TF10-024 Ely Park Improvement	DEV	$29,600
PAW		
TF94-157 Community Park Development	DEV	$169,900
SOUTH HAVEN		
TF887 South Shore Recreation Area	ACQ	$601,000
TF95-093 Dyckman & Packard Beach	DEV	$84,000
TF10-097 South Beach Improvements	DEV	$250,000
TF11-144 Elkeburg Park Improvements	DEV	$254,800
TF12-096 South Beach Park Extension	DEV	$665,000
TF12-114 Van Buren Trail Connection Dev.	DEV	$217,400
SOUTH HAVEN AREA RECREATION AUTHORITY		
TF14-211 Pilgrim Haven Development Project	DEV	$50,000
SOUTH HAVEN TOWNSHIP		
TF06-210 Deerlick Creek Park Acquisition	ACQ	$1,000,000

VAN BUREN COUNTY TOTAL $ 9,681,800

Washtenaw County

The area west of Detroit was known to North American Indians as *Wash-ten-ong*, meaning "land beyond", or "a further district". Washtenaw County is named in European corruption of that name. It was set off as a county in 1815 from parts of Oakland and Wayne County and formally established in 1826, along with counties, five in the lower tier of Lower Peninsula counties and Chippewa County in the Upper Peninsula.

Ann Arbor's Leslie Environmental Center was developed with the help of MNRTF grant TF96-132, and the Nature House was built through a grant from Michigan Consolidated Gas Company. On December 15, 2004, the Michigan Oil And Gas Association presented the Award of Excellence to the Environmental Center for outstaying use of and MNRTF Grant. Facility Director Kristen Levisohn and Ann Arbor Mayor John Hietftje hold the Award in the inset photo above with MichCon's Paul Ganz - representing MOGA and MichCon, and Ann Arbor Convention and Visitors Bureau President Mary Kerr.

With 710 square miles, Washtenaw County is 26th largest county and 6th largest in population with 344,791 residents.

Since oil was discovered there in 1953, 231 holes have been drilled in the search for oil and gas. Washtenaw County has produced 1,157,227 barrels of oil and 19.852 billion cubic feet of natural gas, ranking 50th and 36th respectively among the 64 oil or gas producing Michigan counties.

Washtenaw County has received $23,275,314 in 52 Michigan Natural Resources Trust Fund grants, ranking 6th in number of grants received and 7th in grant dollars awarded.

WASHTENAW COUNTY active or closed MNRTF Projects

Project	Type	Amount
ANN ARBOR		
TF02-113 Addition to Dolph Nature Area	ACQ	$688,000
TF624 Johnson-Greene Parkland	ACQ	$250,000
TF88-132 Hawkins Property	ACQ	$281,250
TF90-373 Black Pond Property Acq.	ACQ	$875,000
TF91-274 Sias Parcels A and B	ACQ	$321,000
TF91-275 Gunn Property Acquisition	ACQ	$517,600
TF92-115 Ganzhorn Subdivision Lots	ACQ	$87,300
TF92-116 Evergreen Subdivision Lots	ACQ	$37,400
TF92-117 Furstenberg Park	DEV	$375,000
TF95-225 Renovate Neighborhood Parks	DEV	$70,000
TF95-227 Main Street Property Acquisition	ACQ	$726,000
TF96-130 Southeast Area Park Addition	ACQ	$293,250
TF96-132 Leslie Environmental Center	DEV	$500,000
TF98-089 Scarlett-Mitchell Addition	ACQ	$575,500
TF11-013 Gallup Park Livery & Site Renovations	DEV	$300,000
TF11-014 Veterans Memorial Park Skate Park	DEV	$300,000
DNR - EXECUTIVE OFFICE		
TF04-180 Cedar Lake Outdoor Center Development	DEV	$261,000
DNR - FISHERIES DIVISION		
TF906 Huron River/Belleville Lake	ACQ	$300,000
DNR - PARKS & RECREATION DIVISION		
TF70-614 Park Lyndon/Waterloo/Pinc.	ACQ	$500,000
HURON-CLINTON METROPOLITAN AUTHORITY		
TF10-040 Hudson Mill Hike/Bike Trail Development	DEV	$500,000
TF14-129 Hudson Mills Metropark Property	ACQ	$75,000
PITTSFIELD TOWNSHIP		
TF00-339 Lillie Park South and East Development	DEV	$386,720
TF03-042 Central Area Rural Preserve - Phase I	DEV	$340,800
TF09-013 Hickory Woods Park Development	DEV	$300,000
TF95-164 Lillie Park	DEV	$187,500
TF99-196 Lillie Park Restoration/Redevelopment	DEV	$219,724
SALINE		
TF99-016 Curtiss Park Improvements	DEV	$99,470
SCIO TOWNSHIP		
TF08-144 Sloan Property Parkland Acquisition	ACQ	$1,405,000
SUPERIOR TOWNSHIP		
TF96-117 Cherry Hill Nature Preserve	ACQ	$420,000
UNIVERSITY OF MICHIGAN		
TF71-036 Colonial Point Forest	ACQ	$435,000

VILLAGE OF DEXTER		
TF09-028 Mill Creek Park Development	DEV	$450,000
WASHTENAW COUNTY		
TF08-060 Rolling Hills Pk. Accessibility Enhancements	DEV	$96,000
TF411 Parker Mill Co. Park	ACQ	$250,000
TF89-033 Rolling Hills Park	DEV	$375,000
TF93-010 Pierce Lake Park Acquisition	ACQ	$400,000
TF99-323 Park Lyndon Expansion	ACQ	$787,50
TF11-035 Arbor Vistas Preserve Natural Area Connector	ACQ	$2,275,000

Washtenaw Township photo

Two MNRTF grants totaling $471,000 have helped develop Washtenaw County's Rolling Hills Park.

YORK TOWNSHIP		
TF04-005 Sandra Richardson Park Development	DEV	$58,600
YPSILANTI		
TF05-054 Riverside Park Capital Improvement Project	DEV	$80,300
TF11-083 Rutherford Pool Renovation	DEV	$300,000
TF11-120 Ypsilanti Heritage Bridge	DEV	$289,400
TF12-120 River's Edge Linear Park & Trail	DEV	$300,000
YPSILANTI TOWNSHIP		
TF03-114 North Hydro Park Development	DEV	$432,700
TF10-055 Lakeside Park Improvements	DEV	$500,000
TF1051 Ford Lake Acquisition	ACQ	$264,600
TF823 Ford Lake	ACQ	$415,000
TF824 Ford Lake Acquisition	ACQ	$1,190,000
TF86-161 Ford Lk Golf Course-Ph I	DEV	$500,000
TF88-157 North Bay Park Boardwalk	DEV	$375,000
TF90-196 North Bay Development II	DEV	$75,000
TF92-104 Ford Heritage Park	ACQ	$750,000
TF98-154 Hewens Creek Land Acquisition	ACQ	$1,483,700

WASHTENAW COUNTY TOTAL $ 23,275,314

Wayne County

Michigan's earliest established county, Wayne County was named in honor of United States Army General and statesman "Mad" Anthony Wayne 1745-1796, who commanded the first outpost in the Northwest territory that would become Michigan. It was set off as a county and formally established in 1815.

With 614 square miles, Wayne County is 34th largest county and has the state's largest population with 1,820,584 residents.

Michigan Department of Natural Resources photo

MNRTF grants TF09-149, and 10-159, totaling $20,450,000 went to the William G. Milliken State Park and Harbor (formerly Tricentennial Park), the first urban state park and is a showcase of the natural resources collected throughout all of Michigan's state parks. This green area in the heart of the city provides opportunities for picnics, walks and shore fishing. Phase Two, dedicated on October 22, 2009, showcases a wetland area along with new trails and a riverwalk. On hand for the dedication were Michigan Natural Resources Commissioner and longtime Michigan Natural Resources Trust Fund Board member Keith Charters, Michigan Department of Natural Resources Director Rebecca Humphries and former Michigan Governor William G. Milliken, the park's namesake.

Since oil was discovered there in 1943, 152 holes have been drilled in the search for oil and gas. Wayne County has produced 2,267,031 barrels of oil and 15.272 billion cubic feet of natural gas, ranking 43rd and 41st respectively among the 64 oil or gas producing Michigan counties.

Wayne County as an entity has received $76,444,618 in 90 Michigan Natural Resources Trust Fund grants, ranking the county 3rd in number of grants received but is first in grant dollars awarded.

WAYNE COUNTY active or closed MNRTF Projects

BELLEVILLE

TF91-161 Horizon Park Development	DEV	$92,300
TF13-003 Horizon Park Improvements	DEV	$120,700

Brownstown Township photo

MNRTF grants TF1045, and 87-237, totaling $141,000 acquire property for Brownstown Acres, part of Metropark Brownstown on Lake Erie, here looking at Sturgeon Bar Bay.

BROWNSTOWN TOWNSHIP

TF1045 Brownstown Acres Conserv.	ACQ	$93,000
TF87-237 Brownstown Acres	ACQ	$48,000
TF89-052 Huron River Boat Launch	DEV	$228,400

CANTON TOWNSHIP

TF07-064 Lower Rouge River Trail Bridges	DEV	$350,000
TF1069 Heritage Park Exp. formerly Cant.Rec.Ctr.	ACQ	$50,000
TF89-031 Heritage Pk. Dev. formerly Canton Rec.Ctr.	DEV	$195,000
TF97-028 Beatrice L. Coleman Trust Land Acquisition	ACQ	$1,235,500

DEARBORN

TF91-175 Dearborn Herndon Golf Course	DEV	$300,000

TF11-053 Camp Dearborn Non-Motorized Trail	DEV	$268.900
TF12-044 Rogue River Gateway Trail Extension	DEV	$280,000

In September 2000, Detroit City Commission Chairman Gil Hill accepted, on behalf of the City of Detroit, the Michigan Oil And Gas Association Award of Excellence for outstanding use of MNRTF grants in restoring the Belle Isle Canal. MOGA President Frank L Mortl presented the award.

DETROIT

TF413 Marina City Land Acquisition	ACQ	$550,000
TF513 St. Aubin Park	ACQ	$1,500,000
TF87-238 St. Aubin Marina	DEV	$400,000
TF88-180 Mt. Elliott Park	DEV	$375,000
TF89-240 Lake Frances	DEV	$375,000
TF90-351 Mt. Elliott - Phase II	DEV	$375,000
TF93-399 Belle Isle Canal Restoration	DEV	$375,000
TF94-228 Belle Isle Canals-Phase II	DEV	$375,000
TF97-223 Riverside Park Seawall/Promenade	DEV	$500,000
TF03-109 Belle Isle Improvements	DEV	$322,000
TF04-044 In Town Youth Camp at Rouge Park	DEV	$407,000
TF04-176 Dequindre Cut Greenway Improvements	DEV	$393,000
TF05-072 Butzel Playfield Improvements	DEV	$500,000
TF07-055 Butzel Playfield Renovation	DEV	$500,000
TF10-044 Patton Park Improvements	DEV	$500,000
TF10-045 Balduck Park In-Town Youth Camp	DEV	$500,000
TF10-142 Dequindre Cut North Acquisition	ACQ	$375,000
TF11-075 Jayne-Lasky Playfield Improvements	DEV	$300,000
TF11-076 Lipke Playfield Improvements	DEV	$300,000
TF13-027 Inner Circle Greenway – Conrsil Acquisition	ACQ	$3,431,300

TF14-095 Coleman Young Playground Improvements DEV $300,000
TF14-096 Dorais Playfield Improvements DEV $300,000

DNR - EDUCATION & OUTREACH

TF97-183 DNR State Fair Exhibit Development DEV $500,000
TF97-283 State Fair Land Acquisition ACQ $195,000

DNR - FISHERIES DIVISION

TF742 Belleville Lake ACQ $350,000
TF87-078 Belleville Lake Pier DEV $200,000

DNR PARKS & RECREATION DIVISION

TF05-153 Tricentennial State Park and Harbor DEV $500,000
TF09-149 Milliken S.P./Harbor E. Riverwalk DEV $450,000
TF10-159 Milliken State Park Acquisition ACQ$20,000,000
TF14-187 Showcase Trail Critical Gaps ACQ $2,000,000
TF14-176 Belle Isle Natural Resource Improvements DEV $300,000

DNR - STATE FAIR

TF1010 MI Exposition & Fairground ACQ $1,200,000
TF88-017 Fairgrounds Exp Ph. III ACQ $1,000,000
TF898 MI Exposition & Fairground Expansion ACQ $900,000

DNR - WILDLIFE DIVISION

TF93-425 Sibley Road Prairie ACQ $415,800
TF97-190 Stony Island Natural Area ACQ $700,000

DNRE - RECREATION DIVISION

TF10-128 Globe Building Adventure Discov.Ctr. Acq. ACQ $9,000,000
TF10-130 Detroit Riverfront Easements and Acq. ACQ $5,000,000

ECORSE

TF07-106 Ecorse Creek Greenway and Park Dev. DEV $415,000

FLAT ROCK

TF90-074 Hu Roc Park Improvements DEV $105,750
TF91-111 Hu Roc Park Improvements DEV $181,400
TF10-002 Flat Rock-Oakwood Metro Park Connector DEV $447,900

GROSSE ILE TOWNSHIP

TF96-210 Frenchman's Creek Greenway and Preserve ACQ $100,000

HCMA

TF00-069 Lower Huron Metropark Fish. Acc. Boardwalks DEV $180,000
TF95-088 Lake Erie Metropark Shoreline Trl. Phase 2 DEV $375,000
TF99-117 Lake Erie Metropark Marina Point Fish. Site DEV $180,000

INKSTER

TF10-027 Inkster Park Greenway Trail DEV $408,000
TF11-145 Inkster Greenway Trail DEV $192,500

LINCOLN PARK

TF721 Lincoln Park Recreation ACQ $385,000

MELVINDALE

TF86-305 Riverside Acquisition ACQ $8,000
TF876 Riverside Land Acquisition ACQ $35,000

NORTHVILLE

TF94-274 Griswold Land Acquisition ACQ $150,000

NORTHVILLE TOWNSHIP

TF06-010 Coldwater Springs Nature Area-Linear Park DEV $303,800
TF09-174 Linear Park Acquisition ACQ $4,000,000

TF10-140 Linear Park Acquisition - Phase II	ACQ	$3,053,700
REDFORD TOWNSHIP		
TF08-089 Bell Creek Park Non-Motorized Trailway	DEV	$450,000
TF86-188 Glenhurst Golf Course	ACQ	$600,000
RIVER ROUGE		
TF95-172 Belanger Park Redevelopment	DEV	$375,000
SOUTHGATE		
TF88-196 Kiwanis Park	DEV	$25,350
TF98-106 Southgate Nature Center	ACQ	$525,000
TAYLOR		
TF01-143 Northline Road Land Acquisition	ACQ	$66,000
TF1072 Heritage Park-Phase II	ACQ	$60,000
TF727 Sheridan Heritage Park	ACQ	$70,000
TF904 Municipal Golf Course	ACQ	$30,000
TF94-166 Northline Acquisition	ACQ	$66,800
TF96-090 Community Center Park/Pardee Acq.	ACQ	$237,718
TF97-126 Southwest Corner Acquisition	ACQ	$1,500,000
TRENTON		
TF91-191 Rotary Park Improvements	DEV	$75,000
TF99-184 Trenton Linked Riverfront Parks Imp.	DEV	$332,800
WAYNE		
TF90-316 Goudy Park Dev. Project	DEV	$253,000

Canton Township's Heritage Park (formerly Canton Recreation Center) has received $245,000 in two MNRTF grants for acquisition and development of the property.

WAYNE COUNTY		
TF90-843 Holliday Preserve Add.	ACQ	$360,000
TF91-208 Elizabeth Park Riverwalk	DEV	$375,000
TF09-127 Elizabeth Park Riverwalk	DEV	$400,000
TF10-084 Refuge Gateway Boat Dock/Fishing Pier	DEV	$500,000
TF13-049 Elizabeth Park Greenway & Shoreline	DEV	$300,000
TF14-128 Ellsworth Boardwalk & Trailhead Parking	DEV	$200,000
WYANDOTTE		
TF791 Wyandotte Boat Ramp Extension	ACQ	$80,000
TF87-255 Wyandotte Boat Launch	ACQ	$116,000

WAYNE COUNTY TOTAL $ 76,444,618

Wexford County

Wexford County was named for County Wexford, Ireland. It was set off as a county in 1840 and formally established in 1869.

With 565 square miles, Wexford County is 50th largest county and 46th largest in population with 32,735 residents.

MNRTF grant TF02-194, $279,400, improved the Carl Johnson Hunting & Fishing Center at Mitchell State Park, often visited by school groups, such as this Big Rapids field trip June 8, 2011.

Since oil was discovered there in 1952, 189 holes have been drilled in the search for oil and gas. Wexford County has produced 5,722,349 barrels of oil and 39,168 billion cubic feet of natural gas, ranking 34th and 29th respectively among the 64 oil or gas producing Michigan counties. Wexford County has received $3,278,700 in 11 Michigan Natural Resources Trust Fund grants, ranking 50th in number of grants received and 47th in grant dollars awarded.

WEXFORD COUNTY active or closed MNRTF Projects

Project	Type	Amount
CADILLAC		
TF06-018 Clam River Greenway	DEV	$269,500
TF89-071 Lakefront Boat Launch	DEV	$60,800
TF99-245 Lakefront Park Dock Project	DEV	$111,000
DNR - EDUCATION & OUTREACH		
TF02-194 Johnson Center Improvements	DEV	$279,400
DNR – FOREST MANAGEMENT		
TF12-131 Wheeler Creek Property	ACQ	$510,000
DNR - FOREST, MINERAL & FIRE MANAGEMENT		
TF920 Manistee River Land	ACQ	$106,000
TF08-123 Manistee River Deeryard and Bog	ACQ	$600,000
DNR - PARKS & RECREATION DIVISION		
TF08-127 Mitchell State Park Bear Marsh	ACQ	$500,000
TF485 Mitchell State Park	ACQ	$242,000
TF88-198 Mitchell State Park	DEV	$300,000
WEXFORD COUNTY		
TF03-013 CASA All-Sports Park & Natural Rec. Area	DEV	$300,000

WEXFORD COUNTY TOTAL $ 3,278,700

Michigan Oil & Gas History

Beginning in 1886 there was a small amount of oil production in the Port Huron area. The Port Huron Field was abandoned in 1921.

In 1912 and 1913, a group of local capitalists and businessmen formed the Saginaw Valley Development Company to prospect for oil. The group's second attempt, near the center of the city erupted with a spout of oil forty feet high from the mouth of the well and stood solid for four or five minutes. This discovery well, along with eight others nearby, did not pan out commercially.

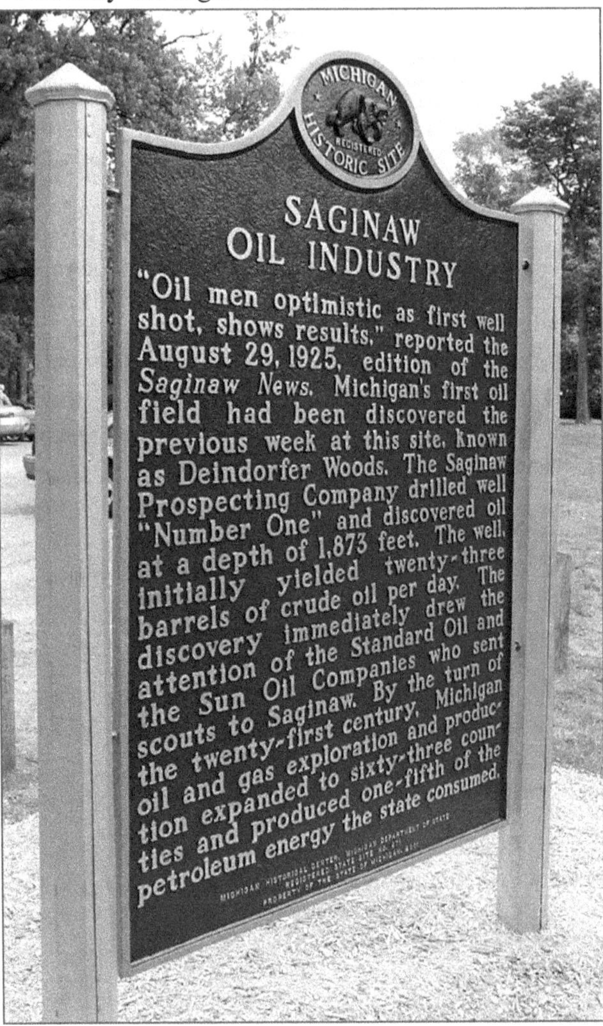

James C. Graves, a chemist by education, worked for the Dow Chemical Company beginning in 1900. Graves closely followed the progress of Dow's brine wells. Graves left Dow to join the Saginaw Chemical Company. He was appointed president of the Saginaw Prospecting Company, formed in 1925 to revive the Saginaw area oil search. A test well was started July 25, 1925, on city-owned property known as Deindorfer Woods on the north side of Weiss Street.

On August 29, 1925, the Saginaw News reported the well's success with a banner headline on a story that said "The well produced an average of 23 barrels of oil per day for a few days, and averaged 17 barrels a day for the first 30 days."

The late 1920s through early 1950s proliferated with relatively shallow oil and gas field finds throughout the Lower Peninsula of Michigan.

The mid-1950s saw the discovery of the Albion-Scipio Trend, which has produced more than 125 million barrels of oil from a single reservoir, qualifying as a major oilfield by worldwide definition.

The late 1960s saw the discovery of the Niagaran Reef Trend, heralding the 1970s tripling of Michigan oil production and multiplying Michigan natural gas production six times.

The early 1980s discovery of deep strata natural gas production, still an emerging frontier, along with the potential of shallower zones and new technologies, signal even greater potential versus any of Michigan's previous petroleum history.

The late 1980s and early 1990s were punctuated by an unprecedented upsurge of drilling activity in the shallow Antrim Shale of Northern Michigan, which continues to be a major factor in Michigan natural gas production through refracturization and other advancing technologies.

The 1990s, with expanded Michigan market pipeline networks, saw Antrim Shale development increased and new horizontal drilling technologies ushered the state into a new era as a substantial natural gas production state. In the late 1990s, modern record low wellhead prices of oil and natural gas devastated the petroleum industry in Michigan and nationwide.

The early 2000s found Michigan petroleum explorers maintaining abbreviated drilling programs while recovering from the price devastations of the late 1990s. Drilling activity in Michigan rebounded, with enhanced wellhead prices for oil and natural gas, averaging more than 475 holes per year 2000-2009, then declined in the 2010-2014 period with a slight 717 holes drilled for an average of 141 holes per year.

Projections are for a slight rise in Michigan holes drilled in 2015.

Appendix A

MUCCs Washington traces history of Pigeon River Controversy & Michigan Natural Resources Trust Fund

(Editor's Note: The late Thomas L. Washington executive director of the Michigan United Conservation Clubs, addressed the May 26, 1988, regular monthly meeting of the Michigan Oil And Gas Association at the Grand Traverse Resort on the Pigeon River development controversy, the Michigan Natural Resources Trust Fund and the unique compromises between the oil industry, "preservationists" and his sportsmen's group which led to inception of the fund.

Following is an edited summary of Washington's remarks – jrw.)

"Thank you very much. It is indeed a pleasure to be here with you this evening to share my thoughts on a subject that is near and dear to my heart – the Michigan Natural Resources Trust Fund.

Over the next few minutes, I'd like to trace the history of this unique land acquisition program, and demonstrate how our two organizations have worked together for more than a decade to see that this landmark piece of legislation has served the people of Michigan. My primary goal is to demonstrate how two special interest organizations, on seemingly opposite sides of an issue, can make a solid commitment to put aside their differences and hammer out an agreement that has lasting benefits for both of their constituencies and society as a whole.

Before I get into that topic, however, I would like to briefly discuss the Michigan United Conservation Clubs, and give you some background on this unique and vital citizen's organization.

Chartered in 1937, the MUCC is a statewide association of citizen conservationists and sportsmen and women who are dedicated to the conservation of our natural resources and the protection of the sportsmen's rights. For more than 50 years, our mission has been to educate our own members, the general public and government officials at all levels about the need to conserve Michigan's abundant forests, waters, air, fish and wildlife resources – all critical elements of our state's unique outdoor heritage.

I emphasize the word "conserve." To the MUCC, conservation means the planned, scientific management of a natural resource to prevent exploitation, destruction or neglect. It should not be confused with the word "preservation," which in our view, mean the locking away of natural resources so they can be enjoyed by only a select few in our society.

As a conservation organization, the MUCC supports the planned, scientific management and wise use of our varied and abundant natural resources. We believe strongly in the multiple-use concept of resource management. It is our view that if our air, water, land, forest, fish and wildlife resources are properly and thoughtfully managed, they can be shared by a wide range of competing interests to benefit everyone in society.

In essence, that is the principal philosophy behind the MUCC. It is a philosophy that we have nurtured since the day in November of 1937, when a small group of sportsmen and conservationists put aside their parochial differences to form, what is today, the largest and most influential statewide conservation organization in the United States.

More than a decade ago, it was MUCC's dedication to this "conservation philosophy" that led to the enactment of a landmark piece of legislation that has contributed immeasurably to our state's rich outdoor heritage and eventually paved the way for the wise and prudent development of Michigan's abundant oil and natural gas resources.

I'm speaking, of course, about the Michigan Natural Resources Trust Fund – a unique program under which the interest earned on state royalties from oil and gas development are used to purchase unique tract of recreational land throughout the state.

As all of you are aware, the idea for the original Kammer Land trust Fund emerged from the bitter, decade-long controversy surrounding plans to develop the rich oil and natural gas resources in the Pigeon River Country State Forest in the early 1970's.

When this complex clash between the oil companies, the so-called "preservationists," sportsmen's groups and the DNR began to unfold, it looked as though it would develop into a battle with plenty of losers and no winters. But now we know that there were winners – more than nine million of them. They are the citizens of Michigan – ourselves, our children and our grandchildren – who enjoy the bounty that came from the agreement forged in the crucible of the Pigeon River controversy.

The seeds that led to this "Conservation Milestone" were sown in 1968, when the Michigan Natural Resources Commission voted to sell leases for hydrocarbon exploration and development within the Pigeon River State Forest to several of your association's member companies. That action touched off a firestorm of local and statewide controversy that sparked years of acrimonious debate and dozens of lawsuits that would drag-on all the way to the United State Supreme court.

All because a small group of preservationists would mistakenly label the Pigeon River Forest "wilderness," and take the fight to preserve their "pristine natural hideaway" to every level of government.

Covering 145 square miles, the Pigeon River Forest is the largest block of publicly-owned wild lands in the Lower Peninsula. Two-thirds of the 90,000 acre forest, which was established in 1919, were purchased with sportsmen's dollars in the form of deer license funds that were earmarked for land acquisition mostly in the late 1920's. Most of the remaining public land within the forest is property that reverted to the state through the non-payment of taxes.

Prior to 1930, most people who lived near the forest area viewed the land as essentially worthless. The timber had been cut and the slash burned, and all that remained were the charred stumps and bare earth of what had been a vast, thriving forest.

In the early 1930's, conservationists, led by P.S. Lovejoy, convinced the then-Department of Conservation to expend a portion of deer hunting revenues to purchase thousands of acres of this barren terrain, which doubled the size of the Pigeon River State Forest. As the years passed, and with the help of the Civilian Conservation Corps, the forest began to regenerate. By 1960, nature had nearly erased the signs of destruction. Healthy populations of deer, bear, bobcat, grouse and coyote thrived in the forest, as did the area's population of transplanted Rocky Mountain elk.

Growing human encroachment and the sale of the oil development leases in 1968 compelled a number of local residents and preservationist groups to push for the development of a comprehensive management plan covering the wildlife, timber and mineral resources within the forest area. Working with numerous interest groups the DNR formulated such a plank, which was adopted by the Natural Resources Commission in 1973.

Conspicuously absent in the forest management plan was any mention of oil and gas development. That portion of the management plan was presented to the Commission in 1975 by then-DNR Director Dr. Howard Tanner. Its detail – and environmental protection provisions – were unprecedented in Michigan history.

It called for the use of directional drilling to reach under environmentally sensitive areas; a reduced number of drilling sites through the use of common facilities; the exchange of seismic information among oil companies and the use of common pipelines. Total disruptions under the plan represented approximately one percent of the land in the southern 1/3 of the forest.

State royalties from exploration and extraction activities were pegged at $130 million, some of which would be used to enhance recreation lands throughout the state. Upon presenting, the oil and gas development plan to the Commission, DNR Director Tanner said:

"Oil and Gas production, while viewed by some as evil, provides our state with a unique opportunity to invest in the future by funding needed resource management programs in the Pigeon river country as well as in other unique and environmentally valuable area of our state."

As the public comment period on this plan dragged on, a series of lawsuits involving the Michigan Oil Company led to a 1975 decision by Ingham County Circuit Judge Thomas Brown that the DNR had the legal authority to deny permits on leased land if the drilling was likely to cause environmental degradation.

Backed by Judge Brown's decision, which the State Court of Appeals let stand, the DNR redrafted and presented its new hydrocarbon development plan to the Commission in September, 1975. The new plan called for the drilling of 7 to 10 test wells only in United 1 and only by Shell Oil Company, the Unit 1 operator. Virtually all of the parties involved in the controversy cried foul – led by various protectionist groups that bitterly opposed any drilling in the forest out of fear that it would damage the environment and conviction that hydrocarbon development was simply not necessary.

Faced with the realization that the controversy was growing, and following careful examination and analysis of the various development proposals, MUCC stepped into the controversy in October of 1975.

At its regular bi-monthly board of directors meeting in Harbor Springs, MUCC directors voted unanimously in favor of a policy supporting rigidly controlled oil and gas drilling in the Pigeon River State Forest with state royalties from the exploration and development activities earmarked for the purchase of state recreation lands. The resolution put the state's largest conservation organization on record in support of "a policy keeping oil exploration and development of out of swamps and other environmentally sensitive areas while at the same time promoting unitized development in the non-sensitive areas."

A key clause in the resolution stipulated that royalties accruing to the Game and Fish Fund from hydrocarbon development in the Pigeon River Country would be placed in trust, with interest to be used to "purchase and enhance" private in-holdings within the state forest. If land was unavailable within the forest, acreage suitable for hunting and fishing in other parts of the state would be purchased for public use.

By actively supporting the development of oil and gas resources in the Pigeon River State Forest, the MUCC publicly reaffirmed its conservation philosophy. The organization sent a clear message to the Commission and the groups opposed to hydrocarbon development that sportsmen, whose license fees had purchased 65 percent of the Pigeon River Forest, were supportive of the thoughtful management and wise use of the forest's timber, wildlife and mineral resources.

Reaction to our proposal from drilling opponents and preservationist groups was both swift and predictable. WE WERE PUBLICY BLASTED FOR COMING OUT IN SUPPORT OF OIL AND GAS DEVELOPMENT IN THE PIGEON RIVER FOREST!

Preservationists howled at our contention that the forest's oil and gas resources could be developed without permanent, irreparable harm to the environment. Newspaper editorials claimed that the MUCC had "caved-in" to the oil and gas development interests. One writer told his readers that MUCC had "sold out," and even suggested that the organization had accepted oil and gas money in exchange for its position. He later publicly retracted that outrageous charge.

Despite the continued whining of oil drilling critics, the concept of allowing strictly controlled hydrocarbon development and using state royalties from drilling activities for recreation land purchase caught the attention of key decision makers in Lansing.

At the outset of the 1976 legislative session, State Senator Kerry Kammer worked with MUCC staff to draft and introduce Senate bill 12518, which established the framework for the recreation land trust fund. In all, 26 senators from both parties co-sponsored the trust fund legislation in the upper chamber.

Further support for the trust fund concept came when then-Governor William Milliken called for the creation of a "Resources Heritage Fund" in his 1976 State of the State message. Actually, the Governor's proposal went one step further by calling for a trust fund made up of royalty fees from hydrocarbon development on all public lands in the state.

In a letter to Governor Milliken, Senator Kammer wrote: "This proposal represents a means by which Michigan can embark upon an ambitious new long range program of recreational land acquisition without increasing the burden of Michigan taxpayers."

Endorsed by the Governor and carrying bi-partisan legislative support, the proposal moved quickly through the legislative process.

During public hearings on the concept, I testified that "royalties can and must be the mitigating factor which makes environmental disruption justifiable." I told the legislators that … "we are prepared to accept short term aesthetic and environmental disruption to achieve the tremendous recreation potentials that these monies can provide."

Looking ahead to our present-day recreation needs near our state's urban centers I told the legislative committees … "It is even conceivable that wild areas in Southern Michigan could be created with these monies even as the Pigeon River Country State forest was created over the last five decades by the application, in large part, of special earmarked monies."

Despite strident opposition from my good friend Senator Joe Mack, then-chairman of the Senate Conservation Committee, the land trust measure was approved by both chambers of the Legislature on June 30th and signed into law by Governor Milliken in early August of 1976.

As everyone in this room knows, the Pigeon River controversy did not end with the signing of that landmark measure. Lawsuits filed by development opponents and countersuits filed by your own companies would drag on for several years. It was not until November 1980 – following months of on-again/off-again negotiations arranged by MUCC – that your companies and the preservationist groups reached a compromise on the Pigeon River issue. On December 16, 1980, Judge Thomas Brown approved a detailed settlement of the dispute which had blocked drilling in the forest since 1977.

In mid-February 1981, the 12 year dispute over hydrocarbon development in the Pigeon River Country State Forest came to a symbolic end when Shell Oil company sank the first section of a 5,000-foot well in the southern third of the forest.

Michigan Oil – the "stuff" that powers our vehicles, heats our homes and helps propel our nation's economy – began flowing from beneath the Pigeon River Forest.

And that Michigan oil also has powered a very successful drive to acquire some of the most valuable and significant tracts of recreation land in this state. Without a doubt, the Recreational Land Trust Fund, and your companies hydrocarbon development activities that make it possible, have been positive developments for Michigan. But that's not to say that the trust fund has not faced problems.

In the late 1970's, when then-state budget director Gerald Miller proclaimed that Michigan's economy was in a "free-fall," the order went out to find new painless sources of revenue to pay state government's mounting bills.

In both chambers of the Legislature and, sadly, in the office of the Governor who signed the historic bill, the cry went forth ..."LET'S RAID THE TRUST FUND!"

Over several years, the Legislature "borrowed" a total of $142 million from the Kammer Land Trust Fund to keep the great ship of state afloat – always with the promise (snicker, snicker) to pay the money back when times were rosy.

As all of you know, not one-penny of that borrowed money has ever been repaid ... which prompted a coalition of groups, led by the MUCC, to fight back and "SAVE THE TRUST FUND."

At MUCC's request several legislators pushed through the House and Senate legislation to-shield the fund within the state constitution. Their actions cleared the way for Proposal B to be placed on the statewide election ballot in November 1984.

With broad-based support from state officials, conservation groups and business interest, Michigan voters by a 2 to 1 margin approved Proposal B, which established the Michigan Natural Resources Trust Fund within the framework of the state constitution. Now the trust fund is off-limits to periodic raids by the Legislature and it continues to build a source of solid funding for future acquisitions of public recreation land.

At the ceremony marking the signing into law of the original Land Trust bill, I called the Kammer Fund measure "one of the most significant pieces of conservation legislation ever enacted by a legislative body in any state. "Over the years my view has not been altered. Thanks to the royalties your companies pay for the developing our state's oil and gas resources, Michigan's outdoor recreation opportunities have improved dramatically over the past decade. And, because of this fund, they'll improve even more in the next decade.

Hindsight is always 20/20, and I probably wouldn't have said this at the time, but … looking back, I think the controversy and the battles were worth the effort. I know that most if not all of you will disagree. The dispute made for a lot of sleepless nights and cost your companies millions of dollars in lost production time and legal fees … but in the end I think we were able to set a good example and prove an important point.

We set a good example by sitting down, parking our lawyers and our rhetoric at the door, looking each other straight in the eye and hammering out an agreement that both sides could eventually live with. No, neither side got everything it wanted, but we came up with a pretty fair compromise. And I'll tell you something … our agreement, and the methods we employed to reach it, are going to be a model for solving similar disputes in the future.

We also proved an important point … one that I stress time and time again.

We proved to the doubters and the cynics, the politicians and the power brokers and to all those who at the first sign of controversy throw their hands in the air and give up, that *we could do it*. We proved that two special interest groups, on seemingly opposite sides of a controversy, can put aside their emotions and their differences and design an agreement that benefits both constituencies and society as a whole.

Thank you."

Appendix B
MICHIGAN PUBLIC ACTS 1976—No. 204

[No. 204]

AN ACT to create a state recreational land acquisition trust fund to be funded by the sale of oil, gas, and mineral leases in the Pigeon river country state forest and in certain other land and from the royalties accruing from the oil, gas, and mineral leases sold in the Pigeon river country state forest and in certain other land; to create the state recreational land acquisition trust fund board of trustees and to prescribe its powers and duties; and to provide for the administration and uses of the fund.

The People of the State of Michigan enact:

318.401 Short title. [M.S.A. 13.1095(21)]

Sec. 1. This act shall be known and may be cited as the "Kammer recreational land trust fund act of 1976".

318.402 Definitions. [M.S.A. 13.1095(22)]

Sec. 2. As used in this act:

(a) "Gas" means casinghead gas, or gas produced incidental to the production of oil.

(b) "Mineral" means an inorganic substance that can be extracted from the earth, except for oil or gas, and includes rock, metal ores, coal, and mineral water.

(c) "Oil" means natural crude oil or petroleum and other hydrocarbons, regardless of gravity, which are produced at the well in liquid form by ordinary production methods and which are not the result of condensation of gas after it leaves the underground reservoir.

318.403 State recreational land acquisition trust fund; creation; administration; duties of state treasurer and department of natural resources; use of interest and earnings. [M.S.A. 13.1095(23)]

Sec. 3. The state recreational land acquisition trust fund is created in the state treasury and shall be administered by the state recreational land acquisition trust fund board of trustees, hereafter called the board, which board shall be a division of the department of natural resources. The state treasurer shall direct the investment of the trust fund. The department of natural resources shall offer its cooperation and aid to the board and shall provide suitable offices and equipment for the board. In compliance with 16 U.S.C. sections 669 to 669i and 16 U.S.C. sections 777 to 777k, the interest and earnings of the fund shall be used exclusively for the purchase of land or rights in land as provided in section 6 for hunting or fishing and recreational purposes including, but not limited to, camping, hiking, picnicking, and swimming, for those expenses authorized in section 7(5), and for the payment of any taxes owed by the state on the land.

318.404 Disposition and use of moneys accruing from royalties or leases; limitation on trust fund. [M.S.A. 13.1095(24)]

Sec. 4. (1) The moneys accruing to the state from the royalties paid by persons extracting oil and gas from the Pigeon river country state forest under leases with the state and from gas, oil, and mineral extractions initiated after the effective date of this act on other lands for which the state has sold mineral, gas, or oil leases; and from the sale of additional oil and gas leases in the Pigeon river country state forest and from other mineral, gas, or oil leases the state enters into after the effective date of this act shall be deposited in the state recreational land acquisition trust fund. Money accrued in this section may be allotted to improve the multipurpose use of the Pigeon river country state forest.

(2) The trust fund shall not exceed the sum of $100,000,000.00, excluding interest. When the trust fund contains the sum of $100,000,000.00, excluding interest, additional moneys accruing to the state from the royalties or leases described in subsection (1) shall be deposited as provided by law, including section 5.

318.405 Limitations on expenditures; mandatory deposit. [M.S.A. 13.1095(25)]

Sec. 5. In any 1 fiscal year, not more than 33-1/3$ of the moneys accruing to the state pursuant to section 4(1) in the previous fiscal year may be used for the purposes for which the interest and earnings of the fund may be used for pursuant to section 3. However, the total expenditure of moneys permitted by this section in a fiscal year shall not exceed $2,500,000.00. In any fiscal year at least 66-2/3% of the moneys accruing to the state pursuant to section 4(1) shall be deposited in the state recreational land acquisition trust fund.

318.406 Easement restricting development of land. [M.S.A. 13.1095(26)]

Sec. 6. The board may acquire an easement from the owner of land in this state which shall restrict the development of the land pursuant to the easement agreement entered into between the parties. The form of the easement agreement shall be approved by the attorney general.

318.407 Board; appointment, qualifications, and terms of members; removal; vacancies; compensation. [M.S.A. 13.1095(27)]

Sec. 7. (1) The board shall consist of 5 members. The members shall include the director of the department of natural resources, the chairman of the natural resources commission, and 3 citizens of the state to be appointed by the governor with the advice and consent of the senate. One of the appointed members shall be from a group representative of sportsmen's associations or interests.

(2) The terms of the appointive members shall be 3 years, except that of those first appointed, 1 shall be appointed for 1 year, 1 shall be appointed for 2 years, and 1 shall be appointed for 3 years.

(3) The appointive members may be removed by the governor for inefficiency, neglect of duty, or malfeasance in office.

(4) Vacancies on the board shall be filled for the unexpired term in the same manner as the original appointments.

(5) The board may incur expenses necessary to carry out its powers and duties under this act and shall compensate its members for actual expenses incurred in carrying out their official duties.

318.408 Board; chairman; administrative procedures; meetings; record of proceedings; reports. [M.S.A. 13.1095(28)]

Sec. 8. (1) The board shall elect its own chairman and establish its own administrative procedures. It shall meet at least bimonthly and shall record its proceedings. All meetings shall be open to the public.

(2) On or before January 15 of each year the board shall report to the governor and to the legislature detailing the operations of the board for the preceding 1-year period. The board shall also make special reports as requested by the governor or the legislature.

318.409 Lands and rights in lands to be acquired; determination; list; estimate of costs; statement of guidelines; legislative approval. [M.S.A. 13.1095(29)]

Sec. 9. (1) The board shall determine which lands and rights in lands within the state should be acquired and shall submit to the legislature in January of each year a list of those lands and rights in lands it has determined should be acquired with fund money, compiled in order of priority.

(2) The list shall be accompanied by estimates of total costs for the proposed acquisitions.

(3) The board shall supply with each list a statement of the guidelines used in listing and assigning the priority of these proposed acquisitions.

(4) The legislature shall approve by law the lands and rights in lands to be acquired with fund money each year.

This act is ordered to take immediate effect.

Approved July 23, 1976.

Appendix C

MNRTF Board Members 1977-2011

1977 - Donald D. Juchartz Chairperson

Howard Tanner - Director of Michigan Department of Natural Resources (DNR), Joan L. Wolfe - Michigan Natural Resources Commission (NRC Representative), Patricia Huxtable, Thomas L. Washington.

1978 – Patricia Huxtable Chairperson

O. J. Scherschligt (Representing DNR Director), Dean Pridgeon (replaced Joan Wolfe as NRC Representative), Donald Juchartz, Thomas Washington.

1979 –Thomas Washington Chairperson

O. J. Scherschligt (Representing DNR Director), Hilary Snell (replaced Dean Pridgeon as NRC Representative), Donald Juchartz, Laura Heuser.

1980 - Donald Juchartz Chairperson

O. J. Scherschligt (Representing DNR Director), Jacob Hoefer (replaced Hilary Snell as NRC Representative), Laura Heuser, Thomas Washington.

1981 – Laura Heuser Chairperson

O. J. Scherschligt (Representing DNR Director), Jacob Hoefer (NRC Representative), Donald Juchartz, Thomas Washington.

1982 –Thomas Washington Chairperson

James Cleary (Representing DNR Director), Jacob Hoefer (NRC Representative), Donald Juchartz, Laura Heuser.

1983 – Donald Juchartz Chairperson

James Cleary (Representing DNR Director), Paul Wendler (replaced Jacob Hoefer as NRC Representative), Laura Heuser, Thomas Washington.

1984 – Laura Heuser Chairperson

James Cleary (Representing DNR Director), Stephen Monsma (replaced Paul Wendler as NRC Representative), Frank Ruswick (replaced Donald Juchartz), Thomas Washington.

1985 – Thomas Washington Chairperson

James Cleary (Representing NRC as of 10/23/85 meeting), Stephen Monsma (NRC Representative through 09/23/85 meeting), Frank Ruswick, Ruth Briney (replaced Laura Heuser), June Kretzschmer.

1986 – Thomas Washington Chairperson

Thomas Anderson (replaced James Cleary as NRC Representative), Frank Ruswick, Ruth Briney, June Kretzschmer.

1987 – Frank Ruswick Chairperson

Thomas Anderson (NRC Representative), Thomas Washington, Ruth Briney, June Kretzschmer.

1988 – Ruth Briney Chairperson

Thomas Anderson (NRC Representative), Thomas Washington, June Kretzschmer, Roy Wilbanks (replaced Frank Ruswick).

1989 – June Kretzschmer Chairperson

Thomas Anderson (NRC Representative), Thomas Washington, Ruth Briney, Roy Wilbanks.

1990 – Thomas Washington Chairperson

Thomas Anderson (NRC Representative), Ruth Briney, Roy Wilbanks, June Kretzschmer.

1991 – Roy Wilbanks Chairperson (resigned 09/19/91)

Thomas Anderson (NRC Representative last meeting 06/19/91), Marlene Fluharty (NRC Representative 08/7/91 meeting only), David Holli (NRC Representative 10/9/91 and 12/9/91 meetings), Ruth Briney, June Kretzschmer, Thomas Washington.

1992 – Ruth Briney Chairperson

David Holli (NRC Representative), June Kretzschmer, Thomas Washington, Keith Charters (appointed 06/4/92; replaced Roy Wilbanks).

1993 – June Kretzschmer Chairperson

David Holli (NRC Representative), Thomas Washington, Keith Charters, William Parfet (replaced Ruth Briney).

1994 – Thomas Washington Chairperson

David Holli (NRC Representative), Keith Charters, William Parfet, Wendy Potts (replaced June Kretzschmer).

1995 – Keith Charters Chairperson

David Holli (NRC Representative), William Parfet, Wendy Potts, Thomas Washington (passed away 11/16/95).

1996 – William Parfet Chairperson

David Holli (NRC Representative last meeting 6/19/96), Keith Charters (NRC Representative balance of year), Nancy Douglas (replaced Keith Charters as regular Board member—whose term expired—beginning at 8/21/96 meeting), Charles Knabusch (replaced Thomas Washington), Wendy Potts.

1997 – Wendy Potts Chairperson (resigned 03/14/97)

Charles Knabusch (resumed Chairperson for Potts 4/16//97; passed away 10/14/97), Keith Charters (NRC Representative), Paul Sabatine (appointed 02/20/97; replaced Nancy Douglas (Chairperson 11/12 and 12/17 meetings), Jim Thompson (appointed 2/20/97; replaced William Parfet), John Rock (replaced Wendy Potts), Gordon Guyer (replaced Charles Knabusch).

1998 – Paul Sabatine Chairperson

Keith Charters (NRC Representative), Jim Thompson, John Rock, Gordon Guyer.

1999 – Paul Sabatine Chairperson

Keith Charters (NRC Representative), Jim Thompson, John Rock (resigned 07/12/99), Gordon Guyer, Frank Wheatlake (appointed 10/19/99; replaced John Rock).

2000 – Jim Thompson Chairperson

Keith Charters (NRC Representative), Gordon Guyer, Frank Wheatlake, Paul Sabatine (resigned September 2000).

2001 – Frank Wheatlake Chairperson

(February through July – resigned July 2001),
Gorden Guyer (Chairperson September through December), Keith Charters (NRC Representative), Kevin Johnson (appointed April 2001; replaced Paul Sabatine), Steven Arwood (appointed 7/12/01; replaced Frank Wheatlake), Jim Johnson.

2002 – Gordon Guyer Chairperson

(February through October – term expired October 1, not reappointed), Kevin Johnson (Chairperson December), Keith Charters (NRC Representative), Steven Arwood, Jim Johnson.

2003 – Kevin Johnson Chairperson

(term expired 10/1/03—not reappointed; last meeting 09/10/03) David Dempsey (appointed 10/1/03; replaced Kevin Johnson), Steven Arwood (Chairperson 10/15/03 meeting), Jim Johnson (Chairperson 12/10/03 meeting), Sam Washington (appointed 12/13/02; replaced Gordon Guyer), Keith Charters (NRC Representative; resigned 03/7/03), Bob Garner (NRC Representative; replaced Keith Charters).

2004 – Jim Johnson Chairperson

Bob Garner (NRC Representative), David Dempsey (resigned 12/8/04), Steven Arwood (resigned 12/9/04), Sam Washington.

2005 – Sam Washington Chairperson

Bob Garner (NRC Representative), Steven Hamp (appointed 1/26/05; replaced Steven Arwood), Lana Pollack (appointed 1/26/05; replaced David Dempsey), Frank Torre (appointed 5/26/05; replaced Jim Thompson, whose term expired 10/1/04).

2006 – Sam Washington Chairperson

Bob Garner (NRC Representative appointed to replace Keith Charters representing general public 09/8/06), Steven Hamp (resigned June 2006), Lana Pollack, Frank Torre, Keith Charters (appointed 06/13/06; replaced Steven Hamp; resigned 09/8/06; appointed as NRC Representative 10/06).

2007 – Bob Garner Chairperson

Keith Charters (NCR Representative), Lana Pollack, Frank Torre, Sam Washington (passed away 10/10/07).

2008 – Bob Garner Chairperson

Keith Charters (NCR Representative), Lana Pollack, Frank Torre, Dennis Muchmore (replaced Sam Washington; appointed 02/5/08).

2009 – Lana Pollack Chairperson

Keith Charters (NCR Representative), Bob Gardner, Frank Torre (reappointed 03/10/09), Dennis Muchmore (Vice-Chairperson).

2010 – Lana Pollack Chairperson (resigned 06/18/10)

Bob Garner (reappointed 03/25/10), Keith Charters (NCR Representative; replaced Lana Pollack 07/1/10), Frank Torre, Dennis Muchmore (Chairperson 08/18/10), Director Rebecca Humphries (DNR Representative – Aug./Oct./Dec. meetings).

2011 – Bob Garner Chairperson

Rodney A. Stokes – Director of Michigan Department of Natural Resources (DNR) (replaced Rebecca Humphries 2/16/11), Keith Charters (NCR Representative), Frank Torre, Samuel Cummings (appoimted 3/1/11, replaced Dennis Muchmore).

2012 – Bob Garner Chairperson

Rodney A. Stokes – Director of Michigan Department of Natural Resources (DNR) (February, April and June Meetings), Keith Creagh Director of Michigan Department of Natural Resources (DNR) (replaced Rodney Stokes August, 2012), Keith Charters (NCR Representative), Frank Torre (term expired 10/1/12), Brad Canale (replaced Frank Torre 11/7/12, attended December meeting).

2013 – Samuel Cummings Chairperson

Keith Creagh - Director of Michigan Department of Natural Resources (DNR), Keith Charters, Brad Canale, Erin McDonough.

2014 – Samuel Cummings Chairperson

Keith Creagh – (DNR), Samuel Cummings, Keith Charters (resigned 12/3/14),,Brad Canale, Erin McDonough.

2015 – Brad Canale Chairperson

Keith Creagh – (DNR), Samuel Cummings, Steve Hamp (appointed 12/9/14), Erin McDonough (Vice-Chairperson)

Appendix D

MICHIGAN ACT 451 OF 1994 (EXCERPT)

NATURAL RESOURCES AND ENVIRONMENTAL PROTECTION ACT (EXCERPT)

324.1902 Michigan natural resources trust fund; establishment; contents; transfer of amount to Michigan state parks endowment fund; receipts; investment; report on accounting of revenues and expenditures; "Michigan state parks endowment fund" defined.

Sec. 1902.(1) In accordance with section 35 of article IX of the state constitution of 1963, the Michigan natural resources trust fund is established in the state treasury. The trust fund shall consist of all bonuses, rentals, delayed rentals, and royalties collected or reserved by the state under provisions of leases for the extraction of nonrenewable resources from state owned lands. However, the trust fund shall not include bonuses, rentals, delayed rentals, and royalties collected or reserved by the state from the following sources:

(a) State owned lands acquired with money appropriated from the former game and fish protection fund or the game and fish protection account of the Michigan conservation and recreation legacy fund provided for in section 2010.

(b) State owned lands acquired with money appropriated from the subfund account created by former section 4 of former 1976 PA 204.

(c) State owned lands acquired with money appropriated from related federal funds made available to the state under 16 USC 669 to 669i, commonly known as the federal aid in wildlife restoration act, or 16 USC 777 to 777l, commonly known as the federal aid in fish restoration act.

(d) Money received by the state from net proceeds allocable to the nonconventional fuel credit contained in section 29 of the internal revenue code of 1986, 26 USC 29, as provided for in section 503.

(2) Notwithstanding subsection (1), until the trust fund reaches an accumulated principal of $500,000,000.00, $10,000,000.00 of the revenues from bonuses, rentals, delayed rentals, and royalties described in this section, but not including money received by the state from net proceeds allocable to the nonconventional fuel credit contained in section 29 of the internal revenue code of 1986, 26 USC 29, as provided for in section 503, otherwise dedicated to the trust fund that are received by the trust fund each state fiscal year shall be transferred to the state treasurer for deposit into the Michigan state parks endowment fund. However, until the trust fund reaches an accumulated principal of $500,000,000.00, in any state fiscal year, not more than 50% of the total revenues from bonuses, rentals, delayed rentals, and royalties described in this section, but not including

net proceeds allocable to the nonconventional fuel credit contained in section 29 of the internal revenue code of 1986, 26 USC 29, as provided in section 503, otherwise dedicated to the trust fund that are received by the trust fund each state fiscal year shall be transferred to the Michigan state parks endowment fund. To implement this subsection, until the trust fund reaches an accumulated principal of $500,000,000.00, the department shall transfer 50% of the money received by the trust fund each month pursuant to subsection (1) to the state treasurer for deposit into the Michigan state parks endowment fund. The department shall make this transfer on the last day of each month or as soon as practicable thereafter. However, not more than a total of $10,000,000.00 shall be transferred in any state fiscal year pursuant to this subsection.

(3) In addition to the contents of the trust fund described in subsection (1), the trust fund shall consist of money transferred to the trust fund pursuant to section 1909.

(4) The trust fund may receive appropriations, money, or other things of value.

(5) The state treasurer shall direct the investment of the trust fund. The state treasurer shall have the same authority to invest the assets of the trust fund as is granted to an investment fiduciary under the public employee retirement system investment act, 1965 PA 314, MCL 38.1132 to 38.1140l.

(6) The department shall annually prepare a report containing an accounting of revenues and expenditures from the trust fund. This report shall identify the interest and earnings of the trust fund from the previous year, the investment performance of the trust fund during the previous year, and the total amount of appropriations from the trust fund during the previous year. This report shall be provided to the senate and house of representatives appropriations committees and the standing committees of the senate and house of representatives with jurisdiction over issues pertaining to natural resources and the environment.

(7) As used in this section, "Michigan state parks endowment fund" means the Michigan state parks endowment fund established in section 35a of article IX of the state constitution of 1963 and provided for in section 74119.

324.1903 Expenditures.

Sec. 1903. (1) Subject to the limitations of this part and of section 35 of article IX of the state constitution of 1963, the interest and earnings of the trust fund in any 1 state fiscal year may be expended in subsequent state fiscal years only for the following purposes:

(a) The acquisition of land or rights in land for recreational uses or protection of the land because of its environmental importance or its scenic beauty.

(b) The development of public recreation facilities.

(c) The administration of the fund, including payments in lieu of taxes on state owned land purchased through the trust fund.

(2) In addition to the money described in subsection (1), 33-1/3% of the money, exclusive of interest and earnings, received by the trust fund in any state fiscal year may be expended in subsequent state fiscal years for the purposes described in subsection (1). However, the authorization for the expenditure of money provided in this subsection does not apply after the state fiscal year in which the total amount of money in the trust fund, exclusive of interest and earnings and amounts authorized for expenditure under this section, exceeds $500,000,000.00.

(3) An expenditure from the trust fund may be made in the form of a grant to a local unit of government, subject to the following conditions:

(a) The grant is used for the purposes described in subsection (1) and meets the requirements of either subdivision (b) or (c).

(b) A grant for the purposes described in subsection (1)(a) is matched by the local unit of government or public authority with at least 25% of the total cost of the project.

(c) A grant for the purposes described in subsection (1)(b) is matched by the local unit of government with 25% or more of the total cost of the project.

(4) Not less than 25% of the total amounts made available for expenditure from the trust fund from any state fiscal year shall be expended for acquisition of land and rights in land, and not more than 25% of the total amounts made available for expenditure from the trust fund from any state fiscal year shall be expended for development of public recreation facilities.

(5) If property that was acquired with money from the trust fund is subsequently sold or transferred by the state to a nongovernmental entity, the state shall forward to the state treasurer for deposit into the trust fund an amount of money equal to the following:

(a) If the property was acquired solely with trust fund money, the greatest of the following:

(i) The net proceeds of the sale.

(ii) The fair market value of the property at the time of the sale or transfer.

(iii) The amount of money that was expended from the trust fund to acquire the property.

(b) If the property was acquired with a combination of trust fund money and other restricted funding sources governed by federal or state law, an amount equal to the percentage of the funds contributed by the trust fund for the acquisition of the property multiplied by the greatest of subdivision (a)(i), (ii), or (iii).

324.1904 Limitation on amount accumulated in trust fund; deposit and distribution of amount.

Sec. 1904. The amount accumulated in the trust fund shall not exceed $500,000,000.00, exclusive of interest and earnings and amounts authorized for expenditure under this part. Any amount of money that would be a part of the trust fund but for the limitation stated in this section shall be deposited in the Michigan state parks endowment fund created in section 74119, until the Michigan state parks endowment fund reaches an accumulated principal of $800,000,000.00. After the Michigan state parks endowment fund reaches an accumulated principal of $800,000,000.00, any money that would be part of the Michigan state parks endowment fund but for this limitation shall be distributed as provided by law.

324.1905 Michigan natural resources trust fund board; establishment; powers and duties of transferred agency; cooperation, aid, offices, and equipment; appointment and terms of members; removal; vacancies; expenses; compensation.

Sec. 1905. (1) The Michigan natural resources trust fund board is established within the department. The board shall have the powers and duties of an agency transferred under a type I transfer pursuant to section 3 of the executive organization act of 1965, Act No. 380 of the Public Acts of 1965, being section 16.103 of the Michigan Compiled Laws. The board shall be administered under the supervision department and the department shall offer its cooperation and aid to the board and shall provide suitable offices and equipment for the board.

(2) The board shall consist of 5 members. The members shall include the director or a member of the commission as determined by the commission, and 4 residents of the state to be appointed by the governor with the advice and consent of the senate.

(3) The terms of the appointive members shall be 4 years, except that of those first appointed, 1 shall be appointed for 1 year, 1 shall be appointed for 2 years, 1 shall be appointed for 3 years, and 1 shall be appointed for 4 years.

(4) The appointive members may be removed by the governor for inefficiency, neglect of duty, or malfeasance in office.

(5) Vacancies on the board shall be filled for the unexpired term in the same manner as the original appointments.

(6) The board may incur expenses necessary to carry out its powers and duties under this part and shall compensate its members for actual expenses incurred in carrying out their official duties.

324.1906 Board; election of chairperson; administrative procedures; conducting business at public meeting; notice; meetings of board; availability of writings to public; reports.

Sec. 1906. (1) The board shall elect a chairperson and establish its administrative procedures. The business which the board may perform shall be conducted at a public meeting of the board held in compliance with the open meetings act, Act No. 267 of the Public Acts of 1976, being sections 15.261 to 15.275 of the Michigan Compiled Laws. Public notice of the time, date, and place of the meeting shall be given in the manner required by Act No. 267 of the Public Acts of 1976. The board shall meet not less than bimonthly and shall record its proceedings. A writing prepared, owned, used, in the possession of, or retained by the board in the performance of an official function shall be made available to the public in compliance with the freedom of information act, Act No. 442 of the Public Acts of 1976, being sections 15.231 to 15.246 of the Michigan Compiled Laws.

(2) Before January 16 of each year, the board shall report to the governor and to the legislature detailing the operations of the board for the preceding 1-year period. The board shall also make special reports as requested by the governor or the legislature.

324.1907 List of lands, rights in land, and public recreation facilities to be acquired or developed; estimates of total costs; guidelines; legislative approval.

Sec. 1907. (1) The board shall determine which lands and rights in land within the state should be acquired and which public recreation facilities should be developed with money from the trust fund and shall submit to the legislature in January of each year a list of those lands and rights in land and those public recreation facilities that the board has determined should be acquired or developed with trust fund money, compiled in order of priority. In preparing the list under this subsection, the board shall give particular consideration to the acquisition of land and rights in land for recreational trails that intersect the downtown areas of cities and villages.

(2) This list shall be accompanied by estimates of total costs for the proposed acquisitions and developments.

(3) The board shall supply with each list a statement of the guidelines used in listing and assigning the priority of these proposed acquisitions and developments.

(4) The legislature shall approve by law the lands and rights in land and the public recreation facilities to be acquired or developed each year with money from the trust fund.

324.1907a Project status; report.

Sec. 1907a.If within 2 years after a parcel of property that is approved for acquisition or development by the legislature has not been acquired or developed in the manner determined by the board and is not open for public use, the board shall report to the standing committees of the senate and the house of representatives with jurisdiction over issues related to natural resources and the environment on the status of the project and the reason why the property has not been purchased or developed in the manner determined by the board.

324.1908 Adopting decisions of state recreational land acquisition trust fund board of trustees; completion of projects; validity and expenditure of appropriations; deposit and appropriation of unexpended funds; appropriation of funds available under former law; deposit of interest and earnings on unexpended money.

Sec. 1908. (1) Beginning on October 1, 1985, the board shall adopt as its own any decision made by the state recreational land acquisition trust fund board of trustees under the Kammer recreational land trust fund act of 1976, former Act No. 204 of the Public Acts of 1976, and shall administer to completion any project pending under that act.

(2) Appropriations made pursuant to former Act No. 204 of the Public Acts of 1976 shall remain valid after October 1, 1985 and may be expended until the projects approved through the appropriations are complete. Any funds appropriated pursuant to former Act No. 204 of the Public Acts of 1976 but unexpended after completion of the projects funded under that act shall be deposited in the trust fund and may be appropriated as natural resources trust funds.

(3) Funds available for appropriation under former Act No. 204 of the Public Acts of 1976 as of October 1, 1985, but not appropriated as of that date, may be appropriated by the legislature under the terms and conditions of that act. Any funds appropriated as provided in this subsection but unexpended after completion of the projects for which the money was appropriated shall be deposited in the trust fund and may be appropriated as natural resources trust funds.

(4) The interest and earnings on money appropriated pursuant to former Act No. 204 of the Public Acts of 1976 or subsection (3) but not expended shall be deposited in the trust fund.

Appendix E
CONSTITUTION OF MICHIGAN (EXCERPT)
Effective September 22, 2002

§ 35 Michigan natural resources trust fund.
Sec. 35.
There is hereby established the Michigan natural resources trust fund. The trust fund shall consist of all bonuses, rentals, delayed rentals, and royalties collected or reserved by the state under provisions of leases for the extraction of nonrenewable resources from state owned lands, except such revenues accruing under leases of state owned lands acquired with money from state or federal game and fish protection funds or revenues accruing from lands purchased with such revenues. The trust fund may receive appropriations, money, or other things of value. The assets of the trust fund shall be invested as provided by law.

Until the trust fund reaches an accumulated principal of $500,000,000.00, $10,000,000.00 of the revenues from bonuses, rentals, delayed rentals, and royalties described in this section otherwise dedicated to the trust fund that are received by the state each state fiscal year shall be deposited into the Michigan state parks endowment fund. However, until the trust fund reaches an accumulated principal of $500,000,000.00, in any state fiscal year, not more than 50 percent of the total revenues from bonuses, rentals, delayed rentals, and royalties described in this section otherwise dedicated to the trust fund that are received by the state each state fiscal year shall be deposited into the Michigan state parks endowment fund.

The amount accumulated in the trust fund in any state fiscal year shall not exceed $500,000,000.00, exclusive of interest and earnings and amounts authorized for expenditure pursuant to this section. When the accumulated principal of the trust fund reaches $500,000,000.00, all revenue from bonuses, rentals, delayed rentals, and royalties described in this section that would be received by the trust fund but for this limitation shall be deposited into the Michigan state parks endowment fund until the Michigan state parks endowment fund reaches an accumulated principal of $800,000,000.00. When the Michigan state parks endowment fund reaches an accumulated principal of $800,000,000.00, all revenues from bonuses, rentals, delayed rentals, and royalties described in this section shall be distributed as provided by law.

The interest and earnings of the trust fund shall be expended for the acquisition of land or rights in land for recreational uses or protection of the land because of its environmental importance or its scenic beauty, for the development of public recreation facilities, and for the administration of the trust fund, which may include payments in lieu of taxes on state owned land purchased through the trust fund. The trust fund may provide grants to units of local government or public authorities which shall be used for the purposes of this section. The legislature shall provide that a portion of the cost of a project funded by such grants be provided by the local unit of government or public authority.

Until the trust fund reaches an accumulated principal of $500,000,000.00, the legislature may provide, in addition to the expenditure of interest and earnings authorized by this section, that a portion, not to exceed 33-1/3 percent, of the revenues from bonuses, rentals, delayed rentals, and royalties described in this section received by the trust fund during each state fiscal year may be expended during subsequent state fiscal years for the purposes of this section.

Not less than 25 percent of the total amounts made available for expenditure from the trust fund from any state fiscal year shall be expended for acquisition of land and rights in land and not more than 25 percent of the total amounts made available for expenditure from the trust fund from any state fiscal year shall be expended for development of public recreation facilities.

The legislature shall provide by law for the establishment of a trust fund board within the department of natural resources. The trust fund board shall recommend the projects to be funded. The board shall submit its recommendations to the governor who shall submit the board's recommendations to the legislature in an appropriations bill.

The legislature shall provide by law for the implementation of this section.

History: Add. H.J.R. M, approved Nov. 6, 1984, Eff. Dec. 22, 1984 ;-- Am. S.J.R. E, approved Nov. 8, 1994, Eff. Dec. 24, 1994 ;-- Am. S.J.R. T, approved Aug. 6, 2002, Eff. Sept. 21, 2002

Appendix F

NATURAL RESOURCES AND ENVIRONMENTAL PROTECTION ACT (EXCERPT)

Act 451 of 1994 – 2010 Amendments by Act 32 2010

324.1909, 324.1910 Repealed. 2010, Act 32, Eff. Oct. 1, 2010. Note: The repealed sections pertained to duties of state treasurer and transfer of writings or documents by department of natural resources and department of treasury.

324.1911 Local public recreation facilities fund.

Sec. 1911.(1) The local public recreation facilities fund is created within the state treasury.

(2) The state treasurer may receive money or other assets from any source for deposit into the local public recreation facilities fund. The state treasurer shall direct the investment of the local public recreation facilities fund. The state treasurer shall credit to the local public recreation facilities fund interest and earnings from local public recreation facilities fund investments.

(3) Money in the local public recreation facilities fund at the close of the fiscal year shall remain in the local public recreation facilities fund and shall not lapse to the general fund.

(4) The department of natural resources shall be the administrator of the local public recreation facilities fund for auditing purposes.

(5) The department of natural resources shall expend money from the local public recreation facilities fund, upon appropriation, only for grants to local units of government for the development of public recreation facilities pursuant to the same procedures of the board and guidelines as apply under section 1907.

U. S. Senator Debbie Stabenow and the author with MNRTF literature at a summer Michigan Association of Counties meeting at Mackinac Island in 2005.

Acknowledgements

A word about content before the obligatory "thank yous".

The photographs which do not bear a photo credit are those I have taken over the years, privately and for the *Michigan Oil & Gas News*.

The oil and gas production statistics in individual county profiles are through 2013 while drilling statistics and Michigan Natural Resources Trust Fund active and completed figures and rankings are through 2014. Population in 2010 is the lastest available from the U.S. Census Bureau.

Rankings of counties in various categories are my own calculations, they are all named with that rank. Any miscalculation, omissions or bollixed interpretation can be laid at my doorstep .... and I would appreciate you for telling me about them.

Now to the "much obligeds"

Certainly the biggest expression of appreciation must go to the Internet for making so much data about practically everything available. Many of the photos of projects are borrowed from government and organizational websites identified in photo credits.

Along those lines, Wikipedia – the free online encyclopedia was invaluable in composing county history information. Another invaluable source of county information was Universal Map Company's *Michigan County Atlas, Second Edition*, an absolutely stunning publication no business or pleasure traveler should be without.

Thanks to Scott Bellinger and Shannon Sak, my successors at the *Michigan Oil & Gas News* magazine, for making updated data available to me in a workable format for the MNRTF project lists I no longer kept up the past few years, and for filling in my photo needs when I couldn't locate a photo I took when still active with them (and for permission to use those photos as well as excerpts from past articles).

Hats off to Linda Harlow of the Grants Management Office of the Michigan Department of Natural Resources, for her gracious cooperation in answering my questions through this process and for furnishing me with a ready-made list of MNRTF Boards of Trustees from 1977 to the present.

Special thanks to Saint Clair County's Nelson Pine River Nature Center Director Sarah Davidson-Nelson, who in the final days before leaving for pregnancy leave, made the effort to photograph and send images of the Nature Center to me in a prompt fashion.

Of course, thanks to my proofreader, keystroker, consultant, editor, and life partner, my wife Mary Lou, who looks uncomfortable when called my lovely assistant, without whom none of it happens.

J.R.W. Mt. Pleasant, Michigan, February 27, 2015

About the Author

JACK R. WESTBROOK is a Mt. Pleasant, Michigan, resident, retired Managing Editor of the Michigan Oil & Gas News weekly magazine and author of four previous historical photo review books for Arcadia Publishing Company: *MICHIGAN OIL & GAS* (2006); *MT. PLEASANT THEN and NOW* (2006); *CENTRAL MICHIGAN UNIVERSITY* (2007); and *ISABELLA COUNTY (Michigan) 1859-2009* (2008). He has self-published: *YESTERDAY'S SCHOOL KIDS OF ISABELLA COUNTY,* with co-author historian/genealogist Sherry Sponseller (2009); *ANOINTED WITH OIL: MY JOURNEY WITH FAITH FROM THE OILFIELDS OF MICHIGAN TO THE LEGISLATIVE HALLS OF WASHINGTON DC and BACK AGAIN*, by C. John Miller as told to Jack R. Westbrook (2010); *THE BIG PICTURE BOOK OF MT. PLEASANT, MICHIGAN: Yesteryears to 2010* (2010); *MICHIGAN NATURAL RESOURCES TRUST FUND* (2011); AT HOME IN EARLIER MT. PLEASANT, MICHIGAN (2012); MID-MICHIGAN HISTORY: THE MT.PLEASANT AREA'S PAST AS SEEN IN THE MORNING SUN & MT. PLEASANT MONTHLY MAGAZINE PHOTO FEATURES (2013); THE WEBER FAMILY OF BEAL CITY MICHIGAN (2014); and MID-MICHIGAN HISTORY 2 (2015).

Westbrook's first work of fiction, *KAISA*: A NOVEL OF MICHIGAN'S COPPER MINING & OIL AND GAS EXPLORATION AND PRODUCTION INDUSTRIES; CALUMET; HOLLAND; MT. PLEASANT; MACKINAC ISLAND AND JEKYLL ISLAND, GEORGIA was published in August of 2013 and he is now working on a second novel "MURDER IN THE MICHIGAN OILPATCH."

MNRTF Contacts

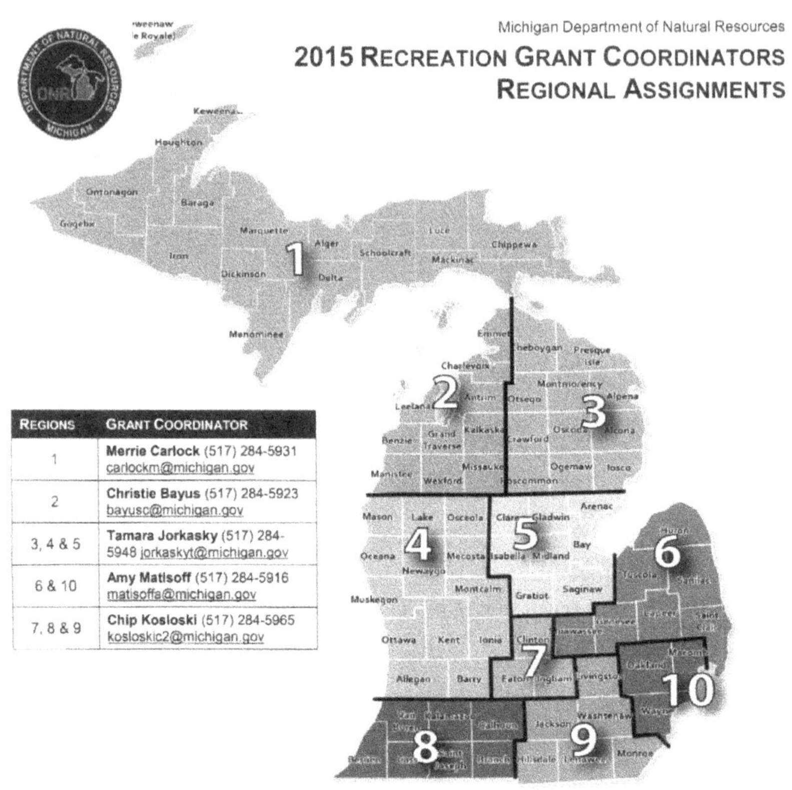

REGIONS	GRANT COORDINATOR
1	**Merrie Carlock** (517) 284-5931 carlockm@michigan.gov
2	**Christie Bayus** (517) 284-5923 bayusc@michigan.gov
3, 4 & 5	**Tamara Jorkasky** (517) 284-5948 jorkaskyt@michigan.gov
6 & 10	**Amy Matisoff** (517) 284-5916 matisoffa@michigan.gov
7, 8 & 9	**Chip Kosloski** (517) 284-5965 kosloskic2@michigan.gov

ADDITIONAL GRANTS MANAGEMENT CONTACTS	
Steven J. DeBrabander, Manager, (517) 284-5930, debrabanders@michigan.gov **Linda Harlow**, Assistant to the Manager and MNRTF Board Secretary, (517) 284-7268, harlowl@michigan.gov	
Jon Mayes, Unit Manager, Recreation Grants (517) 284-5954, mayesj@michigan.gov **Christie Bayus**, Program Manager, LWCF/Marine Safety/ Recreation Passport Programs (517) 284-5923, bayusc@michigan.gov **Kammy Frayre**, Program Manager, Invasive Species Grant Program and Conversions Officer (517) 284-5970, frayrek1@michigan.gov	**Michelle Ballard**, Grants Payment Officer, LWCF/Marine Safety/ Recreation Passport Programs (517) 284-5974, ballardm3@michigan.gov **Lance Brooks**, Grants Payment Officer, Aquatic Habitat and Wildlife Habitat Grant Programs (517) 284-5971, brooksl@michigan.gov **Kelly Parker**, Program Manager, Dam Management, Aquatic Habitat, Wildlife Habitat Grant Programs (517) 284-5957, parkerk4@michigan.gov **Janet Liesman**, Financial Specialist, MNRTF (517) 284-5951, liesmanj@michigan.gov

The above is reproduced from the Michigan Department of Natural Resources Grants Management website. To access this and other MNRTF information go to www.michigan.gov/dnr then click on the word *Grants* on the left and, finally, click on the phrase *Michigan Natural Resources Trust Fund.*

www.ingramcontent.com/pod-product-compliance
Lightning Source LLC
Chambersburg PA
CBHW060048100426
42742CB00014B/2735

* 9 7 8 0 9 8 4 0 3 6 1 8 9 *